CASES AND ISSUES FOR
PHILIPPINE
COMPARATIVE STUDY

Facts, Laws, and Opinions of a U.S. State Court of Appeal

Marcelino C. Maxino, LL.M., Esq.

Portions of Philippine Notes
co-written with
M. Mikhail Lee L. Maxino, LL.M., Esq.

DEDICATION

This work is dedicated to my wonderful family—wife Remy; children Warren, Mikhail, Ivy, Wilbur, and Linus; children-in-law Zaldy and Yolanda; and grandchildren Abigail, Mykaela, and Marc—all whom I love dearly and from whom I draw my inspiration.

I also dedicate this work to my late father and my 101-year old surviving mother, who taught me how life should be lived.

Above all, I dedicate this work to God Almighty, to Whom I owe all that I am, and all that I have.

Copyright © 2004 Marcelino C. Maxino
All rights reserved.

No part of this book may be used or reproduced or distributed in any form, or by any means, or stored in a database or retrieval system, without the prior written permission of the author.

Published by Ulyssian Publications, an imprint of Pine Orchard Inc.

Book design by Pine Orchard. Visit us on the internet at www.pineorchard.com

Printed in Canada.

9 8 7 6 5 4 3 2 1

ISBN 1-930580-54-1

Library of Congress Control Number: 2004107588

CONTENTS

ACKNOWLEDGMENTS 5
THE AUTHOR 6
INTRODUCTION 9

I. At-Will Employment;
Implied Covenant of Good Faith
Bliss v. BT North America, Inc. 13

II. Contracting with Corporation;
Civil Standard of Review
Chuk v. Yen 25

III. Contracting with Unlicensed Contractors;
Arbitration
Sunshine Western v. Hearrean 37

IV. Child Endangerment
People v. Blomquist 48

V. Termination of Parental Rights
In Re Leslie R. 58

VI. Protective Sweep;
"Bounty Hunter"
People v. Villa 69

VII. Lawyer's Fiduciary Duty to Client
Hoffman v. Heagerty 78

VIII. Trial by Jury v. Trial by Judge;
Criminal Standard of Review;
Sanitized Evidence
People v. Castaneda 94

IX. Prior Conviction Evidence;
Identification Evidence;
Removal of Juror
People v. Lasoya 104

X. Jury Nullification;
Jury Instructions;
Cruel and Unusual Punishment
People v. Olson 126

XI. Drunk Driving Law;
     Due Process;
     Equal Protection
               People v. Ireland 143

XII. Wireless Phones and Federal Preemption
               People v. Stevens 158

XIII. Right to Counsel: Self-Representation
               People v. Lattimore 167

XIV. Right to Counsel: Change of Circumstances
               People v. Mitchell 180

XV. Right to Counsel: Civil Case;
     Punitive Damages;
     Statement of Decision;
     Attorney Fees
               Tran v. Nguyen 202

XVI. Ineffective Assistance of Counsel;
      Disclosure of Surveillance Location
               People v. Garza 216

XVII. Harmless Error;
       Unavailability of Witness for Trial;
       Right of Confrontation;
       In-Court Identification
               People v. Lang 227

XVIII. Search and Seizure;
        Public Search of Crotch Area;
        Payment of Fees as Condition of Probation
               People v. Jones 257

XIX. Piracy of Intellectual Property;
      Standard of Review on Preliminary Injunctions
               DVD CCA v. Bunner 272

ACKNOWLEDGMENTS

This project is largely a family affair. My wife, Remy, inspires me no end and spares no sacrifice to give me all I need to write this book. My eldest son, Warren, served me hot coffee to perk me up each time my concentration level ebbed. My second son, Mikhail, reviewed the manuscript, gave valuable suggestions, and wrote portions of the notes relating to Philippine law and jurisprudence. My daughter, Ivy, retrieved my old files, found me a publisher, put together the production package, ran errands to make sure I had no excuse not to complete this work, and handles the marketing and distribution arrangements with my wife. My two youngest sons, Wilbur and Linus, provided financial assistance. I thank all my children for their inspiration, assistance, contribution, and support.

My brother, Vicente, reviewed the manuscript and gave invaluable suggestions. Carmen Miraflor, a dear friend from college days, and now with Stanford University, wrote press releases and continues to help in many ways. Carmen was also among the first to suggest that I write a book. I thank my brother Vicente and Carmen for their help and support.

THE AUTHOR

I immigrated to the United States in November 1985. I was 47 years old. Before that, I had been teaching law at Foundation University and Silliman University, both in Dumaguete City, for a combined period of 23 years. I had also been a dean of the School of Law of Foundation University for six years, and the president of that university for another six years.

I was fortunate, and privileged, to be associated for a long time with the late Dr. Vicente Guzman Sinco, the founder and first president of Foundation University. Dr. Sinco was the country's foremost authority in constitutional law. He was a professor of constitutional law at the College of Law of the University of the Philippines, then the illustrious and incomparable dean of that college of law, and finally the president of the university. Dr. Sinco was the greatest legal mind I was ever privileged to meet. I consider my long association with Dr. Sinco the most academically enriching and rewarding years of my life. That great man and scholar greatly influenced my thinking on many social, educational, legal, and political issues.

I was educated and trained in civil law in the Philippines. However, I did studies in the United States that provided me some understanding of common law. I was a DeWitt Fellow at the University of Michigan, Ann Arbor, Michigan, in 1964-1965, where I completed my Master of Laws degree. I was also a Fellow at the Academy of American and International Law, International and Comparative Law Center, Southwestern Legal Foundation, in Dallas, Texas, in the summer of 1965.

Two weeks into my entry to the U.S., I got a job as a legal assistant in the Law Offices of Richard T. Bowles in Walnut Creek, California. (The firm later became the Law Offices of Bowles and Verna when Mike Verna joined as a partner.) As a legal researcher for Rick Bowles, I was exposed to common law and the California legal system in greater detail. My job as a legal researcher for Rick Bowles, and my exposure to American law at the University of Michigan, contributed in no small measure to my passing the California bar examination on my first attempt in February 1987. Rick Bowles was very supportive of my desire to become a licensed California attorney. Although I had worked for him for only 13 months, he generously gave me a whole month of paid leave to allow me to prepare for, and take, the California bar examination. I am ever grateful to Rick Bowles.

I am also ever grateful to a kind heart, Kenneth Jacobson, Esq., of Pleasant Hill, California, for my passing the California bar examination. Ken and I did not know each other before. One autumn day in 1986, as I was playing golf by myself in a little 9-hole golf course in Walnut Creek, Ken joined me from the threesome behind that he was with. As we were trying to know each other, Ken asked me what I was doing for a living. I told him I was a legal assistant to Rick Bowles, and that I was a licensed attorney in the Philippines. Ken asked me if I was intending to get a California license. I told him I was, but that I needed to take the California bar examination first. He asked when I was going to do that. I told him I did not know because I still had to save money to buy the review materials and to pay the examination fee. Ken, who had passed the bar two years before, said he still had his review materials and would be happy to lend them to me. I asked Ken when I could borrow his materials. He said he would gather them when he got home. The next day, Ken came to my home in Concord to deliver the review materials. God truly works in mysterious ways!

After passing the California bar examination, I left Bowles and Verna, with the firm's blessings, and practiced law on my own in the Bay Area cities of Concord, Walnut Creek, and San Francisco. A year later, I competed for judicial attorney job openings at the Sixth District Court of Appeal in San Jose. Justice Eugene M. Premo took me in as his first chambers attorney. I learned much from Justice Premo. I owe to him, more than to any other man, the state of knowledge I presently have on California law.

During my first few months as judicial attorney, I often wondered if I had not overestimated my abilities in applying for the job. Many of the cases I was reviewing raised issues that were absolutely foreign to me. Some of the lawyers' briefs were helpful, but some were not. Fortunately, Presiding Justice Nat Agliano timely instituted weekly issue tracking meetings for judicial attorneys. In those meetings, attorneys compared notes and discussed the issues they were working on. These discussions allowed me to learn more about my own issues and made my task less daunting.

I retired from the California Court of Appeal in July 2001 after serving that court as judicial attorney for 13 years. I was lead attorney when I retired. In the 13 years that I was with the court, I had drafted for the court more than 500 opinions. Some of those opinions were published opinions, but most were not.

While working as a judicial attorney for the California Court of Appeal, I was also, on the side, a reader for, and consultant to, the Committee of Bar Examiners of the State Bar of California. In this latter capacity, I read and graded answers to the California bar examinations. I did this for 14 years. In the last few years of my consultancy to the Committee of Bar Examiners, I was invited to submit essay questions for the California bar examination in the area of criminal law and procedure. I was honored by the invitation, and, for five years, submitted essay questions to the Committee of Bar Examiners.

My experience as an examiner and reader/grader for California's Committee of Bar Examiners allowed me to compare California's system of preparing and administering bar examinations, and of reading and grading essay answers to those examinations, with the Philippine system. I will have to say that I think the California system is far more efficient, reliable, and fair.

INTRODUCTION

The 19 cases in this book were selected because, first, they involve issues that are appropriate for comparative law study, and, second, the facts giving rise to those issues appeal, in my view, to human interest. It is my hope that this book will reach not only the students and practitioners of Philippine law, but also the general public whose interest may not go beyond reading the book for leisure, or for picking up a little of the law to learn.

Not all Philippine readers are familiar with the federal setup of the United States, given the centralized, unitary system of government that the Philippines has. In the United States, there are two sets of laws. One set is the federal law. In this set are the acts passed by the United States Congress and signed into law by the president of the United States. Another set of laws is the laws passed by each of the 50 states of the United States. In this set are the acts passed by the legislatures of the 50 states and signed into law by the governors of those states. The laws of a state are for that state only. California, for example, is not bound by the laws of New York, and the citizens of California are not subject to the laws of New York, unless they happen to be in New York.

Each state has a constitution of its own, separate and distinct from the constitutions of the other states, and separate and distinct from the federal constitution of the United States. The constitution of a state binds only the government and citizens of that state. The federal constitution, however, which is what is meant when one speaks of the Constitution of the United States, is the supreme law of the entire United States, and binds all 50 states and all the citizens of those states. If there is a conflict between the U.S. Constitution and a state constitution, the U.S. Constitution prevails.

Likewise, federal laws bind all American citizens, regardless of their state of residence. If there is a conflict between federal law and state law, federal law prevails.

The U.S. Congress cannot legislate just on any matter. It can legislate only on matters specified under the U.S. Constitution, or necessarily implied from the powers specified. When the states of the

Union decided to form a federation more than a hundred years ago, they transferred to the federation only certain specified powers, and retained to themselves all other powers not transferred. The U.S. Congress cannot exercise powers not given to it by the states.

There is no attempt in this book to suggest that one system is better than the other. The book merely points out differences. It cannot be denied, however, that people learn from each other only because they are different from each other. Two people who know exactly the same things have nothing to learn from each other. Because differences provide opportunities for learning, I have, where appropriate, offered suggestions to help enrich and improve the Philippine system.

Some of the opinions in this book were published at the California Appellate Reports, the official publication for opinions of the California Courts of Appeal that are certified for publication. However, many of the opinions reproduced in this book were not published. The fact that an opinion is unpublished does not mean that it is less interesting, or less important, or less researched, than a published opinion. It only means, most often, that the issues involved are not new, or that the fact pattern giving rise to those issues is not significantly different to require extension of an existing rule to a new fact pattern.

There is a practical reason not to publish every case decided by the courts of appeal. Were the rule different, there would not be enough shelves and space in law libraries to house them. The indiscriminate publication would be wasteful and unnecessary, and would exact undue burden on the consumers of the courts' opinions without any redeeming advantage. If all the issues that a new case addresses are the same issues that earlier cases had settled, publication of the new opinion only adds to the volume without saying anything new. Unpublished opinions cannot be cited, but they are part of the public record.

Why, then, should a court of appeal bother taking a case that does not raise new issues? The answer is, because it is required to do so. It is required to do so because the fact that the case does not raise new issues does not mean that the trial court committed no errors.

The court of appeal reviews the case for errors, but only for errors of law. Errors of fact are not appealable.

There is, under California law, a right of appeal to the courts of appeal from decisions of the trial courts (called Superior Courts). Because appeal to the courts of appeal is a right, the courts of appeal are bound to review the cases appealed to them.

There is no similar duty to review cases on the part of the California Supreme Court. Decisions of the courts of appeal are not appealable to the California Supreme Court. A party who is not satisfied with the decision of a court of appeal may go to the Supreme Court only by a petition for review, not by appeal. In the vast majority of cases, such petitions do not reach first base; they are denied summarily. The Supreme Court grants review only in the following cases: (1) where there is conflict among the courts of appeal and it is necessary to settle the conflict to secure uniformity of decision or to settle important questions of law; (2) where the court of appeal acted without jurisdiction of the cause; or (3) where, because of disqualification or other reasons, the decision of the court of appeal lacks the concurrence of the required majority of qualified judges. (Rule 29)

The cases where these grounds exist are not many. That explains why only very, very few of the cases decided by the courts of appeal reach the Supreme Court. In the overwhelming majority of the cases, the decision of a court of appeal is final. It is usually the last decision on the case.

There is a difference in the kind of review that a California court of appeal does from the kind of review that the Philippine Court of Appeals does. The California court of appeal reviews only questions of law. Questions of fact cannot be reviewed because those questions are not appealable. The jury is the sole trier of fact, and the jury's finding of the facts is final. In the Philippines, on the other hand, the Court of Appeals reviews questions of fact. Questions of law may also be reviewed, but only when they are combined with questions of fact. Pure questions of law are appealable only to the Philippine Supreme Court. Because the California court of appeal reviews only questions of law, the jurisdiction it exercises is comparable more to the jurisdiction of the Philippine Supreme Court than to the jurisdiction of the Philippine Court of Appeals.

What is the work of a judicial attorney? He mainly assists the court in reviewing the cases that are appealed to his court. He does the legal research and writes memoranda to the court. The memorandum is in the form of the court's opinion so that if the court approves the attorney's recommendations and the way in which the proposed opinion is written, it is convenient to make the attorney's draft opinion the court's official opinion.

I do not know of any other Filipino attorney who served as judicial attorney for the appellate courts of California during my time, or before. If no other Filipino lawyer had served as attorney for a California appellate court, I am the more honored to publish this book. But it's not just honor. Knowing that what I share with the Filipino readers is something that they may not be able to find elsewhere in Philippine writings also lends some sense of duty.

I.
Bliss v. BT North America, Inc.
(Unpublished)

Bliss is an unpublished civil case. It addresses contract issues. It is relevant to Philippine jurisprudence in that it demonstrates an approach to terminating employment contracts that is vastly different from the Philippine approach. In California, as in the United States in general, employment contracts are terminated without participation by, let alone permission from, the Department of Labor. Employment, or the termination thereof, is a matter between the employer and the employee. If the employment is at will, the employer can terminate the employment at any time with or without cause. Even if the employment is for a definite term, the employer can still terminate the employment before the expiration date by buying out the contract, which means paying the employee the value of the unserved term of the contract. The government does not interfere.

In the Philippines, the rule is different. There is no such thing as employment at will. The Philippine employer cannot terminate an employment contract with an indefinite term without just cause. Even if the contract is for a definite term, Philippine law disregards the term agreement if the employee has been engaged to perform activities that are usually necessary or desirable in the usual business or trade of the employer. In such a case, the employee is regarded as a regular employee with an indefinite term.

Fixed term employment is recognized in Philippine law only when it is not entered into to preclude acquisition of tenurial security by the employee. The criteria under which term employment will be tested for purposes of security tenure analysis are:

(1) The fixed period or employment was knowingly and voluntarily agreed upon by the parties without any force, duress, or improper pressure being brought to bear upon the employee and absent any other circumstances vitiating his consent; or

(2) It satisfactorily appears that the employer and the employee dealt with each other on more or less equal terms with no moral dominance exercised by the former or the latter.

The Filipino lawyer will note that at the beginning of the discussion part of the opinions, there is always a statement of the applicable standard of review. This is not common practice in the Philippines. We hardly see in the opinions of Philippine appellate courts a clear statement of the standard of review. Without a clearly defined standard of review, it is difficult for the appellant to know just exactly what he needs to do to carry his burden of showing reversible error. It is also difficult for counsel to evaluate his client's chances of winning the appeal. If counsel does not know what the standard of review is, he cannot fashion his argument to specifically address the standard. If he cannot do this, he has to use a shotgun-type of argument that spreads lead everywhere, but not analytically focused and concentrated enough to be of greatest value to the reviewing court. A shotgun approach unduly consumes and wastes the time of the appellate court. Also, without a clearly defined standard of review, counsel cannot properly weigh for his client the costs of pursuing the appeal, which are quite certain, against the hoped-for outcome of the appeal, which is uncertain.

The memorandum opinion that I submitted to the court in *Bliss* is reproduced below. As a uniform format for this book, the opinions of the court are printed in a different font to identify the narratives from the cases. The opinions are reproduced in the exact language of the court, but no opening quotation marks are used. Except for the font style printed in this book, the opinions appear in exactly the same way they appeared when filed with the clerk of the court.

Most of the footnotes in *Bliss*, and in all the other cases, are part of the opinions of the court. However, I have added a few footnotes that were not originally in the opinions to explain certain terms or rules. Where such new footnotes are added, they are so indicated.

The opinion in *Bliss v. BT North America* follows:

FACTS

In June 1984, plaintiff Bliss was hired by Tymshare Inc. (hereafter, Tymshare) as a senior scientist in its hardware development group. At that time, Tymshare was in the process of being acquired or had recently been acquired by McDonnell Douglas Corporation (hereafter, MDC). Subsequent to its acquisition by MDC, Tymshare became Tymnet.

In November 1989, British Telecommunications plc (hereafter, British Telecom) acquired Tymnet from MDC. Following this acquisition, Tymnet became BT Tymnet Inc. (hereafter, BT Tymnet).

Prior to the takeover, British Telecom sent out identical employment offers to the Tymnet employees, a pertinent portion of which reads: "As with your current status with McDonnell Douglas, your employment with British Telecom is also one of employment-at-will. This employment agreement supersedes any previous employment agreements."

On November 8, 1989, plaintiff accepted British Telecom's offer. Plaintiff's acceptance reads: "I accept employment with BT Tymnet Inc. under these terms and conditions." (Hereafter, defendant's employment offer and plaintiff's acceptance thereof will be known as the November agreement.)

On January 15, 1990, BT Tymnet laid off plaintiff. Plaintiff's discharge was part of a large-scale reduction in defendant's work force in the United States. Defendant had decided, as a result of increased competition, to shift its development efforts away from proprietary hardware, which the company could no longer support, and toward software. Plaintiff, who was working in the hardware division, was one of the approximately 170 employees, comprising more than 10 percent of defendant's total U.S. work force, whose positions were eliminated.

The reduction of defendant's work force continued even after plaintiff's discharge. Between January 1990 and September 1991, the size of the hardware support and development staff had been further reduced from 75 to less than 35 employees.

Since plaintiff's discharge, there had been no hiring in the hardware unit, except for one contractor who was hired at a junior position that was at least three salary grades lower than plaintiff's grade level.

In April 1991, defendant BT North America, Inc. succeeded to the interest of BT Tymnet.

On April 6, 1992, plaintiff filed the instant complaint for breach of the employment agreement and the implied covenant of good faith and fair dealing. On March 4, 1993, defendant moved for summary judgment, which the trial court granted on April 12, 1993.

In granting summary judgment, the court stated: "I think there is a statute of limitations barred. Time starts to run when plaintiff knows that he is being terminated and there is more than two years before he files the action. I don't think there is any material issue of fact as to whether there is an at will contract, and I don't think there is a problem with good cause since there was a reduction in force."

STANDARD OF REVIEW

"The purpose of summary judgment is to penetrate evasive language and adept pleading and to ascertain, by means of affidavits, the presence or absence of triable issues of fact. [Citation.]" (Molko v. Holy Spirit Assn. (1988) 46 Cal.3d 1092, 1107.) "A defendant is entitled to summary judgment if the record establishes as a matter of law that none of the plaintiff's asserted causes of action can prevail. [Citation.]." (Ibid.)

In AARTS Productions, Inc. v. Crocker National Bank (1986) 179 Cal.App.3d 1061, 1064-1065, and again in Barisich v. Lewis (1990) 226 Cal.App.3d 12, 15-16, we stated the standard of review for appeals from summary judgment, as follows: "Since a summary judgment motion raises only questions of law regarding the construction and effect of the supporting and opposing papers, we independently review them on appeal, applying the same three-step analysis required of the trial court. [Citations.] First, we identify the issues framed by the pleadings since it is these allegations to which the motion must respond by establishing a complete defense or otherwise showing there is no factual basis for relief on any theory reasonably contemplated by the opponent's pleading. [Citations.] [¶] Secondly, we determine whether the moving party's showing has established facts which negate the opponent's claim and justify a judgment in movant's favor. [Citations.] The motion must stand self-sufficient and cannot succeed because the opposition is weak. [Citations.] A party cannot succeed without disproving even those claims on which the opponent would have the burden of proof at trial. [Citations.] [¶] When a summary judgment motion prima facie justifies a judgment, the third and final step is to determine whether the opposition demonstrates the existence of a triable, material factual issue. [Citation.]" (179 Cal.App.3d at pp. 1064-1065.)

DISCUSSION

Applying the foregoing standard of review, we identify the main issues in this case, as framed by the pleadings, to be as follows:

1. Whether plaintiff's employment contract was at will.

2. Whether plaintiff's claim of an implied-in-fact agreement with MDC raises triable issues of fact.

3. Whether plaintiff's claim of breach of the implied covenant of good faith and fair dealing raises triable issues of fact.

4. Whether plaintiff's claimed causes of action are barred by the statute of limitations.

At-Will Employment

The parties do not dispute that on November 8, 1989, plaintiff accepted defendant's employment offer. That employment offer, which was in letter form, reads as follows: "Dear Prospective Employee: [¶] As you know, British Telecom is in the process of acquiring the Tymnet, Payment Systems and ACS businesses of McDonnell Douglas. Subject to the completion of the acquisition, I have great pleasure in offering you employment in the new company, BT Tymnet Inc., which we anticipate will be effective November 18, 1989. [¶] Your salary and job title with British Telecom will be the same as that which you last earned and held with McDonnell Douglas, subject to periodic reviews and adjustments. Your basic employee benefits will be as described in the attached Employee Benefits Transaction booklet. As with your current status with McDonnell Douglas, your employment with British Telecom is also one of employment-at-will. This employment agreement supersedes any previous employment agreements. In signing, you also agree no one is authorized to make a different employment agreement with you unless it is signed by an executive of British Telecom. [¶] Please indicate your acceptance of this offer by dating and signing on the lines below and returning this letter and the enclosed employee proprietary information agreement signed by you to Human Resources or your supervisor on or before November 18, 1989, the anticipated first day of employment with British Telecom."

Plaintiff's acceptance, which was written below the letter, reads: "I accept employment with BT Tymnet Inc. under these terms and conditions."

On its face, plaintiff's employment contract was clearly at will. "Few principles of our law are better settled, than that '[t]he language of a contract is to govern its interpretation, if the language is clear and explicit. . . .' [Citations.]" (Brandt v. Lockheed Missiles & Space Co. (1984) 154 Cal.App.3d 1124, 1129-1130.)

The question is whether other terms can be read into the contract.

Implied-in-Fact Agreement Not Triable Issue

Plaintiff claims that notwithstanding the express at-will provision of the contract, there were "oral and implied-in-fact terms and agreements" which showed that his employment was not terminable "except upon good cause and then only after reasonable warnings and reasonable opportunities to improve were given." He claims that his "five years of employment, numerous promotions, assurances of continued employment, and policies and procedures providing for progressive discipline created an implied-in-fact agreement between plaintiff and the Tymnet subsidiary of McDonnell Douglas." Plaintiff also asserts that the phrase "as with your current status with McDonnell Douglas" in the November agreement refers to his implied-in-fact agreement with MDC, and argues that there is thus raised the triable issue of what the terms of the implied agreement were.

We first note that plaintiff's alleged implied-in-fact agreement was not with defendant, but with plaintiff's previous employer, MDC. Therefore, unless defendant had assumed MDC's obligations thereunder, the alleged implied agreement would be irrelevant to determining what plaintiff's rights are under the November agreement. Nothing in the record indicates that defendant had agreed to be bound by any employment contract plaintiff might have had with MDC. To the contrary, the November agreement explicitly provides that "[t]his employment agreement supersedes any previous employment agreements."

By agreeing to supersede any prior employment agreement with the November agreement, plaintiff and defendant clearly intended to make the November agreement their only agreement on the matters therein covered. The writing was therefore an integration of the parties' agreement on the subject of when either party thereto may terminate the employment relationship. As such, parol evidence is inadmissible to contradict its terms. (Malmstrom v. Kaiser Aluminum & Chemical Corp. (1986) 187 Cal.App.3d 299, 314-316.)

As here, the contract in Malmstrom provided that it was to "'supersede all previous agreements by and between Employer and Employee.'" As plaintiff does now, Malmstrom contended that there was an oral agreement that his employment would continue "so long as he satisfactorily performed his job." (187 Cal.App.3d at p. 313.) The court held that the superseding language of the written contract showed that the contract was integrated, and therefore any oral evidence contradicting its terms was inadmissible under the parol evidence rule. Said the court: "California law presumes a written contract supersedes all prior or contemporaneous oral agreements. [Citations.] Parol evidence is admissible to establish the terms of the complete agreement of the parties only if the written agreement is not the complete and final embodiment of that agreement. [Citation.]" (Id. at p. 314.)

The Malmstrom court also noted that the superseding language "is clear on its face" and that "the alleged oral agreement is completely inconsistent with the terms of the written contract." (187 Cal.App.3d at p. 315.) It then concluded: "We hold that the contract is a contract for employment terminable at will and that, since the contract is integrated and provides that it supersedes all prior agreements, evidence of an implied agreement which contradicts the terms of the written agreement is not admissible. 'There cannot be a valid express contract and an implied contract, each embracing the same subject, but requiring different results.' [Citation.]" (Id. at p. 316.)

In Tollefson v. Roman Catholic Bishop (1990) 219 Cal.App.3d 843, 855-856, the court, addressing the same question, stated: "Indeed, there simply cannot exist a valid express contract on one hand and an implied contract on the other, each embracing the identical subject but requiring different results and treatment. [Citations.] Consequently, . . .

an employee's allegations of an implied-in-fact contract for continuing employment and benefits cannot rebut that employee's status as an at-will employee [citation] . . . ." Tollefson also held that "lengthy service combined with promotions and salary increases are natural occurrences for an employee who remains with an employer for a substantial length of time and do not evince or create an implied agreement for permanent employment, terminable within the context of nonrenewal only upon just cause. [Citation.]" (Id. at p. 856, fn. omitted.)

Similarly, in Gerdlund v. Electronic Dispensers International (1987) 190 Cal.App.3d 263, 277, the court stated that "[n]o obligation can be implied . . . which would result in the obliteration of a right expressly given under a written contract."

Significantly, the alleged implied-in-fact agreement in Malmstrom was between Malmstrom and his current employer. If oral evidence was there inadmissible to prove an implied agreement between the parties thereto, there is greater reason to exclude such evidence in this case where the party against whom the evidence is intended to be offered was not privy to the alleged implied agreement.

Granting arguendo that the "at will" provision of plaintiff's employment contract could be contradicted by parol evidence of an alleged implied-in-fact agreement that plaintiff had with MDC, and granting further that plaintiff's true agreement with defendant was that plaintiff could only be terminated for cause, plaintiff's layoff by reason of the large-scale reduction in defendant's work force was a valid cause for termination. It was held in Malmstrom v. Kaiser Aluminum & Chemical Corp., supra, 187 Cal.App.3d at page 321 citing Clutterham v. Coachman Industries, Inc. (1985) 169 Cal.App.3d 1223, 1227, that the elimination of the employee's position to reduce the working staff because of the depressed condition of the business, is a "fair and honest cause or reason, regulated by good faith" to terminate the employee.

In his opposition to defendant's summary judgment motion, plaintiff does not dispute the large-scale reduction of defendant's work force and that his position was one of those eliminated by the reduction.

Moreover, we stated in Slivinsky v. Watkins-Johnson Co. (1990) 221 Cal.App.3d 799, 806, that "[e]ven if the reduction in force were a pretextual ground for terminating Slivinsky's employment, it would not be actionable with an at-will employment contract unless 'the employer's motivation for [a] discharge contravenes some substantial public policy principle . . . .' [Citation.]" As in <u>Slivinsky</u>, plaintiff here has not demonstrated any public policy violation.

In any event, because the alleged implied-in-fact agreement was not in writing, any cause of action based thereon is subject to the two-year statute of limitations. Code of Civil Procedure section 339 provides that the statute of limitations for "[a]n action upon a contract, obligation or liability not founded upon an instrument of writing" is two years. Here, plaintiff was laid off January 15, 1990. He did not file the instant complaint until more than two years later on April 6, 1992. Clearly, the statute of limitations had run. Plaintiff's contention that the two-year period did not commence to run until he received his last salary on May 15, 1990, because it was only after that date that he suffered damage, is disingenuous. Since plaintiff's cause of action is for wrongful termination, that cause of action accrued at the time his employment was allegedly wrongfully terminated, regardless of when he received his last salary.

Plaintiff also argues mistake on the basis that in indicating the employment to be at will, the letter stated that it was to be "[a]s with your current status with McDonnell Douglas," and that his current employment status with McDonnell Douglas was not at will. Assuming that defendant was mistaken in believing that plaintiff's employment with MDC was at will, the mistake was on defendant's part; therefore, only defendant can invoke the mistake to question the contract. If plaintiff knew of the mistake at the time the contract was entered into but did nothing to correct it, he is bound by that mistake and is estopped to question it. If he did not know of the mistake, then his acceptance of the offer was on the terms therein specified, one of which was the terminability of the employment at will. Therefore, in any event, plaintiff cannot claim mistake to release himself from the effects of the contract. As stated in <u>Chan</u> v. <u>Drexel Burnham Lambert, Inc.</u> (1986) 178 Cal.App.3d 632, 641: "'As a general rule, a party is bound by the provisions of an agreement which he signs, even though he does not read them and signs unaware of their existence.' [Citation.]"

On this record, we conclude that defendant's showing has established plaintiff's employment contract with defendant to be at will, and that plaintiff's claim of an implied-in-fact agreement to the contrary fails to raise any triable issue of fact.

Implied Covenant of Good Faith and Fair Dealing Not Triable Issue

Plaintiff argues that even if he was an at-will employee, he may still bring an action for breach of the implied covenant of good faith and fair dealing based on defendant's failure to follow its own personnel policies and procedures regarding layoff, rehire, and recall.

In support of this argument, plaintiff alleges that his employment was terminated in retaliation for his participation in October 1989 in a "skip-level" review of his direct supervisor, David Alcorn. A "skip-level" review is one where the supervisor of the manager being reviewed would convene with the employees who directly reported to the manager and would solicit their evaluation of him. In this particular "skip-level" review, plaintiff was one of several employees who were asked by Bill Euske, a vice-president and Alcorn's supervisor, to evaluate Alcorn.

Plaintiff also alleges that defendant breached the implied covenant of good faith and fair dealing "by its continued refusal to re-hire him as required by the company's policies, procedures, and practices."

There is no question that "'[e]very contract imposes upon each party a duty of good faith and fair dealing in its performance and its enforcement.' [Citation.]" (Foley v. Interactive Data Corp. (1988) 47 Cal.3d 654, 683.) However, this duty "is designed to effectuate the intentions and reasonable expectations of parties reflected by mutual promises within the contract. [Citation.]" (Slivinsky v. Watkins-Johnson Co., supra, 221 Cal.App.3d at p. 806.) Therefore, "'what that duty embraces is dependent upon the nature of the bargain struck between [the parties] and the legitimate expectations of the parties which arise from the contract.' [Citation.]" (Brandt v. Lockheed Missiles & Space Co., supra, 154 Cal.App.3d at p. 1129.)

Where the employment relationship is strictly at will, "[t]he 'legitimate expectations' of employee and employer . . . can be no more than the continuation of employment until one party or the other decides to terminate the relationship. When that decision is made, "'. . . the privilege [to terminate] is absolute, and the presence of ill will or improper motive will not destroy it." [Citation.]' [Citation.]" (Hejmadi v. AMFAC, Inc. (1988) 202 Cal.App.3d 525, 547.)

Because continuous employment is not a benefit of the agreement in an at-will employment relationship, good cause is not required to terminate the relationship. The Supreme Court made this point clear in Foley v. Interactive Data Corp., supra, 47 Cal.3d at page 698, footnote 39: "[W]ith regard to an at-will employment relationship, breach of the implied covenant cannot logically be based on a claim that a discharge was made without good cause. If such an interpretation applied, then all at-will contracts would be transmuted into contracts requiring good cause for termination, and Labor Code section 2922 would be eviscerated. This is not to say that the Legislature could not impose such a requirement in every employment contract. It has not done so, however, and the implied covenant should not be read as uniformly imposing such a contractual term. Thus, in Wagenseller v. Scottsdale Memorial Hosp., supra, 710 P.2d at page 1040, the court properly stressed, '[w]hat cannot be said is that one of the agreed benefits to the at-will employee is a guarantee of continued employment or tenure.' Because the implied covenant protects only the parties' right to receive the benefit of their agreement, and, in an at-will relationship there is no agreement to terminate only for good cause, the implied covenant standing alone cannot be read to impose such a duty. [Citation.]"

In Wallis v. Farmers Group, Inc. (1990) 220 Cal.App.3d 718, 737, the court, noting that "the Supreme Court in Foley laid to rest the notion that the implied covenant of good faith and fair dealing somehow created an independent source of job security rights," stated: "'After all, when an employment relationship is—as a matter of agreement—terminable at will, terminating an employee without good cause does not deprive the employee of the benefits of the agreement.' [Citation.]"

In light of the foregoing, we conclude that plaintiff's allegation of breach of the implied covenant of good faith and fair dealing does not, in the setting of this case, raise triable issues of fact.

DISPOSITION

The judgment is affirmed. Defendant is awarded costs on appeal as the prevailing party herein.

The dispositive portion of the opinion awarded costs to the defendant as the prevailing party in the appeal. Awarding costs to the prevailing party is not a matter of discretion, but of law, because, in California, as in many other states of the Union, the rule on appellate costs is: Loser pays. Awarding mandatory costs to the prevailing party discourages frivolous appeals.

II.
Chuk v. Yen
(Unpublished)

Chuk is another contract case, involving the question of whether the corporation was bound by the agreement between Chuk, a third party who agreed to invest in the corporation, and Yen, who formed the corporation but was not a stockholder of record, although he was the corporation's vice president. This was a hard opinion to write, not because the law was not clear, because it was, but because, as a human interest story, considerations of justice and equity seem to lean on Chuk's favor. To this day, I wonder what the results might have been had Chuk raised the issue of piercing the corporate veil. "Piercing the corporate veil" is a legal doctrine that permits the court to go beyond the corporation to its stockholders or owners on the basis that the corporation is not a true corporation but merely a facade created to shield the owners from liabilities. Because it is not a true corporation, it has no legal personality of its own separate and distinct from the individual personalities of its owners and stockholders. Accordingly, the owners or stockholders cannot hide behind the corporate shield, and are liable for their acts. I had thought of asking the parties to file supplemental briefing, but I had no basis to make the request.

California appellate courts cannot address issues that are not raised and briefed by the parties. If the court thinks an issue is important, perhaps even dispositive, but the issue is not briefed, the only way for the court to reach the issue is to ask for supplemental briefing. The reason is to give the parties the opportunity to brief and argue the issue. But if the issue was not tried below, and there is nothing in the record that touches on the issue, there would be nothing for the parties to brief. This was the situation in *Chuk*.

The question of what review standard to apply played a crucial role in *Chuk*. Although the California courts of appeal review questions of law only, this does not mean that we do not look at the facts in the record. We need to know the facts because the question of whether the judgment of the trial court is supported by substantial evidence is a question of law, not of fact. If we find that the judgment is supported by substantial evidence, we have to affirm the judgment, even if we might have reached a different judgment had we been the trial court.

We applied the substantial evidence standard of review in *Chuk*. The application of that standard, which requires deference to the findings of the trial court, dictated the flow of the analysis. Because there was substantial evidence in the record to support the judgment of the trial court, Chuk lost the appeal. Tough, indeed, but *dura lex, sed lex*. (The law may be hard, but it's the law.)

The opinion in *Chuk v. Yen* follows:

FACTS

Chuk and Yen had been best friends for years. They first met in Taiwan in 1965 when they attended National Taiwan University and were members of the same mountain climbing club. Yen completed his bachelor's degree in chemistry in 1968, and Chuk completed his mechanical engineering degree a year later.

After college, Chuk and Yen pursued different careers. Following one year of military service in the Taiwan air force, Yen immigrated to the United States. He spent five years at the University of Chicago where he completed a master's degree and a Ph.D. He then went to the University of California in Berkeley where he pursued seven months of post-doctorate work in chemistry. Thereafter, Yen worked for several companies, the last of which was Xerox at its research center in Palo Alto. Yen is now a United States citizen.

Chuk, on the other hand, pursued a career in business. He established a number of companies in Hong Kong, Taiwan, and California. By 1985, Chuk had established and managed 12 new companies. Chuk also attended Northrop University near Los Angeles where he completed a master's degree in international management. In November 1988, Chuk immigrated to Canada, of which he is now a citizen.

Chuk and Yen had not seen each other since their college days in Taiwan until 1977 or 1978, when Chuk met Yen while on a trip to California. Since then, Chuk has stayed in Yen's home many times, and the Yens have also stayed in Chuk's home overseas. It was normal for Chuk to stay in Yen's home whenever he visited California.

In January 1983, while Chuk was visiting the United States and staying in Yen's home, Yen told him about his pellicle invention[1] and his project of trying to commercially produce and market pellicles. Yen explained to Chuk what a pellicle was and how it was produced. Yen showed Chuk a small room (approximately 600 square feet) which a friend had allowed him to use, and in which Yen was making his pellicles.

Yen told Chuk that MLI had been losing money. For the fiscal year ended October 1982, MLI had sold $20,000 worth of pellicles only; this was a loss of approximately $19,000. Yen discussed with Chuk his plan to move the company to another site, and what it would cost to make that move.

Yen and Chuk talked about Chuk investing in MLI. They agreed that Chuk would invest $50,000 and that this amount would represent a 10 percent share in the interest of MLI. (Hereafter, the agreement to invest $50,000 in exchange for a 10 percent share in MLI's stock will be known as the Chuk/Yen agreement.)

Mrs. Yen was not present when the Chuk/Yen agreement was entered into. However, when Mrs. Yen was told of the agreement later that day, she agreed thereto on condition that Chuk would not interfere in the operations of the company. Chuk agreed to the no-interference condition and, in fact, never interfered in the operations of MLI.

MLI is a California corporation that was organized and registered in 1981 to manufacture and market Yen's pellicle invention. At the time of the Chuk/Yen agreement, and even until the trial of this case, Yen was not a stockholder of record of MLI. The stockholders of record were Mrs. Yen, Mrs. Yen's parents, and Mrs. Yen's brother. The total number of shares outstanding at the time of the Chuk/Yen agreement was 13,000. Of this number, 7,000 were in the name of Mrs. Yen. The other 6,000 shares were owned by Mrs. Yen's parents and Mrs. Yen's brother.

Yen did not make himself a stockholder of record because, at the time of the formation of MLI in 1981, he was working with Xerox and he was afraid that if stock was issued in his name Xerox would find out

---

1 Chuk's definition of a pellicle, accepted by respondents, is: "A pellicle is a protective device composed of a thin, transparent membrane adhered to a metal frame and is used to protect photomask surfaces from harmful particle contamination by placing the pellicle over the photomask during the semiconductor chip manufacturing process."

and would not like it. Yen testified, however, that Mrs. Yen's stockholding was their community property. Although not a stockholder of record, Yen was MLI's vice president in January 1983. The president was Mrs. Yen.

MLI's articles of incorporation authorize the corporation to issue one million shares, and only one kind of stock. MLI's by-laws are not part of the record of this appeal. There is no showing if such by-laws were in fact presented as evidence in this case. Consequently, we are unable to determine what specific powers and duties Yen had as vice president under MLI's bylaws.

There is also no evidence on record as to who composed MLI's board of directors at the time of the Chuk/Yen agreement, or if any governing board had at all been constituted at that time. There is no evidence that, at the time of the Chuk/Yen agreement, Yen was authorized by corporate resolution or other form of express corporate authorization to sell any stock of MLI to Chuk.

Pursuant to the Chuk/Yen agreement, Chuk paid his $50,000 investment a few days later. He remitted it directly to MLI's bank account by wire transfer from Hong Kong. MLI used the money to move its site to a new location and to purchase new equipment.

At the time of the Chuk/Yen agreement, MLI was a start-up company. The Yens had put in approximately $20,000. There is no evidence of the amount Mrs. Yen's parents and Mrs. Yen's brother had invested at that time. The company was struggling financially, and the Yens had not been drawing salaries.

After Chuk's $50,000 investment, MLI started becoming profitable. For the fiscal year which ended October 31, 1983, MLI's sales improved to $709,000. This permitted the Yens to draw compensation in the amount of $82,000. In addition, the company generated a profit of $12,000.

For the fiscal year which ended October 31, 1984, MLI's sales further improved to $4 million, generating a profit of $362,000 after payment of $1,150,000 to Yen and Mrs. Yen. For the six-month period ended April 30, 1985, MLI's sales amounted to $2.8 million.

In May 1985, Yen retained the investment banking firm of Sutro & Co. Incorporated for the purpose of trying to sell MLI. Sutro & Co.

thereafter told Yen that it was very confident it could sell MLI for at least $10 million.

No certificates of stock were issued to Chuk. In 1985, Chuk asked Yen for a stock certificate. Yen told Chuk the issuance of his stock certificate was "delayed in the company's lawyer's office."

ISSUE

The dispositive issue in this case is whether MLI was bound by the Chuk/Yen agreement.

STANDARD OF REVIEW

The parties disagree on the standard of review to apply. Chuk contends this cause should be reviewed de novo because the facts relating to the Chuk/Yen agreement are undisputed and hence the legal significance of those facts present an issue of law. Respondents, on the other hand, contend that the correct standard is the substantial evidence standard because, contrary to Chuk's claim, the facts underlying the Chuk/Yen agreement are in fact disputed.

We think there is sufficient dispute on the material facts to require application of the substantial evidence standard of review. The critical issue of fact is whether Yen acted on behalf of the corporation or on his own behalf when he contracted with Chuk to accept Chuk's $50,000 investment in exchange for 10 percent of MLI's stock.

Chuk claims that Yen acted on behalf of MLI; respondents, on the other hand, claim that Yen acted on his own behalf. Because "[t]he existence of agency is a question of fact for the trial court" (Burr v. Capital Reserve Corp. (1969) 71 Cal.2d 983, 995), the parties' disagreement on this issue sufficiently precludes de novo review.

However, to the extent that certain facts are not disputed, we will review them as raising only questions of law, in which event we will not be bound by the substantial evidence rule. Instead, we will review them as we review all questions of law: according to our own independent determination.

There is no question that whenever the issue on appeal is sufficiency of evidence, our power as an appellate court "begins and ends with a determination as to whether there is any substantial evidence, contradicted or uncontradicted, which will support the conclusion reached by the [trier of fact]." (Crawford v. Southern Pacific Co. (1935) 3 Cal.2d 427, 429.) Moreover, in determining the presence of substantial evidence, "[a]ll of the evidence most favorable to the respondent must be accepted as true, and that unfavorable discarded as not having sufficient verity, to be accepted by the trier of fact. If the evidence so viewed is sufficient as a matter of law, the judgment must be affirmed." (Estate of Teel (1944) 25 Cal.2d 520, 527.)

However, "[s]ubstantial evidence 'is not synonymous with "any" evidence. To constitute sufficient substantiality to support the verdict, the evidence must be "reasonable in nature, credible, and of solid value; it must actually be 'substantial' proof of the essentials which the law requires in a particular case."' [Citation.]" (Osborn v. Irwin Memorial Blood Bank (1992) 5 Cal.App.4th 234, 284.)

DISCUSSION
MLI Not Bound by Chuk/Yen Agreement

In the first of its three statements of decision, the trial court stated: "On the basis of an intentionally vague personal agreement with defendant Chris Yen, plaintiff's own evidence shows no intent to bind the corporation, and the corporation never became a party to their agreement. Plaintiff's own evidence, corroborated by defendant's testimony, establishes a best-friends, informal entrustment of $50,000 to be used by defendant Chris Yen in his wife's corporation in his discretion. Plaintiff expressly avoided any binding subscription contract, preferring to allow Chris Yen to manage his investment for their mutual benefit. Agreement with Mrs. Yen was specifically avoided, and no terms or conditions of the investment were sought except giving plaintiff a 10% interest in their venture, to be managed solely by Chris Yen in his discretion—a discretion controlled, pursuant [to] the express agreement of the two parties, solely by the good faith and fairness of both of them as best friends entering into a close confidential relation."

This finding of fact, particularly the finding that there was "no intent to bind the corporation, and the corporation never became a party to their agreement," if sustained, disposes the issue on appeal.

Accordingly, we will review the record to determine if it is supported by substantial evidence.

The rule is settled that "[o]fficers have only such powers as are stated in the bylaws, or given them expressly by the directors, or by acquiescence of the directors. [Citations.]" (9 Witkin, Summary of Cal. Law (9th ed. 1989) Corporations, § 114, p. 613.)

It is not controverted that Yen entered into the Chuk/Yen agreement without the prior knowledge and express authority of MLI. There is no evidence that, prior to the Chuk/Yen agreement, MLI's board of directors had convened to consider any proposal to sell corporate stock to MLI, or that Yen had discussed the matter individually with any member of MLI's governing board.

Nor is there anything in the record to demonstrate implied authority. As stated, MLI's bylaws are not part of the record, and no evidence was introduced to define the powers and authority of Yen's office. In the absence of anything expressly defining the powers and duties of Yen's office, no implied authority can be deduced.

We likewise find nothing in the record to support any claim of ostensible authority. There is ostensible authority when "a corporation allows its officers to conduct its business and third persons act upon the apparent authority thus shown." (Fowler Gas Co. v. First Nat. Bank (1919) 180 Cal. 471, 477.) The apparent authority must derive from the corporation's conduct—not from the conduct of the individual transacting with the third party. (Burr v. Capital Reserve Corp., supra, 71 Cal.2d at p. 995.) To establish apparent authority there must be evidence that the corporation "intentionally or by want of ordinary care" caused a third party to believe that the person he or she is dealing with is clothed with corporate authority. (Id. at p. 996.)

Chuk presented no such evidence. The record does not show any conduct on the corporation's part which Chuk could have taken as authorizing Yen, on behalf of MLI, to sell to him any portion of MLI's stock. Indeed, there is nothing in the record to show that prior to the Chuk/Yen agreement Chuk had any dealings with MLI.

Chuk was not without experience in transactions involving sale of corporate stock. To the contrary, he had long and wide experience in such matters. He had organized and managed 12 corporations of his own in Taiwan, Hong Kong, and California. He therefore knew or should have known that any person selling corporate stock must have the authority of the corporation to do so.

Even Yen's conduct evinced no attempt to mislead Chuk into believing that Yen was acting for MLI. Chuk's own testimony does not show that when he entered into the Chuk/Yen agreement he thought he was contracting with MLI. Chuk merely testified that he agreed with Yen to buy 10 percent of MLI stock; he did not testify that he thought he was buying the stock from MLI or that Yen had claimed to possess authority to represent MLI in the deal.

Because Yen had neither express nor implied nor ostensible authority from MLI to sell MLI stock to Chuk, MLI did not become a party to the Chuk/Yen agreement and was not bound thereby.

Chuk claims, however, that there was subsequent ratification because MLI accepted Chuk's $50,000 investment, and the minutes of MLI's board of directors' meeting in October 1983 (hereafter, October minutes) showed that MLI had accepted and recognized Chuk as a stockholder of MLI. We disagree.

Acceptance by MLI of Chuk's $50,000 investment was not inconsistent with any private agreement between Chuk and Yen for Chuk to invest in MLI stocks in the manner found by the trial court, i.e.: "a best-friends, informal entrustment of $50,000 to be used by defendant Chris Yen in his wife's corporation in his discretion." The fact that MLI was not a party to the contract did not preclude Chuk and Yen from agreeing to invest in MLI stocks or Chuk from remitting his investment directly to MLI's account.

Because, as found by the trial court and demonstrated by the record, Chuk and Yen never intended to bind the corporation and made no attempt to do so, the corporation had nothing to ratify. Ratification is the subsequent adoption or affirmance by the corporation of an act that an individual has assumed to do on behalf of the corporation without previous authority. (1 Marsh & Finkle, Marsh's Cal. Corporation Law (3d. ed., 1993 supp.) § 928, p. 650.)

The same is true of the October minutes. Because the absence of any intent to bind the corporation provided the corporation with nothing to ratify, the October minutes cannot be considered an act of ratification.

Moreover, although "[t]he usual conduct which will establish ratification is voluntary <u>acceptance of the benefits of the transaction by the principal</u> . . . the acquiescence or acceptance of benefits must be with <u>full knowledge of the material facts</u>, and at the time the principal learns of the unauthorized act he must be in a position to reject it and restore the things received." (2 Witkin, Summary of Cal. Law, <u>supra</u>, Agency and Employment, § 89, pp. 89-90.) "The principal must have full knowledge of the material facts at the time of the act of ratification. No ratification by acceptance of benefits results in the absence of such knowledge [citation], and even an express ratification may be rescinded for lack of it. [Citation.]" (<u>Id</u>. at § 92, p. 91.)

Civil Code section 1589 is to the same effect: "A voluntary acceptance of the benefit of a transaction is equivalent to a consent to all the obligations arising from it, <u>so far as the facts are known, or ought to be known</u>, to the person accepting." (Emphasis added.)

Thus it has been held that ratification by voluntary acceptance of benefits "only applies where it is shown that the principal had full knowledge of the acts which it is claimed were ratified." (<u>Bourne</u> v. <u>Root</u> (1932) 125 Cal.App. 461, 464.)

Here, the Chuk/Yen agreement was itself vague on material facts. It is not clear, for example, whether the 10 percent was a straight sale of 10 percent of the outstanding stock, which at that time was 13,000 shares, or whether it was a subscription contract to 10 percent of MLI's authorized stock, which the articles of incorporation had set at one million shares. If the agreement was a subscription contract, it is not clear what the full consideration or the manner of payment was to be.

It is also not clear what kind of stock Chuk was to receive. MLI's articles of incorporation authorize MLI to issue only one kind of stock. However, it is evident that Chuk's stock was to be of a different kind than those held by the other shareholders in that, unlike the stocks of the other shareholders, Chuk's stock was not to allow him to interfere in the business of the corporation. Did this mean that Chuk's stock was to be nonvoting? If so, did the Chuk/Yen agreement include an understanding to amend MLI's articles of incorporation so that MLI could issue more than one class of shares?

These facts were material to understand the import of the Chuk/Yen agreement. But as neither Chuk nor Yen had evinced a clear understanding of what the Chuk/Yen agreement provided in regard thereto, MLI's board of directors cannot be charged with full knowledge thereof at the time the acts of ratification were supposedly performed. Therefore, there was no valid ratification.

In any event, while the October minutes showed that Chuk owned 10 percent of the corporate stock and was named a director of MLI, there is also evidence that the October minutes merely reflected a "scheme" for future action that was never implemented. The presence of contrary evidence does not permit us to reweigh the evidence and substitute our judgment for that of the trial court.

For the same reasons that we reject Chuk's ratification argument, we hold that the doctrine of estoppel does not here apply. There cannot be estoppel against the corporation where the acceptance by the corporation of Chuk's investment was not inconsistent with Chuk and Yen agreeing between themselves to invest in MLI stock without any intent on their part to make MLI a party to that agreement.

The fact that Mrs. Yen subsequently consented to the Chuk/Yen agreement does not compel the conclusion that MLI became a party thereto. Mrs. Yen was the wife of Yen. There is testimony that although Yen was not a named stockholder of MLI, the stocks in Mrs. Yen's name were in fact the Yens' community property. Therefore, any conformity by Mrs. Yen to the Chuk/Yen agreement was not inconsistent with the consent that a wife might have given to her husband concerning a decision affecting their community property.

Because we find substantial evidence to support the trial court's conclusion that the agreement was a private agreement between Chuk and Yen which did not bind MLI, the other issues raised by Chuk in this appeal, except the joint venture and cost award issues, are moot.

No Joint Venture

Chuk contends that, alternatively, the Chuk/Yen agreement was a joint venture and, therefore, he is entitled to the remedies of a joint venturer. We disagree.

The record shows that following the trial of this case Chuk moved to amend his complaint in order to allege a joint venture agreement as conforming to proof. The trial court denied the motion on the basis that Chuk had neither pleaded nor proved a joint venture agreement.

The rule is settled that a denial of a motion to amend should be reversed only if the trial court abused its discretion. (City of Stanton v. Cox (1989) 207 Cal.App.3d 1557, 1563.) Here, we find no abuse of discretion. Chuk waited more than five years before making his motion to amend; he asserted no new facts in support of the motion; and he waited until after trial to file the motion, without demonstrating any justifiable excuse for the delay.

In any event, the undisputed facts do not support a joint venture. "A joint venture exists where there is an 'agreement between the parties under which they have a community of interest, that is, a joint interest, in a common business undertaking, an understanding as to the sharing of profits and losses, and a right of joint control.' [Citations.]" (Bank of California v. Connolly (1973) 36 Cal.App.3d 350, 364.) Here, it is undisputed that Chuk had agreed to not interfere in the operations of MLI. Chuk, therefore, did not have a "right of joint control" over the "common business undertaking."

Cost Award

Chuk contends that the cost award of $45,655.50 for two expert witnesses under Code of Civil Procedure sections 998 and 2034[2] and the award of $7,981.25 as special master fees should be stricken. We disagree.

On the expert witness fees, Chuk claims that the award was unauthorized because the two expert witnesses were not disclosed and did not testify at trial. Citing Evers v. Cornelson (1984) 163 Cal.App.3d 310, 317, Chuk argues that the "costs of the services of expert witness" that section 998, subdivision (c), allows are costs for the services of potential witnesses. Chuk reasons that because Barrington Consulting Group (hereafter, Barrington) and Trademark & Licensing Associates (hereafter, TLA) were not disclosed, they were not potential witnesses.

---

[2] Further statutory references in this case are to the Code of Civil Procedure unless otherwise stated.

Chuk's reliance on Evers is misplaced. Evers held that an expert witness does not need to testify at trial in order to permit a party utilizing his or her services to recover costs under section 998; it is enough if the expert witness "at least aided in the preparation of the case for trial," so long as the expert is a potential witness. (Evers v. Cornelson, supra, 163 Cal.App.3d at p. 317.) And an expert witness "was potentially an expert witness whose services were obtained in preparation for trial." (Ibid.)

Here, there is evidence that respondents hired Barrington as a potential witness on financial matters although they presented only one witness at trial. Likewise, there is evidence that respondents retained TLA to provide expert testimony on patent royalties in response to Chuk's allegation that MLI had improperly paid Yen excessive royalties on his patents. Indeed, Dr. Plummer testified that he utilized the work product of both Barrington and TLA in giving his expert testimony.

As to the special master fees, Chuk contends that Superior Court Judge Cliff did not have jurisdiction to award special master fees because Judge Stewart had earlier issued an order of reference to special master for discovery matters in which the court ordered that "[t]he Special Master's fees shall be paid one-half each by Plaintiff and Defendants." Chuk argues that Judge Cliff's order constituted a total reversal of Judge Stewart's order and, as a matter of law, Judge Cliff had no jurisdiction to reverse Judge Stewart.

The argument is untenable. As held in Winston Square Homeowner's Assn. v. Centex West, Inc. (1989) 213 Cal.App.3d 282, 293: "A special master having been appointed by the court, his or her fee is analogous to the award of '[f]ees of expert witnesses ordered by the court.' [Citations.] The expense of court-appointed experts is first apportioned and charged to the parties, and then the prevailing party's share is allowed as an item of costs. [Citation.]"

We think it quite clear that on this record the trial court committed no error and abused no discretion in awarding the questioned costs.

DISPOSITION

The judgment is affirmed. Respondents are awarded costs on appeal as the prevailing party herein.

III.
Sunshine Western v. Hearrean
(Unpublished)

Sunshine addresses the issue of the validity and enforceability of work contracts entered into by unlicensed contractors. In California, contractors must obtain a state license before engaging in business. Unlicensed contractors have virtually no rights under the law. Contracts entered into by unlicensed contractors are void as to them. They cannot enforce and sue on those contracts. The purpose of the law is to protect the public from contractors who may not be adequately funded, bonded, or competently trained and equipped. There is no similar licensing requirement in the Philippines, and contracts entered into by unlicensed contractors are not subject to the same unenforceability sanctions.

Sunshine also discusses some aspects of arbitration practice in California. It is heartening to note that arbitration, as a form of alternative dispute resolution, is now gaining headway in the Philippines. Because of docket backlog in Philippine courts, resort to arbitration should drastically cut dispute time. However, for this mode of dispute resolution to succeed, the parties to the dispute must have absolute trust and confidence in the fairness and competence of the arbitrators. This means creating a pool of arbitrators whose reputation for probity, integrity, and competence is unassailable. When arbitration, as a form of alternative dispute resolution, gets accepted by litigants, it can be more effective than court proceedings. Arbitration is much faster, simpler, less combative, less expensive, and less stressful.

The opinion in *Sunshine v. Hearrean* follows:

FACTUAL BACKGROUND

In June 1988, Roy Hearrean and his wife Elda purchased the Santa Clara Airport Plaza Hotel. After the purchase, Hearrean redesigned and renovated the hotel. The renovation involved the construction of a nine-story tower which housed function rooms and suites. Hearrean, a licensed general contractor, utilized his wholly-owned company, State Wide Investors, Inc., to administer and supervise the renovation.

Respondents sought bids for the various aspects of the construction. R. P. Richards, Inc. (hereafter, RPR) submitted a bid for the construction of the heating, ventilation, and air conditioning (hereafter, HVAC) and plumbing systems. Respondents accepted RPR's bid. When respondents presented the contract to RPR for signature, RPR informed respondents that it was unable to execute the contract, but that appellant, who was RPR's non-union arm, would be executing the contract and performing the work. Pressed by the necessity to maintain the construction schedule, respondents gave the subcontracting job to appellant.

Respondents' contract with appellant provided for appellant to construct the HVAC and the plumbing mechanical systems. The HVAC contract cost was $513,000, while the plumbing contract cost was $460,962. Unknown to respondents at the time, appellant did not have an HVAC contractor's license (C-20); appellant's license was as a plumbing contractor (C-36).[3] Appellant represented in the contract that it was licensed to perform the scope of the work defined in the contract, which included HVAC installation.

Appellant had no previous experience in a project of the type, size, or scale it had undertaken for respondents. Appellant was principally a residential plumbing contractor and had never had a commercial or high-rise hotel project prior to the contract.

When the HVAC system was first tested, there was a considerable noise problem, particularly in the hotel's meeting rooms and ballrooms. Appellant had failed to install the insulation system that was necessary to attenuate the sound. As a result, respondents hired another HVAC contractor to remedy the problem.

During the course of the construction, disputes arose between respondents and appellant concerning the quality of appellant's work and delays in the completion of the construction. Respondents claimed that appellant's lack of proper experience and financial capability resulted in delays and substandard quality of performance. Appellant denied respondents' claims.

After the renovation was completed, respondents withheld payment to appellant, claiming that appellant's delays and defective performance had resulted in respondents having to incur additional

---

[3] RPR had both a plumbing contractor's license and an HVAC contractor's license.

costs and expenses, and to suffer loss of income from the delayed opening of the hotel.

In November 1990, appellant filed the instant action. Respondents answered and cross-complained, alleging breach of contract and negligence by appellant.

Respondents petitioned the court to compel arbitration pursuant to the arbitration clause of the contract. Appellant filed no opposition. The court granted the petition.

Following a lengthy arbitration, the arbitrator issued his statement of decision and award. The arbitrator denied appellant's claims on the basis that appellant had no HVAC license throughout the course of performance of its work. The arbitrator also denied respondents' claims on their cross-complaint on the basis that the balance of contract owing to appellant was sufficient to offset the damages incurred by respondents.

At the arbitration hearing, appellant did not question the arbitrator's jurisdiction to decide the license issue. To the contrary, appellant introduced evidence to support its position that it was properly licensed to perform the HVAC scope of the contract, arguing that its plumbing license covered HVAC contracting "supplementally and incidentally."

On or about January 4, 1993, appellant moved for reconsideration and, in the alternative, to reopen the hearing for new testimony and evidence. The arbitrator denied appellant's motion.

After the arbitrator had confirmed the finality of his decision, appellant moved in superior court to declare the arbitrator's decision invalid, contending that because appellant was not properly licensed the contract was void and nonexistent, and because the contract was nonexistent, there was no arbitration provision that could be enforced; consequently, the arbitrator was without authority to decide the license issue. The court denied appellant's motion, and confirmed and granted the arbitrator's award.

On April 1, 1993, the court entered judgment decreeing that appellant was to take nothing by way of its complaint, and that respondents take nothing by way of their cross-complaint. The parties were to bear their respective costs.

This appeal ensued.

DISCUSSION

There is only one central issue in this appeal: the legal effects of the contract entered into between respondents and appellant, in light of the arbitrator's finding that appellant, during the entire performance of the HVAC work, was not properly licensed pursuant to Business and Professions Code section 7031.[4] As a corollary issue, appellant contends the arbitrator was without jurisdiction to declare the contract illegal.

For the reasons discussed hereunder, we hold that the bar of section 7031 applied to appellant only; respondents were not similarly barred. Therefore, the arbitration clause was enforceable, and the arbitrator did not exceed his jurisdiction in deciding the license issue.

Section 7031 provides, in relevant part: "(a) Except as provided in subdivision (d), no person engaged in the business or acting in the capacity of a contractor, may bring or maintain any action, or recover in law or equity in any action, in any court of this state for the collection of compensation for the performance of any act or contract for which a license is required by this chapter without alleging that he or she was a duly licensed contractor at all times during the performance of that act or contract, regardless of the merits of the cause of action brought by the person . . . ."

Appellant argues that a contract entered into in violation of section 7031 is illegal and void; and because it is void, it cannot confer upon the arbitrator the power and jurisdiction to arbitrate any dispute arising from the contract. Further, appellant contends that the issue of the legality of a contract is in any event a purely judicial question, and therefore the arbitrator exceeded his powers when he ruled the contract invalid. None of these contentions has merit.

On the illegality issue, appellant relies on the 1949 case of <u>Loving & Evans</u> v. <u>Blick</u> (1949) 33 Cal.2d 603. In that case, the copartnership of Loving and Evans entered into a contract with Blick for the repair and remodeling of Blick's premises. The contract was on "a cost plus ten percent (10%) basis," and provided that any controversy between the parties should be submitted to arbitration. Loving had a contractor's license, but his partner Evans did not. The partnership itself, as a business

---

[4] Further statutory references in this case are to the Business and Professions Code unless otherwise stated.

entity, did not possess a contractor's license. After the work was completed, Blick paid the partnership some amount of money, but the partnership claimed that an additional amount was due. The dispute was submitted to arbitration. The arbitrator found for the partnership and awarded it the balance due. Upon the partnership's application, the superior court confirmed the arbitrator's award. The Supreme Court reversed the trial court, noting that because the partnership was not licensed to engage in the contracting business, "[t]here can be no question but that this case presents a clear violation of the statutes regulating the contracting business." (Id. at p. 607.)

The court stated: "'[A] contract made contrary to the terms of a law designed for the protection of the public and prescribing a penalty for the violation thereof is illegal and void, and no action may be brought to enforce such contract' [citations]; and that 'whenever the illegality appears, whether the evidence comes from one side or the other, the disclosure is fatal to the case.' [Citations.]" (33 Cal.2d at pp. 607-608.)

The court further stated that "[t]he question of the validity of the basic contract being essentially a judicial question, it remains such whether it is presented in a proceeding 'for an order directing . . . arbitration' under section 1282 of the Code of Civil Procedure or in a proceeding 'for an order confirming' or 'vacating an award' under sections 1287 and 1288 of said code. If it is presented in a proceeding under said section 1282 and it appears to the court from the uncontradicted evidence that the contract is illegal, the court should deny the petition 'for an order directing the parties to proceed to arbitration.' If it is presented in a proceeding under said section 1287 or 1288 and similar uncontradicted evidence is offered, the court should deny confirmation and should vacate any award granting relief under the illegal contract upon the ground that the arbitrator exceeded his powers in making such award." (33 Cal.2d at p. 610.)

Loving & Evans is distinguishable. There, the arbitrator decided in favor of the unlicensed contractor. The award therefore permitted the unlicensed contractor to enforce an unenforceable contract, contrary to the clear language and intent of section 7031. The court applied the illegal contract doctrine to strike down the confirmation award.

That is not the situation here. The arbitrator's award in this case does not result in enforcing an illegal contract; to the contrary, it precisely precludes the enforcement of such contract. Hence, whereas the arbitrator's award in Loving & Evans disserved the ends of section 7031, the award in this case serves those ends.

This distinction is critical. To apply Loving & Evans to this case would produce the very result that Loving & Evans disapproved. It would, in effect, make appellant's violation of the law its own excuse for the violation.

Appellant has failed to cite any case wherein Loving & Evans has been applied to affirm an award made in favor of the unlicensed contractor or to reverse an award made against the unlicensed contractor. In fact, the courts have refused to apply Loving & Evans where to do so would permit the unlicensed contractor to recover in a section 7031 violation.

In Lewis & Queen v. N. M. Ball Sons (1957) 48 Cal.2d 141, for example, where the unlicensed subcontractor sued the licensed general contractor to recover payment for work done after the state had paid the general contractor, the court refused to allow the unlicensed subcontractor to recover, stating: "Since plaintiff did not comply with the statute, it cannot 'bring or maintain any action in any court of this State for the collection of compensation. . . .' [Citations.]" (Id. at p. 150.)

Responding to the unlicensed subcontractor's contention that justice required that the general contractor be compelled to turn over to the unlicensed contractor that part of the proceeds attributable to the unlicensed contractor's labor, the court continued: "One answer to this contention is that, even in the absence of a provision such as section 7031, the courts generally will not enforce an illegal bargain or lend their assistance to a party who seeks compensation for an illegal act. The reason for this refusal is not that the courts are unaware of possible injustice between the parties, and that the defendant may be left in possession of some benefit he should in good conscience turn over to the plaintiff, but that this consideration is outweighed by the importance of deterring illegal conduct. Knowing that they will receive no help from the courts and must trust completely to each other's good faith, the parties are less likely to enter an illegal arrangement in the first place. [Citations.] [¶] . . . Section 7031 represents a legislative determination that the importance of deterring unlicensed persons from engaging in the contracting business outweighs any harshness between the parties, and that such deterrence can best be realized by denying violators the right to maintain any action for compensation in the courts of the state [citation]." (48 Cal.2d at pp. 150-151.)

Because of the deterrent purpose of section 7031, the court concluded that while unlicensed contractors cannot maintain an action to enforce the contract, the persons with whom they contract may do so. "[W]hen the Legislature enacts a statute forbidding certain conduct for the purpose of protecting one class of persons from the activities of another, a member of the protected class may maintain an action notwithstanding the fact that he has shared in the illegal transaction. The protective purpose of the legislation is realized by allowing the plaintiff to maintain his action against a defendant within the class primarily to be deterred. In this situation it is said that the plaintiff is not in pari delicto. [Citations.]" (48 Cal.2d at p. 153.)

The Lewis & Queen view that section 7031 does not make the contracting parties in pari delicto was also the view the court took in Domach v. Spencer (1980) 101 Cal.App.3d 308, 312: "The bar of Business and Professions Code section 7031 applies by its terms only to the person acting in the capacity of a contractor and not to a member of the public. To apply that statute to members of the public would defeat its purpose by providing a shield from litigation for an unlicensed builder due to the fortuity that he had been paid. Such an interpretation is supported by neither the statutory nor decisional law of this state and is unwarranted."

Furthermore, the bar of section 7031 applies regardless of whether the property owner knew that the contractor was not licensed. (Pickens v. American Mortgage Exchange (1969) 269 Cal.App.2d 299, 302.)

However, the bar of section 7031 does not preclude the unlicensed builder from setting up the defense of nonpayment in an action brought by the property owner against the unlicensed contractor. (Culbertson v. Cizek (1964) 225 Cal.App.2d 451, 473.) In Culbertson, the court held that "although Cizek was found not to hold the required contractor's license, the foregoing statute and rule of law do not prevent him from offsetting as a defense against sums due the plaintiffs any amounts that would otherwise be due Cizek under his contract. [Citations.]" (Ibid.) The court explained that "[t]he philosophy of these cases permits the unlicensed contractor to assert his counterdemands defensively as it were, to the end of reducing in whole or in part the claims against him but without authorizing an affirmative judgment in the contractor's favor for an excess. [Citation.]" (Id. at p. 473, fn. omitted.)

In light of all the foregoing, we conclude that appellant's claim of illegality under section 7031 did not preclude respondents from enforcing the arbitration clause of the contract, did not preclude the arbitrator from conducting the arbitration hearing and making his award thereon, and did not preclude the trial court from confirming the arbitration award.

There now only remains appellant's contention that even if the arbitration agreement is valid the arbitrator exceeded his jurisdiction when he decided the issue of the legality of the contract. Appellant argues that "the illegality of a contract is a matter for the court to decide, not the arbitrator."

First, Loving & Evans did not hold that the arbitrator cannot decide questions of law. All Loving & Evans said was: "[T]he rules which give finality to the arbitrator's determination of ordinary questions of fact or of law are inapplicable where the issue of illegality of the entire transaction is raised in a proceeding for the enforcement of the arbitrator's award. When so raised, the issue is one for judicial determination upon the evidence presented to the trial court, and any preliminary determination of legality by the arbitrator, whether in the nature of a determination of a pure question of law or a mixed question of fact and law, should not be held to be binding upon the trial court." (Loving & Evans v. Blick, supra, 33 Cal.2d at p. 609.)

Clearly, to argue that the lack of finality of the arbitrator's decision on a point of law amounts to excess of jurisdiction is impermissible non sequitur. Neither logic nor statute supports such a leap in reasoning.

Moreover, the rigidity of the Loving & Evans opinion has been relaxed over time. In Ericksen, Arbuthnot, McCarthy, Kearney & Walsh, Inc. v. 100 Oak Street (1983) 35 Cal.3d 312, decided eight years after Loving & Evans, the court narrowed substantially the application of Loving & Evans by holding that fraud-in-the-inducement cases are arbitrable. In a long footnote, the court explained: " Ericksen relies on cases which have held that when the issue of illegality of the contract has been raised, judicial determination is required, and the arbitrator's decision on legality does not bind the court. [¶] In Loving & Evans v. Blick (1949) 33 Cal.2d 603, this court dealt with an agreement which, because it had been executed by an unlicensed contractor in violation of statute, was unenforceable. [Citation.] The plurality opinion by Justice Spence asserted that it would violate public policy to allow a party to enforce through arbitration what it could not enforce through litigation. [Citation.] The plurality declared that the court, and not the arbitrator, must determine the issue of illegality of the entire transaction [citation]; it cited earlier cases holding that the power of the arbitrator to determine the rights of the parties is dependent upon a valid contract; in the absence of a valid contract no such rights can arise and the arbitrator has no power to determine 'such nonexistent rights.' [Citations.] [¶] [] The illegality cases are distinguishable. As the Loving plurality noted, it would violate public policy to allow a party to do through arbitration what it cannot do through litigation. Also, it has been recognized that a claim of illegality in an incidental clause of the contract, that falls short of affording grounds for revocation of the entire contract, is subject to arbitration. [Citation.] Arbitrators can decide questions of law [citation], and 'It is of the very nature of the arbitration process that it should not be halted upon the claim the arbitrators will make an illegal award.' [Citation.]" (Id. at pp. 316-317, fn. 2.)

In holding that legality issues outside of the Loving & Evans variety are arbitrable, the Ericksen court stated: "California courts have observed in other contexts the dangers inherent in committing preliminary issues to the courts. 'If participants in the arbitral process begin to assert all possible legal or procedural defenses in court proceedings before the arbitration itself can go forward, "the arbitral wheels would very soon grind to a halt."' [Citation.] Referring preliminary issues to the courts can cause '"serious delay and confusion, thus robbing the arbitration procedure of much of its value to the parties."' [Citation.] And, we have recently warned against 'procedural gamesmanship' aimed at undermining the advantages of arbitration. [Citation.] A statutory interpretation which would yield such results is not to be preferred. [¶] . . . In this state, as under federal law [citation], doubts concerning the scope of arbitrable issues are to be resolved in favor of arbitration. [Citations.]" (35 Cal.3d at p. 323.)

In any event, appellant misperceives the arbitrator's finding. The arbitrator did not declare the contract invalid. He simply found that appellant did not possess the proper license to perform the HVAC work, and that "the failure to have an HVAC license precludes Sunshine from asserting any claim in this proceeding under the provisions of Business and Professions Code [section] 7031." In other words, from the arbitrator's finding that appellant was not properly licensed, the bar of section 7031 merely followed as a matter of law. The arbitrator did not have to declare the contract invalid for section 7031 to apply, and in fact he did not do so.

Moreover, it is evident that section 7031 considers the issue of whether a contractor is licensed or not as an issue of fact. Subdivision (c) of that section clearly sets forth the evidentiary requirement to determine that issue: "If licensure or proper licensure is controverted, then proof of licensure pursuant to this section shall be made by production of a verified certificate of licensure from the Contractors' State License Board which establishes that the individual or entity bringing the action was duly licensed in the proper classification of contractors at all times during the performance of any act or contract covered by the action. Nothing herein shall require any person or entity controverting licensure or proper licensure to produce a verified certificate. When licensure or proper licensure is controverted, the burden of proof to establish licensure or proper licensure shall be on the licensee."

But even if the question was one of law, the arbitrator's determination was still final and binding on the parties and the court. "[I]t is the general rule that, with narrow exceptions, an arbitrator's decision cannot be reviewed for errors of fact or law. In reaffirming this general rule, we recognize there is a risk that the arbitrator will make a mistake. That risk, however, is acceptable for two reasons. First, by voluntarily submitting to arbitration, the parties have agreed to bear that risk in return for a quick, inexpensive, and conclusive resolution to their dispute. [Citation.] As one commentator explains, 'the parties to an arbitral agreement knowingly take the risks of error of fact or law committed by the arbitrators and that this is a worthy "trade-off" in order to obtain speedy decisions by experts in the field whose practical experience and worldly reasoning will be accepted as correct by other experts.' [Citation.] 'In other words, it is within the power of the arbitrator to make a mistake either legally or factually. When parties opt for the forum of arbitration they agree to be bound by the decision of that forum knowing that arbitrators, like judges, are fallible.' [Citation.]" (Moncharsh v. Heily & Blase (1992) 3 Cal.4th 1, 11-12.)

We conclude the trial court committed no error in confirming the arbitration award.

DISPOSITION

The judgment is affirmed. Respondents are awarded costs on appeal as the prevailing party herein.

IV.
People v. Blomquist
(Unpublished)

Blomquist is included in this collection because of its unusual facts. The legal issues are quite straightforward. *Blomquist* is about parents who refused to take their sick child to a doctor because they did not trust doctors and believed that there were betters ways of treating ailments than using drugs. The question is whether the refusal to seek medical help, which resulted in the deterioration of the child's health, constituted child endangerment, child abuse, and torture, which are serious offenses.

The opinion in *People v. Blomquist* follows:

FACTS

Father and Ethel Mae Blomquist (hereafter, Mother) are the parents of 10-year-old Steven. (Hereafter, Father and Mother will collectively be called Parents.) In December 1991, Steven fell ill. Parents thought the ailment was flu. In fact, Steven had Addison's disease, an ailment involving gradual failure of the adrenal glands. The symptoms included lethargy, physical weakness, and vomiting.

Parents did not take Steven to a doctor. Parents did not trust doctors; they believed there were better ways of dealing with illness than using drugs.

In February 1992, Parents started attending classes on healing through nutrition taught by a holistic "doctor" named Bud Keith. Keith held himself out as an expert in "pneumiatrics," a theory of healing based on nutrition principles found in the bible. Parents accepted Keith's teachings, and changed the family's eating habits: heavier meals, with foods such as red meat and potatoes, in the morning; lighter meals of chicken or tuna for lunch; and salad and fruit for supper. Certain exercises and food supplements were also prescribed for Steven.

The dietary changes and exercise regimen did not improve Steven's health. As Steven's health deteriorated, Father began to believe that Steven's problem was mental, born out of Steven's rebelliousness toward Parents. Father believed that the matter had developed into a contest of wills between him and Steven, and that Steven was manipulating his illness and vomiting. Keith suggested "aversion therapy," pursuant to which Steven was required to eat his own vomit. The theory was, if Steven was required to eat what he vomited, he would stop vomiting. When Steven could not eat all that he had vomited, Parents would save the rest for later.

Father would spank Steven if Steven did not eat his vomit. Father at first used a belt and a small branch of a tree to spank Steven, then later abandoned those items in favor of a wooden spoon.

Mother kept a daily record of Steven's misconduct which she would give to Father when Father returned home from work. If there was only one item on the list at the end of the day, Steven would receive 10 spanks. If the record listed more items, Steven would be spanked around 50 times. Steven thought that on June 26, 1992, the day he was taken to the hospital, Father had spanked him with the wooden spoon about 100 times. One or two days earlier, Father had also spanked Steven about 75 times.

At about 10 p.m. of June 26, 1992, while Father was walking down the hall of the Blomquist home, he heard Steven coughing, which indicated that Steven was about to vomit. Father entered Steven's room and saw Steven lean over one side of the bed as if to throw up; he then leaned back and stopped breathing. Father gave Steven CPR and called out for his other children to call 911. Scott, Steven's older brother, made the call.

What happened on the night of June 26 was not the result of the spankings that Steven had received. It was a full-scale manifestation of Addisonian crisis, a stage in which the patient virtually stops breathing and develops dangerously abnormal heart rhythms.

The emergency team that responded to Scott's 911 call took Steven to the hospital. The failure of Steven's adrenal glands was life threatening. However, Steven responded to treatment. After more than a month of hospitalization, Steven was released from the hospital and was able to fully recuperate. Steven is now in foster care.

Following the June 26 Addisonian crisis, Parents were charged with child endangerment (now § 273a, subd. (a); count 1), torture (§ 206; count 2), and child abuse (§ 273d; counts 3 & 4). Count 3 related to acts of child abuse committed between June 1, 1992 and June 25,

1992. Count 4 related to acts of child abuse committed on June 26, 1992.

Father was convicted as charged, and Mother was convicted of one count of felony child endangerment and three counts of misdemeanor child endangerment.

The jury's special verdict stated that the torture conviction in count 2 was based upon the same act or acts as the child abuse conviction in count 4.

The trial court sentenced Father to a total prison term of six years and four months for the child endangerment and child abuse convictions. Pursuant to section 654, the trial court stayed execution of the sentence for the torture conviction, which was for life imprisonment with possibility of parole.

CONTENTIONS

Father appeals the torture conviction only. He contends section 206 is unconstitutionally vague in the absence of a saving construction of the intent element, and that his conviction under that statute deprived him of due process of law.

The People cross-appeal that part of the judgment staying execution of the sentence for the torture conviction, contending that section 654 did not give the trial judge discretion to stay execution of that sentence.

DISCUSSION
Father's Appeal

Father's contention that section 206 is unconstitutionally vague is without merit.

Section 206 provides: "Every person who, with the intent to cause cruel or extreme pain and suffering for the purpose of revenge, extortion, persuasion, or for any sadistic purpose, inflicts great bodily injury as defined in Section 12022.7 upon the person of another, is guilty of torture. [¶] The crime of torture does not require any proof that the victim suffered pain."

On the torture offense, the trial court instructed the jury, as follows: "Every person who, with the intent to cause cruel or extreme pain and suffering for the purpose of revenge, persuasion, or for any sadistic purpose, inflicts great bodily injury upon the person of another, is guilty of the crime of torture, in violation of section 206 of the Penal Code. [¶] Great bodily injury means a significant or substantial physical injury. Minor, trivial or moderate injuries do not constitute great bodily injury. [¶] The crime of torture does not require any proof that the perpetrator intended to kill the other person or the person upon whom the injury was inflicted suffered pain. [¶] In order to prove such crime, each of the following elements must be proved: [¶] One, a person inflicted great bodily injury upon the person of another; [¶] and two, the person inflicting the injury did so with specific intent to cause cruel or extreme pain and suffering for the purpose of revenge, persuasion, or for any sadistic purpose."

In arguing vagueness, Father cites to the jury's action on the third day of deliberations of sending the court a note asking for definitions of the terms "specific intent" and "extreme pain." Father argues that by requesting the court to further define "extreme pain," the jurors "put their collective finger on the central constitutional defect in section 206: the phrase 'cruel or extreme pain and suffering' fails to provide meaningful guidance to jurors as to the specific intent required as an element of the crime. The 'ordinary meaning' of the phrases 'cruel pain and suffering' and 'extreme pain and suffering' simply have no objective content."

We are not persuaded. The record shows that upon receipt of the jury's question the court consulted with counsel, following which, the court sent the following written response to the jury: "The term 'specific intent' is defined as follows: When the definition of a crime consists of only the description of a particular act, without reference to intent to do a further act or achieve a future consequence, we ask whether the defendant intended to do the proscribed act. This intention is deemed to be a general criminal intent. When the definition refers to defendant's intent to do some further act or achieve some additional consequence, the crime is deemed to be one of specific intent. The phrase 'extreme pain' is defined in the common ordinary meaning of those words. If further clarification is required, please indicate so to the Court."

Mother's attorney requested that the term "extreme pain" be also defined, and submitted to the court the dictionary definition of "extreme." The court refused the request, explaining: "The reason the court is basically telling them that there is no specific legal definition of the term extreme pain is because that is, in fact, my understanding of the law. [¶] And in fact, I think that's consistent with Mr. Kroeber's [Mother's attorney's] position, because Mr. Kroeber proposes to define the term by resorting to a standard English dictionary, which is consistent with the court's response to the jury question that it is defined in its common, ordinary meaning of those words. [¶] And I think it's further clarified in my response by saying, if further clarification is required, please indicate so to the court. If, after they understand that there's no—that this is not a term of art, but rather a phrase that is to be construed in its common, ordinary meaning, if they then don't know what the common, ordinary meaning of that phrase is, then, as I've indicated to counsel in chambers, and I'll indicate it for the record, I'm then fully prepared to give them an English dictionary definition of that phrase, particularly the word extreme. [¶] I don't think we need to define pain. I think the focus is on the word extreme. But I think they're looking for this to be some type of a term of art like great bodily injury or like serious bodily injury, these phrases which have specific meanings in the law. Extreme pain just means extreme pain."

We believe the court correctly perceived that in seeking clarification the jury simply wanted to know if the term "extreme pain" was to be understood in a sense different from the ordinary meaning of the words. When the court instructed the jury that the term was to be understood in its ordinary meaning, and the jury did not thereafter resubmit its request for further clarification after being told to do so if it needed the ordinary meaning of the words explained to it, the inference is clear that the court's response sufficiently answered the jury's question and that the jury reached its verdict on the torture charge on the basis of its understanding of the words "extreme pain" in their ordinary meaning.

Indeed, as observed by the court, the fact that Mother's counsel used the dictionary meaning of "extreme" in his proffered definition of the term suggested lack of need to define the word beyond the court's instruction that the term was to be understood in its ordinary meaning. Juries are presumed to know the ordinary meaning of common terms; otherwise, every word in an instruction will have to be defined; every word in the definition will have to be further defined; and so on ad infinitum. As stated in Foss v. Oliver J. Olson & Co. (1967) 250 Cal.App.2d 44, 52: "'Since jurors are presumed to possess ordinary intelligence and to be capable of understanding the meaning and use of words in their common and ordinary application, the trial judge is not required to define simple words and phrases employed in an instruction. [Citation.]' [Citation.]"

Father argues that "cruel pain" and "extreme pain" are open-ended terms, and therefore are unconstitutionally vague if not defined. We disagree.

The phrase "cruel pain" is constitutionally clear. (People v. Barrera (1993) 14 Cal.App.4th 1555, 1563-1564.) In holding that "cruel" in the definition of torture "withstands a challenge based upon vagueness," Barrera stated: "Section 206 enjoys 'presumptive validity,' and '". . . is sufficiently certain if it employs words of long usage or with a common law meaning 'notwithstanding an element of degree in the definition as to which estimates might differ.' [Citations.]'" [Citation.]" (Ibid.)

Barrera further explained: "'Torture' has a long-standing, judicially recognized meaning: [¶] 'Torture has been defined as the "Act or process of inflicting severe pain, esp. as a punishment in order to extort confession, or in revenge." (Webster's New Int. Dict. (2d ed.).) The dictionary definition was appropriately enlarged upon . . . in People v. Heslen, 163 P.2d 21, 27 in the following words: "Implicit in that definition is the requirement of an intent to cause pain and suffering in addition to death. That is, the killer is not satisfied with killing alone. He wishes to punish, execute vengeance on, or extort something from his victim, and in the course, or as the result of inflicting pain and suffering, the victim dies. That intent may be manifested by the nature of the acts and circumstances surrounding the homicide." . . . [¶] 'In determining whether the murder was perpetrated by means of torture the solution must rest upon whether the assailant's intent was to cause cruel suffering on the part of the object of the attack, either for the purpose of revenge, extortion, persuasion, or to satisfy some other untoward propensity. The test cannot be whether the victim merely suffered severe pain since presumably in most murders severe pain precedes death.' (People v. Tubby (1949) 34 Cal.2d 72, 76-77.) [¶] Torture combines a specific state of mind with a particular type of violent conduct causing significant personal injury. To require, as Barrera argues, an inquiry into the duration of the pain experienced or the manner in which it was inflicted incorrectly shifts the emphasis from the perpetrator. (See People v. Wiley (1976) 18 Cal.3d 162, 173.) It is even more significant that section 206 does not require proof the victim suffered pain. As written, section 206 continues the Tubby definition." (14 Cal.App.4th at pp. 1563-1564.)

Likewise, in People v. Talamantez (1985) 169 Cal.App.3d 443, 457, the court rejected the vagueness challenge to section 206, concluding: "'Cruel' is the equivalent of 'extreme' or 'severe' pain in the definition of torture," and hence "the use of the word 'cruel' by the trial court . . . did not render unconstitutionally vague the definition of torture. [Citation.]"

Father's reliance on People v. Superior Court (Engert) (1982) 31 Cal.3d 797, is misplaced. In Engert, the court addressed a vagueness challenge to section 190.2, subdivision (a)(14), which attempted to create a special circumstance in murder when murder was committed in a manner that was "'especially heinous, atrocious, or cruel.'" (31 Cal.3d at p. 801.)

In finding subdivision (a)(14) of section 190.2 unconstitutionally vague, Engert stated: "It is difficult to assign any specific content to the pejoratives contained in subdivision (a)(14). Webster's New International Dictionary (2d ed.) defines heinous as '[h]ateful; hatefully bad; flagrant; odious; atrocious; giving great offense.' Atrocious is defined as '[s]avagely brutal; outrageously cruel or wicked. . . .' Cruel is defined as '[d]isposed to give pain to others; willing or pleased to hurt or afflict; savage, inhuman, merciless.' Depravity is defined as 'corruption; wickedness.' The terms address the emotions and subjective, idiosyncratic values. While they stimulate feelings of repugnance, they have no directive content. The adverb 'especially' adds nothing except greater uncertainty. The term 'especial' is defined by Webster as '[n]ot general; distinguished among others of the same class as exceptional in degree.' [¶] None of these terms meets the standards of precision and certainty required of statutes which render persons eligible for punishment, either as elements of a charged crime or as a charged special circumstance." (31 Cal.3d at pp. 801-802.)

Engert is distinguishable. In Talamantez, the court distinguished Engert as "focusing its attention primarily on the word 'especially' as it modified 'heinous, atrocious, cruel.'" (169 Cal.App.3d at p. 457.) Talamantez added: "Since all murder, by definition, would be heinous, atrocious and cruel, the Engert court found the use of the word 'especially' unconstitutionally vague; it would lead to guesswork as to when and how the finding could be made." (Ibid.)

A further distinction was made in People v. Lynn (1984) 159 Cal.App.3d 715. In Lynn, the court stated, at pages 730-731: "Engert declared unconstitutional the use of the word 'cruel' in the context of subdivision (a)(14) taken as a whole. Engert did not address the constitutionality of the word 'cruel' standing alone . . . . Solitary use of the word 'cruel' was upheld against vagueness and due process challenges in People v. McCaughan (1957) 49 Cal.2d 409, 414-417."

We agree with Lynn that "cruel" as a word standing alone is not vague; and we agree with Talamantez that in the context in which "cruel" is used to define the crime of torture under section 206, it is not unconstitutionally vague.

"Extreme" is likewise not a vague term. Indeed, the Supreme Court used the word to define torture in People v. Steger (1976) 16 Cal.3d 539. Steger defined "murder by means of torture under section 189" as "murder committed with a wilful, deliberate, and premeditated intent to inflict extreme and prolonged pain." (Id. at p. 546.)

Although Steger employed the word "prolonged" to accompany "extreme" in defining murder by torture, the absence of "prolonged" in section 206 did not make "extreme" vague. By using the word "extreme" to define the pain in torture murder, the Steger court necessarily accepted "extreme" as a clear enough word to describe pain.

We conclude section 206 is not unconstitutionally vague, and that the failure of the trial court to define "extreme pain" did not deprive Father of his due process rights under the United States and California Constitutions.

In light of this conclusion, Father's contention that torture be defined in terms of "extreme and prolonged pain" to save section 206 from unconstitutional vagueness, is moot.

IV. Child Endangerment

People's Cross-Appeal

The People contend the trial court erred in staying the execution of the sentence for the more serious crime of torture. We disagree.

It is true that in People v. Superior Court (Himmelsbach) (1986) 186 Cal.App.3d 524, 540, we held that "the trial court had no authority under section 654 to stay execution of the sentence imposed upon the most seriously punishable offense arising from an indivisible course of conduct." Other appellate courts have, however, reached the contrary conclusion that a trial court has discretion to stay the greater offense and impose sentence on the lesser. (See, e.g.: People v. Wesley (1970) 10 Cal.App.3d 902 [1st Dist., Div. 2]; People v. Devaney (1973) 33 Cal.App.3d 630 [1st Dist., Div. 1]; People v. Mendevil (1978) 81 Cal.App.3d 84 [2d Dist., Div. 2]; People v. Bradley (1981) 115 Cal.App.3d 744 [4th Dist., Div. 1]; People v. Avila (1982) 138 Cal.App.3d 873 [3d Dist.]; People v. Barela (1983) 145 Cal.App.3d 152 [2d Dist., Div. 4]; People v. Cole (1985) 165 Cal.App.3d 41 [1st Dist., Div. 3]; People v. Salazar (1987) 194 Cal.App.3d 634 [4th Dist., Div. 3]; People v. Thompson (1989) 209 Cal.App.3d 1075 [5th Dist.]; People v. Thompson (1992) 7 Cal.App.4th 1966 [2d Dist., Div. 7].)

We are now persuaded that the position held by the other appellate courts expresses the correct view. We agree with the court's reasoning in People v. Salazar, supra, 194 Cal.App.3d at page 639: "[D]iscretion to sentence on the greater or lesser crime is vital to a trial court's proper exercise of its sentencing mandates: '[A] sentencing judge is required to base his decision on the statutory and rule criteria . . . and not on his subjective feeling about whether the sentence thus arrived at seems too long, too short, or just right.' [Citation.] The analysis should be the same when the court is faced with a sentencing choice under Penal Code section 654. The court should impose sentence on the offense which is most appropriate for the defendant's conduct and not simply the one carrying the greatest penalty. Only in this way will a defendant's punishment 'be commensurate with his culpability' and the purpose of Penal Code section 654 fulfilled. [Citation.]"

We therefore hold that in this case the trial court did not err in staying the sentence for the torture conviction.

DISPOSITION

The judgment is affirmed.

V.
In Re Leslie R.
(Unpublished)

Terminating parental rights and putting up a child for adoption because of parental misconduct is not common in the Philippines. There are provisions for terminating parental authority in the Family Code of the Philippines (Articles 228-233), but actual cases of termination of parental authority for parental abuse are rare, if any. Much may have to do with culture and traditions, and with our natural resistance to drastic changes in our cultural habits and belief systems. It is not easy for us to dissolve the biological bonds that bind the parents to their children at the moment of birth. The sacrosanct reverence that we hold toward parent-child relationship is probably one of the strongest pillars in our culture and society. The situations in *In re Leslie* and in the previous case of *Blomquist*, however, may illustrate instances where we may have to forcibly break filial ties to protect the children and remove them from their irresponsible and abusive parents.

In the United States, the overriding consideration is the best interest of the child. The interest of the parents in keeping their children is secondary. Where the best interest of the child requires dissolution of the biologically-based bond between the parents and the child, the court will remove the child from the parents' custody, terminate the parents' parental authority, and put the child up for adoption. In *In re Leslie*, we affirmed the termination of parental authority.

In the Philippines, the Family Code likewise recognizes the best interest of the child to be of overriding importance.

The opinion in *In Re Leslie* follows:

PROCEDURAL AND FACTUAL BACKGROUND

Our original opinion in this case, which affirmed the judgment below, was filed August 19, 1993. On November 17, 1993, the Supreme Court granted review. On February 3, 1994, the high court transferred this matter to us "with directions to vacate decision and to reconsider the cause in light of In re Matthew C. (1993) 6 Cal.4th 386."

Pursuant to the Supreme Court resolution, we hereby vacate our original decision and issue this reconsidered opinion.

Leslie was born on December 25, 1987. On August 3, 1989, Leslie's mother (hereafter, Mother) was arrested on drug charges. A dependency petition was filed on Leslie's behalf, alleging failure to protect, inability to provide support, and neglect of three older siblings as to whom parental rights had been terminated or relinquished. Mother admitted the allegations of the petition, and the court sustained the petition. Leslie was placed in foster care. The court ordered reunification services. On December 15, 1990, Mother agreed to the termination of the reunification services.

At the 12-month review hearing on March 5, 1991, respondent Santa Clara County Department of Family & Children's Services recommended tentative placement of Leslie with Father and his new wife (Donna), subject to certain conditions. Although Father had a long history of crime, violence, incarceration, and alcohol abuse, the social worker recommended that Father be given the opportunity for placement. Father was warned, however, that this was his only opportunity and that no second chance would be given him should he violate the conditions of placement.

On July 22, 1991, Father was arrested for spousal abuse of Donna. Leslie was removed from Father's home and placed with her original foster family. Respondent filed a supplemental petition under section 387, alleging that the most recent disposition had failed to protect Leslie.

On January 6, 1992, the juvenile court, following a contested hearing, sustained the amended supplemental petition and scheduled a permanency planning hearing on May 4, 1992, pursuant to section 366.26.

On February 19, 1992, the court filed an order finding that Father had violated the conditions of placement, that the placement was not effective in protecting Leslie, that Leslie's welfare required removal of physical custody from Father, and that removal from Leslie's foster home placement would be detrimental to Leslie. The court terminated reunification services with Father.

From this order, Father appealed to this court on February 27, 1992. We dismissed the appeal on the ground that the February 19, 1992, order was not appealable.

In May 1992, Father filed a petition for a writ of mandate. Because the petition was untimely filed, we denied it.

On June 9, 1992, the court heard the section 366.26 matter. Neither Father nor Mother appeared. Father, who was serving time at San Quentin State Prison, had waived his appearance.

On September 9, 1992, the court ordered termination of Father's parental rights.

This appeal ensued.

DISCUSSION

The issue in this appeal is whether the juvenile court erred in ordering termination of Father's parental rights. We conclude there was no error.

In In re Matthew C. (1993) 6 Cal.4th 386, 392, the court, quoting Cynthia D. v. Superior Court (1993) 5 Cal.4th 242, 249-250, stated: "'[I]n order to terminate parental rights [at the section 366.26 hearing], the court need only to make two findings: (1) that there is clear and convincing evidence that the minor will be adopted; and (2) that there has been a previous determination that reunification services shall be terminated.' [Citation.] Hence, the proceeding terminating reunification services and setting a section 366.26 hearing is generally a party's last opportunity to litigate the issue of parental fitness as it relates to any subsequent termination of parental rights, or to seek the child's return to parental custody. [Citation.]"

In re Matthew C. also held that "the findings subsumed within the orders made in at least three of the four phases of dependency proceedings," which include the order terminating reunification services, "are reviewable on appeal from an order terminating parental rights." (6 Cal.4th at p. 393.) This ruling settled the conflict among the courts of appeal on the question whether an order terminating reunification services is reviewable on appeal from the final order terminating parental rights. (Ibid.)

In reviewing the order terminating reunification services as to Father in this case, we first look at the pertinent language of section 366.26. Subdivision (b)(1) of that section provides that the juvenile court, in order to provide stable and permanent homes for the dependent children of the court, shall "[p]ermanently sever the rights of the parent or parents and order that the child be placed for adoption," and subdivision (c)(1) adds that the severance be made "only if it determines by clear and convincing evidence that it is likely that the minor will be adopted." Subdivision (c)(1) of that section further provides that "[i]f the court so determines, the findings pursuant to subdivision (b) of Section 361.5 that reunification services shall not be offered, or the findings pursuant to subdivision (e) of Section 366.21 that the whereabouts of a parent have been unknown for six months . . ., or pursuant to Section 366.21 or Section 366.22 that a minor cannot or should not be returned to his or her parent or guardian, shall then constitute a sufficient basis for termination of parental rights unless the court finds that termination would be detrimental to the minor . . . ."

Father contends that since "no adverse findings under any of the code sections cited in section 366.26(c)(1) were ever entered against [him] during the history of this case . . . respondent failed to prove an essential sufficient basis for the termination of [Father's] parental rights." Father is mistaken.

It is true that as to Father, there were no section 361.5, 366.21, or 366.22 proceedings,[5] and therefore no adverse findings against him under those sections. However, there was a section 387 proceeding involving Father and adverse findings were made against him in that proceeding. The question is whether the adverse findings in the section 387 proceeding may be considered the functional equivalent of adverse findings in a section 361.5, 366.21, or 366.22 proceeding for purposes of terminating parental rights under section 366.26. We hold that they can.

Section 366.21, provides in relevant part: "(e) At the review hearing held six months after the initial dispositional hearing, the court shall order the return of the minor to the physical custody of his or her

---

[5] Combined section 366.21/366.22 hearings were conducted as to Mother, resulting in the termination of reunification services as regards her.

parents or guardians unless, by a preponderance of the evidence, it finds that the return of the child would create a substantial risk of detriment to the physical or emotional well-being of the minor. . . . The failure of the parent or guardian to participate regularly in any court-ordered treatment programs shall constitute prima facie evidence that return would be detrimental. In making its determination, the court shall review the probation officer's report, shall review and consider the report and recommendations of any child advocate appointed pursuant to Section 356.5, and shall consider the efforts or progress, or both, demonstrated by the parent or guardian and the extent to which he or she cooperated and availed himself or herself of services provided; shall make appropriate findings pursuant to subdivision (a) of Section 366; and where relevant, shall order any additional services reasonably believed to facilitate the return of the minor to the custody of his or her parent or guardian. . . . [¶] (f) At the review hearing held 12 months after the initial dispositional hearing, the court shall order the return of the minor to the physical custody of his or her parent or guardian unless, by a preponderance of the evidence, it finds that return of the child would create a substantial risk of detriment to the physical or emotional well-being of the minor. . . . The failure of the parent or guardian to participate regularly in any court-ordered treatment programs shall constitute prima facie evidence that the return would be detrimental. . . . [¶] (g) If a minor is not returned to the custody of a parent or guardian at the hearing held pursuant to subdivision (f), the court shall do one of the following: [¶] (1) Continue the case for up to six months for another review hearing, provided that the hearing shall occur within 18 months of the date the child was originally taken from the physical custody of his or her parent or guardian. The court shall continue the case only if it finds that there is a substantial probability that the minor will be returned to the physical custody of his or her parent or guardian within six months or that reasonable services have not been provided to the parent or guardian. . . . (h) In any case in which the court orders that a hearing pursuant to Section 366.26 shall be held, it shall also order the termination of reunification services to the parent."

Section 366.22, subdivision (a) likewise provides in relevant part: "When a case has been continued pursuant to paragraph (1) of subdivision (g) of Section 366.21, the court, at the 18-month hearing, shall order the return of the minor to the physical custody of his or her parent or guardian unless, by a preponderance of the evidence, it finds that return of the child would create a substantial risk of detriment to the physical or emotional well-being of the minor. . . . The failure of the parent or guardian to participate regularly in any court-ordered treatment programs shall constitute prima facie evidence that return would be detrimental. In making its determination, the court shall review the probation officer's report and shall review and consider the report and recommendations of any child advocate appointed pursuant to Section 356.6 and shall consider the efforts or progress, or both, demonstrated by the parent or guardian and the extent to which he or she cooperated and availed himself or herself of services provided."

As may be noted, the purpose of the review hearings under sections 366.21 and 366.22 is basically to determine whether the return of the child to the parent would "create a substantial risk of detriment to the physical or emotional well-being of the minor." (§ 366.21, subd. (f).) If there is no such substantial risk, the minor is required to be returned to the parent. On the other hand, if the court finds, by a preponderance of the evidence, that the return of the child would create such a substantial risk, the court should not return the child, but should proceed with any of the alternative courses of action set forth in those sections, among which is to order the termination of reunification services and set the case for a section 366.26 hearing.

Significantly, "[t]he failure of the parent or guardian to participate regularly in any court-ordered treatment programs shall constitute prima facie evidence that return would be detrimental." (§§ 366.21, subds. (e) & (f); 366.22, subd. (a).) Moreover, "[i]n making its determination, the court shall review the probation officer's report and shall review and consider the report and recommendations of any child advocate appointed pursuant to Section 356.6 and shall consider the efforts or progress, or both, demonstrated by the parent or guardian and the extent to which he or she cooperated and availed himself or herself of services provided." (§ 366.22, subd. (a).)

Section 387, on the other hand, states: "An order changing or modifying a previous order by removing a minor from the physical custody of a parent, guardian, relative, or friend and directing placement in a foster home, or commitment to a private or county institution, shall be made only after noticed hearing upon a supplemental petition. [¶] (a) The supplemental petition shall be filed by the probation officer in the original matter and shall contain a concise statement of facts sufficient to support the conclusion that the previous disposition has not been effective in the rehabilitation or protection of the minor. . . ."

Clearly, section 387 envisions a situation where the court had returned the minor to the physical custody of the parent or guardian, and subsequent events have shown that decision to be inimical to the best interests of the child. The statute provides a mechanism to rectify the previous order and save the minor therefrom. That mechanism is a supplemental petition which permits the court to conduct further hearings and, thereafter, change or modify the previous order by removing the minor from the physical custody of the parent or guardian, and making whatever dispositions it may deem necessary to serve and protect the best interests of the child.

Because the purpose of a section 387 proceeding is precisely to allow the court to change or modify a previous custody order that had resulted in detriment to the interests of the child, it would be absurd to suggest that in a section 387 hearing, the juvenile court cannot undo what it improvidently did in the previous proceeding, and cannot take any of the alternative courses of action it could have taken at the 12-month or 18-month review hearing to safeguard the child's best interest, such as terminating reunification services and setting the case for a section 366.26 hearing. Such a suggestion would render section 387 meaningless. "The cardinal rule of statutory construction is to ascertain and give effect to the intent of the Legislature. [Citation.]" (Young v. Haines (1986) 41 Cal.3d 883, 894.)

The language in section 366.26 which states that the findings in a section 361.5, 366.21, or 366.22 hearing shall "constitute a sufficient basis for termination of parental rights" cannot be construed to exclude findings in a section 387 proceeding. (§ 366.26, subd. (c)(1).) Nothing in the language of section 366.26 suggests exclusivity in this regard. Additionally, because the supplemental petition under section 387 is intended to change or modify an order that was issued in an earlier

361.5, 366.21, or 366.22 review hearing, the section 387 hearing partakes of the nature of the hearing whose outcome it seeks to change or modify, and, therefore, is also, in a real sense, a section 361.5, 366.21, or 366.22 hearing, albeit supplemental, within the meaning of section 366.26.

Therefore, our conclusion in the prior appeal (In re Leslie R. (Mar. 10, 1993) H009533 [nonpub. opn.]) that the section 387 hearing in this case was the functional equivalent of an 18-month review hearing, was correct, and we make the same conclusion here.

There now remains the question whether the trial court's findings in the section 387 hearing is supported by substantial evidence.

In his opening brief, Father argues that the lack of a section 361.5, 366.21, or 366.22 hearing in this case results in "failure to adduce proof of a sufficient basis for the section 366.26(c)(1) order terminating appellant's parental rights . . . ." Because Father's contention raises a sufficiency of evidence issue, we must review it under the substantial evidence standard.

The rule is settled that whenever the issue on appeal is sufficiency of evidence, our power as an appellate court "begins and ends with a determination as to whether there is any substantial evidence, contradicted or uncontradicted, which will support the conclusion reached by the [trier of fact]." (Crawford v. Southern Pacific Co. (1935) 3 Cal.2d 427, 429.) In determining the presence of substantial evidence, "[a]ll of the evidence most favorable to the respondent must be accepted as true, and that unfavorable discarded as not having sufficient verity, to be accepted by the trier of fact. If the evidence so viewed is sufficient as a matter of law, the judgment must be affirmed." (Estate of Teel (1944) 25 Cal.2d 520, 527.)

We cannot, on appeal, reweigh the evidence. (Estate of Teel, supra, 25 Cal.2d at p. 527.) "It is the province of the [trier of fact] to resolve conflicts in the evidence and to determine the credibility of witnesses." (Fredette v. City of Long Beach (1986) 187 Cal.App.3d 122, 127.) "When two or more inferences can be reasonably deduced from the facts, the reviewing court is without power to substitute its deductions for those of the trial court." (Crawford v. Southern Pacific Co., supra, 3 Cal.2d at p. 429.)

In the instant case, the court had found, inter alia, by clear and convincing evidence, that Father was arrested for spousal abuse; that Father "violated the terms of the Family Maintenance Agreement in that he no longer resides with the minor's stepmother Donna Wofford; he failed to provide verification of twice weekly attendance at AA meetings; he failed to provide verification that he had an AA sponsor; further, the minor does not want to live with her father as she states she is scared of her father and that her father is mean; further, the minor's father is presently incarcerated." The court further found that "the Family Maintenance Program was not effective in the protection of the minor;" that the minor's welfare required removal of physical custody from Father because of substantial danger to her physical health; that reasonable efforts had been made to prevent the removal; and that removal from her current placement in a foster home would be detrimental.

Our review of the record shows such findings to be supported by substantial evidence. Respondent had submitted to the court, among other documents, the following: (1) the reporter's transcript from a hearing in the matter of Leslie R. dated October 16, 1991; (2) the court report dated August 20, 1991, prepared by the social worker; (3) the home study report of Doris Wofford (Leslie's paternal grandmother) prepared by the social worker; (4) an addendum report dated August 13, 1991 prepared by the social worker; (5) a memorandum dated November 25, 1991, prepared by the social worker which included, as an attachment thereto, the psychological evaluation by Dr. Michael Jones. In addition, the court heard testimony from Dr. Michael Jones, Rosemary Orne, Doris Wofford, and Father.

The foregoing documents and the testimonial evidence established that: (1) Father had a long history of crime, violence, incarceration, and alcohol abuse. (2) Notwithstanding such history, the trial court, upon recommendation of the social worker, gave Father reunification opportunities by ordering, at the 12-month review hearing, the return of Leslie to Father under certain conditions. (3) Among the conditions were: Father and Leslie should reside in the home of Donna; Father should attend AA/NA meetings twice a week, and should obtain proof of attendance, sponsorship and successful participation in such meetings; Father should enroll in and complete a parent education class that addresses the needs of preschool age children; and Father should not use alcohol or illegal drugs. (4) On or about July 22, 1991, Father was arrested for spousal abuse. (5) Father violated the terms of the Family Maintenance Agreement in that, following his arrest, he no longer resided with Donna; he failed to provide verification of twice weekly attendance at AA meetings; and he failed to provide verification that he had an AA sponsor. (6) Leslie does not want to live with Father because Father is "mean" to her and she is "scared" of Father. Father "spank[ed] [Leslie] and forc[ed] her to drink yucky beer, which made her sick."

As so established, the evidence was sufficient to support the trial court's decision to terminate reunification services as to Father. It follows that there was sufficient basis for the juvenile court to terminate Father's parental rights at the subsequent section 366.26 hearing.

Significantly, the juvenile court made its findings on the basis of "clear and convincing evidence," which was more than what sections 361.5, 366.21, or 366.22 require. As may be noted, the review hearings under sections 366.21 or 366.22 only require the court to find by a "preponderance of the evidence" that the return of the child to the parent or guardian "would create a substantial risk of detriment to the physical or emotional well-being of the minor." (§ 366.26, subd. (e).) Because the juvenile court used a higher standard of proof than is required for a section 366.21 or 366.22 hearing, it is all too clear that had the proceeding been a plain review hearing under sections 366.21 or 366.22 instead of the supplemental hearing that it was under section 387, the court would have undoubtedly found that returning Leslie to Father would have created "a substantial risk of detriment to the physical or emotional well-being" of Leslie. (§ 366.21, subd. (e).) Therefore, had it been error to conduct a section 387 hearing in lieu of an 18-month review hearing, the error would be harmless.

Father's claim that no reunification services were provided to him is not supported by the record. The court returned Leslie to Father following the 12-month review precisely to afford Father reasonable opportunities for reunification. Father simply failed to fulfill his responsibilities. As the court stated: "[W]e did give him reasonable services. I returned the child to his home. The child was in his home approximately four months. The child would probably still be there but for some other incident that happened."

On this record, we conclude the trial court committed no error in terminating reunification services as to Father and in terminating Father's parental rights.

DISPOSITION

The judgment is affirmed.

VI.
People v. Villa
(Unpublished)

Villa is a "bounty hunter" case. The term "bounty hunter" no longer refers to Western characters who used to hunt down outlaws during the days of the old Wild West. Rather, it now refers to a private citizen who is hired by a bondsman to locate an accused who has jumped bail so that the accused could be arrested and surrendered to the court, and thus prevent the bondsman's bailbond from being forfeited to the state. When a bondsman puts up bail for the accused, the condition of the bond is that the bondsman physically produce the body of the accused in court for trial. When the bondsman cannot produce the body of the accused because the accused has jumped bail, the bondsman violates the condition of the bond. The bond may thus be forfeited to the state.

In *Villa*, the accused (Villa) jumped bail. The bondsman employed a "bounty hunter" (Okane) to track down Villa. Okane found Villa and reported Villa's whereabouts to the sheriff's office. A team of sheriff deputies was dispatched to arrest Villa.

The principal issue on appeal was the legality of the protective sweep of the garage that was made by a late-arriving deputy after Villa had been arrested. A "protective sweep" is a quick and limited search of the premises conducted for the purpose of protecting the safety of the arresting officers. When the late-arriving deputy made a protective sweep of the garage, he saw methamphetamine and assorted paraphernalia for the manufacture of that drug. The question is whether the methamphetamine and the drug paraphernalia are admissible evidence. Villa contended that the protective sweep was illegal because Okane was a "bounty hunter" who was motivated by economic interest when he supplied information to the sheriff's office about Villa's location and the risk Villa posed to the safety of the officers. Because Villa was an unreliable informant, the information he gave was untrustworthy. Therefore, the information did not give the officers sufficient specific facts to warrant a reasonable belief that the premises where Villa was arrested posed a danger to their safety. Absent the required knowledge of specific facts, the protective sweep was unjustified. Because the protective sweep was unjustified, the evidence discovered by reason of that impermissible conduct was "fruit of the poisonous tree," and therefore inadmissible.

I do not think we have "bounty hunter" jurisprudence in the Philippines.

The opinion in *People v. Villa* follows:

> Defendants Juan Francisco Villa and Gabriel Sanchez Padilla were charged by information with possession of methamphetamine for sale (Health & Saf. Code, § 11378; count 1),[6] possession of ephedrine with intent to manufacture methamphetamine (§ 11383, subd. (c); count 2) and manufacture of methamphetamine (§ 11379.6, subd. (a); count 3). The information further alleged that the amount of methamphetamine possessed by defendants in count 1 exceeded four kilograms; that Villa was personally armed with a firearm during the commission of the crimes; and that Villa was on bail when he committed the crimes.
>
> Defendants filed a motion to suppress evidence, which was denied by the court.
>
> Villa pleaded guilty to all the charges and admitted all the enhancing allegations.
>
> Padilla, on the other hand, pleaded guilty to the count 1 charge and admitted the weight clause. The remaining charges against Padilla were dismissed.
>
> The court sentenced Villa to an aggregate prison term of five years. Padilla was sentenced to three years in state prison.
>
> We affirm.
>
> ## FACTS
>
> On March 29, 1995, Tim Okane, employed as a "bounty hunter" by a bondsman, contacted Deputy Sheriff Carlos Dona and told Dona that Villa was wanted in Siskiyou County for jumping bail on a charge of possession of marijuana for sale. Villa's bail bond was $100,000. Okane told Dona that Villa was a flight risk, was in possession of a firearm at the time of his previous arrest, might be in the company of other wanted persons, and was "a dope dealer" who was "associated with other dope

---

[6] Further statutory references in this case are to the Health and Safety Code unless otherwise noted.

dealers." Okane further told Dona that, according to Villa's wife, Villa could be found at 14645 Palomino Drive, San Jose. Okane also told Dona that he (Okane) had driven by the Palomino Drive address and had seen Villa's van parked at that address. Okane showed Dona a photograph of Villa. Dona verified the warrant information supplied to him by Okane and received confirmation from Siskiyou County that the warrant was existing and that the bail bond amount of $100,000 was correct.

Dona consulted his supervisor, Sergeant Larry Latham, for advice on how to proceed. It was arranged that Dona and other sheriff deputies, including Deputies Rowberry, Wulfing, and Gagne would meet at a staging site close to the Palomino Drive address.

When Dona arrived at the Palomino address, he saw the van that Okane had described to him in the driveway. The sheriffs agreed that Dona, Wulfing, and Gagne would approach the house from the front and that Rowberry and another deputy would cover the back of the house.

Dona knocked on the front door. Villa opened the door. Dona identified himself, told Villa he had a warrant for his arrest, and arrested Villa. Padilla, who was sleeping on the floor of the living room approximately eight feet from the door, was also arrested. The arrest of Villa and Padilla was without incident. A radio dispatch was sent to the deputies covering the back of the house that "we have the subject."

Wulfing and Gagne took control of defendants. Dona made a protective sweep of the bedrooms to make sure no one else was present. Wulfing found a gun in the living room under the bedding where Villa had been sleeping.

Meanwhile, while covering the back of the house, Rowberry saw at least three cars parked in that part of the house. Rowberry checked the cars to make sure they were not occupied. Rowberry found no one inside. One of the cars showed a path of flattened grass, which indicated to Rowberry that the path had been recently driven.

When Rowberry heard that the other deputies "[had] the subject," he entered the kitchen through its unlocked door to look for other persons who might be in the house. Finding no one in the kitchen, Rowberry entered the garage through an open door. As he entered the garage,

Rowberry smelled a chemical odor and saw assorted paraphernalia which led him to believe that the garage was used as a laboratory for the manufacture of methamphetamine. Inside a stove, Rowberry found what he believed to be methamphetamine.

The deputies turned over further investigation of the premises to the narcotics task force. The narcotics task force secured a search warrant and served it on defendants. The task force seized numerous items of evidence.

Defendants questioned below, as they now do on appeal, the admissibility of the evidence seized by the narcotics task force, arguing that "the evidence obtained from the garage should have been suppressed because it was seized pursuant to a search warrant which was obtained based on evidence obtained pursuant to an unlawful search."

In denying defendants' motion to suppress and concluding that the deputies had a reasonable basis for conducting the protective sweep, the trial court stated: "[T]here [was] a clear showing that the police had reason to believe that there was more than one person in the house besides Mr. Villa, that they also had reason to believe that the people in the house accompanying Mr. Villa might be dangerous and might cause a safety risk to them."

CONTENTIONS

Villa contends that "[t]he protective sweep of the house was illegal because the deputies did not possess sufficient specific facts to warrant a reasonable belief that the residence harbored persons posing a danger to those on the arrest scene."

Padilla likewise contends that "[b]ecause the police did not have a reasonable belief that the house in which Villa was located harbored additional individuals who posed a danger to the police, all evidence obtained as a result of the protective [sweep] must be suppressed."

DISCUSSION

Because Villa's and Padilla's contentions relate to the same issue, we will discuss them together.

Defendants first argue that the information provided by Okane was unreliable, and hence did not justify the protective sweep. We disagree.

Okane was neither a police officer nor a paid informer; he was a plain citizen. The fact that he was employed by Villa's bondsman as a "bounty hunter" did not make him a police officer or a paid informer, and did not divest him of his status as a plain citizen. Accordingly, the rules concerning the degree of reliance which the police may place on information supplied by plain citizens apply to the information that the police received from Villa in this case.

In People v. Ramey (1976) 16 Cal.3d 263, 268-269, the court stated: "The courts have recognized a distinction between informers who are virtual agents of the police and 'citizen informants' who are chance witnesses to or victims of crime. The former are often criminally disposed or implicated, and supply their 'tips' to the authorities on a recurring basis, in secret, and for pecuniary or other personal gain. The latter are innocent of criminal involvement, and volunteer their information fortuitously, openly, and through motives of good citizenship. [Citation.] Because of these characteristics, the requisite showing of reliability in the case of a citizen informant is significantly less than that demanded of a police informer. [Citations.] [¶] It may therefore be stated as a general proposition that private citizens who are witnesses to or victims of a criminal act, absent some circumstance that would cast doubt upon their information, should be considered reliable."

Elaborating this point, the court, in People v. Kershaw (1983) 147 Cal.App.3d 750, 756, explained: "In the case of confidential citizen informers, the mere fact that they make their identity known to the police is, itself, some indication of their honesty. [Citation.] A further indication of reliability is that by identifying themselves to the police they expose themselves to potential liability for malicious prosecution or false reporting of a crime if their information proves to be false. [Citation.] Furthermore, by identifying themselves, these citizen informers afford the police the opportunity to check on matters affecting their credibility such as the existence of a criminal record and whether they had previously supplied information to the police."

In People v. Lombera (1989) 210 Cal.App.3d 29, 32, the court held that "a citizen informant is presumptively reliable even though reliability has not previously been tested so that corroboration of their information is unnecessary when it is based upon the informant's personal observations of the commission of a crime. [Citation.]"

In the instant case, the bondsman stood to lose the amount of the bail bond by Villa's act of jumping bail. The bondsman's situation was not therefore materially different from that of private citizens described in Ramey as "victims of a criminal act" who, "absent some circumstance that would cast doubt upon their information, should be considered reliable." (16 Cal.3d at p. 269.) Okane, as the bondsman's employee and agent, stood on the same footing of reliability in this sense as his employer. The fact that Okane expected reward or compensation for his work, as all employees and agents do, was not of itself a "circumstance that would cast doubt upon [his] information." (Ibid.)

We are not therefore persuaded by Padilla's argument that Okane was "inherently unreliable" because he had "a vested economic interest in capturing Villa."

Moreover, Okane's reliability as an informant was buttressed by the fact that the information he supplied to Dona concerning the existence of the warrant for Villa's arrest, the amount of the bailbond, and the nature of Villa's underlying charge, which was for possession for sale of marijuana, was subsequently verified to be true. Additionally, Okane's other information was confirmed: Villa was indeed found at the 14645 Palomino Drive address, and his van was parked at that address.

Because there was ample corroboration for Villa's information to Dona, the police could reasonably rely on such information, and hence the trial court did not err in concluding that such reliance was reasonable.

The Harvey-Remers[7] rule relied on by Padilla is inapposite. That rule applies only when information is furnished by one officer to another. Here, as stated, Okane was not a police officer.

Defendants further contend that the protective sweep of the garage was unjustified, and thus illegal. The contention is without merit.

A "protective sweep" is a "quick and limited search of premises, incident to an arrest and conducted to protect the safety of police officers or others. It is narrowly confined to a cursory visual inspection of those places in which a person might be hiding." (Maryland v. Buie (1990) 494 U.S. 325, 327.)

---

[7] People v. Harvey (1958) 156 Cal.App.2d 516; Remers v. Superior Court (1970) 2 Cal.3d 659.

In <u>Maryland</u> v. <u>Buie</u>, the court, addressing the question of "what level of justification is required by the Fourth and Fourteenth Amendments before police officers, while effecting the arrest of a suspect in his home pursuant to an arrest warrant, may conduct a warrantless protective sweep of all or part of the premises," stated: "We conclude that the Fourth Amendment would permit the protective sweep undertaken here if the searching officer 'possesse[d] a reasonable belief based on "specific and articulable facts which, taken together with the rational inferences from those facts, reasonably warrant[ed]" the officer in believing' [citations], that the area swept harbored an individual posing a danger to the officer or others." (494 U.S. at p. 327.)

In adopting this standard, the <u>Buie</u> court found "instructive" its pronouncement in <u>Terry</u> v. <u>Ohio</u> (1968) 392 U.S. 1, 20, that although an on-the-street frisk for weapons "'constitutes a severe, though brief, intrusion upon cherished personal security,' [citation] such a frisk is reasonable when weighed against the 'need for law enforcement officers to protect themselves and other prospective victims of violence in situations where they may lack probable cause for an arrest.' [Citation.]" (494 U.S. at p. 332.)

The <u>Buie</u> court also relied on its holding in <u>Michigan</u> v. <u>Long</u> (1983) 463 U.S. 1032, 1049-1050, that "'[T]he search of the passenger compartment of an automobile, limited to those areas in which a weapon may be placed or hidden, is permissible if the police officer possesses a reasonable belief based on "specific and articulable facts which, taken together with the rational inferences from those facts, reasonably warrant" the officer in believing that the suspect is dangerous and the suspect may gain immediate control of weapons.' [Citation.]" (494 U.S. at p. 332.)

Comparing the facts in <u>Buie</u> to those in <u>Terry</u> and <u>Long</u>, the <u>Buie</u> court stated: "In <u>Terry</u> and <u>Long</u> we were concerned with the immediate interest of the police officers in taking steps to assure themselves that the persons with whom they were dealing were not armed with, or able to gain immediate control of, a weapon that could unexpectedly and fatally be used against them. In the instant case, there is an analogous interest of the officers in taking steps to assure themselves that the house in which a suspect is being, or has just been, arrested is not harboring other persons who are dangerous and who could unexpectedly launch an attack. The risk of danger in the context of an arrest in the home is as great as, if not greater than, it is in an on-the-street or roadside investigatory encounter. A Terry or Long frisk occurs before a police-citizen confrontation has escalated to the point of arrest. A protective sweep, in contrast, occurs as an adjunct to the serious step of taking a person into custody for the purpose of prosecuting him for a crime. Moreover, unlike an encounter on the street or along a highway, an in-home arrest puts the officer at the disadvantage of being on his adversary's 'turf.' An ambush in a confined setting of unknown configuration is more to be feared than it is in open, more familiar surroundings." (494 U.S. at p. 333.)

Echoing the same concern for officer safety in effecting arrests on the "adversary's turf," the California Supreme Court, in People v. Glaser (1995) 11 Cal.4th 354, 367-368, citing Buie, stated: "The police interest in protecting against violence during the search of a home for narcotics has been widely recognized. 'In the narcotics business, "firearms are as much 'tools of the trade' as are most commonly recognized articles of narcotics paraphernalia.'" [Citation.] The danger is potentially at its greatest when, as here, the premises to be searched are a private home, rather than a place of public accommodation as in Ybarra. '[B]ecause of the private nature of the surroundings and the recognized propensity of persons "engaged in selling narcotics [to] frequently carry firearms to protect themselves from would-be robbers," [citation] the likelihood that the occupants [of a residence] are armed or have ready accessibility to hidden weapons is conspicuously greater than in cases where, as in Ybarra, the public freely enters premises where legal business is transacted.' [Citation.] As the United States Supreme Court observed in Maryland v. Buie (1990) 494 U.S. 325, involving the legality of a protective sweep during an in-home arrest, the dangers are particularly acute when an officer seeks to serve a warrant in a suspect's house. The officer is 'at the disadvantage of being on his adversary's "turf." An ambush in a confined setting of unknown configuration is more to be feared than it is in open, more familiar surroundings.' [Citation.]" (Footnote omitted.)

Here, up to the point of Rowberry's entry through the kitchen door, Rowberry knew that most of the information supplied by Okane to the police had been corroborated: there was an outstanding warrant for Villa's arrest for possession for sale of marijuana; the warrant was issued in Siskiyou County; Villa's bond was for $100,000; Villa had jumped bail; Villa was found at the address given by Okane; and Villa's van was parked outside that address.

In addition, Rowberry saw at least three more vehicles parked in the residence's back yard, one of which had apparently been "recently driven in," as shown by the flatted grass on its path. The presence of these other vehicles further corroborated Okane's information that Villa might be in the company of other persons, thereby increasing the danger to which Rowberry and his fellow deputies had exposed themselves.

Defendants argue that because Villa was arrested without incident and the defendants cooperated with the police after their arrest, Rowberry's protective sweep was unjustified. The argument is non sequitur. There is no evidence that Rowberry knew prior to his entry to the kitchen and the garage that defendants had been arrested without incident. Rowberry testified that he entered the house through the kitchen door after he had heard something to the effect that "we have the subject." On cross-examination, Rowberry explained that his understanding of the radio message he received was that his fellow deputies "had the suspect, not that [the subject] was in custody." Explaining further, Rowberry said that "we have the subject" could have simply meant that "the subject is at the residence and they have located him."

And even if Rowberry had known that defendants had been arrested without incident, such fact did not dispel the possibility of the presence of other persons in the garage and of the danger that such persons could pose to him and his fellow deputies.

We conclude that on this record the trial court did not err in finding the protective sweep reasonable and in admitting into evidence the challenged seized items.

DISPOSITION

The judgment is affirmed.

VII.
Hoffman v. Heagerty
(Unpublished)

Hoffman is instructive on the duty of a lawyer to avoid litigation if other less costly avenues for the client are available. The relationship between the lawyer and his client is of the highest kind of fiduciary relationship, so much so that the lawyer is required in that relationship to subordinate his own interests to those of his client. In *Hoffman*, the lawyer did not adequately explore alternative strategies of handling his client's cause, such as reasonable settlement. He rejected reasonable offers of settlement and went on filing one lawsuit after another, which jacked up his attorney fees, until the cost of his attorney fees became unreasonably excessive. Also, the lawyer did not advise his client of what the costs of litigating the lawsuits could amount to, thereby putting his client completely in the dark. In short, the lawyer dragged his client into unnecessary lawsuits without the client's knowing consent. Knowing or informed consent is not just any consent; it is that kind of consent that is given only after the client has been fully advised of what he is going into in terms of costs, risks of success or failure, time consumption, stress of litigation, and all relevant considerations the client needs to know before making the decision to proceed with expensive litigation.

In *Hoffman*, the trial court found that the filing of indiscriminate lawsuits caused Heagerty to incur more attorney fees than necessary. Much of the expenses for attorney fees could have been saved had Hoffman pursued other avenues of promoting and protecting Heagerty's interests. The filing of unnecessary, ineffective lawsuits, which served Hoffman's economic interests more than Heagerty's, constituted breach of Hoffman's fiduciary duties to his client. Accordingly, the court allowed Heagerty to recover from Hoffman the attorney fees she had incurred for the unnecessary lawsuits.

The opinion in *Hoffman v. Heagerty* follows:

FACTS

From October 28, 1988 to November 11, 1993, Hoffman represented Heagerty in various transactions and litigation, including matters related to Heagerty's property in Woodside, California (hereafter, Woodside), which is the property involved in this appeal. For the legal services Hoffman rendered to Heagerty relating to Woodside during this period, Hoffman billed Heagerty a total of $1,053, 833.80, of which $796,144.38 had been paid. The present collection action is for the unpaid balance of $257,689.42, plus damages, attorney fees, and costs.

The events underlying Woodside started in 1986 when Heagerty's husband, Dr. Jerry Heagerty, a veterinarian, was diagnosed for terminal cancer. Dr. Heagerty, who was given only a few years to live, and who as a child had been raised in a ranch, wanted to spend the rest of his life in a farm. The Heagertys moved to Oroville and decided to sell their Woodside residence. Dr. Heagerty also sold his veterinary practice. Dr. Heagerty died two years later in 1988.

The Heagertys listed Woodside with Bill Sereni, a broker friend of Dr. Heagerty. Sereni, Dr. Heagerty, Robert Catalano, and Calvin Gunn, were all members of the Mounted Patrol, a volunteer search and rescue group on horseback working with the San Mateo County Sheriff's office. (RT 594-595) During the listing period, Catalano, a personal injury attorney, approached the Heagertys and offered to take the property on a lease, with option to purchase. The terms of the option lease gave Catalano the right to buy Woodside for $1,200,000 after Dr. Heagerty's death. Sereni, who suggested the lease option idea, advised the Heagertys to accept the offer, pointing out the tax advantages of the proposal, particularly the savings on capital gains tax. (RT 593-596) The Heagertys accepted the offer.

In mid-1988, prior to Dr. Heagerty's death, Catalano was in dire need of funds. Catalano indicated to the Heagertys his intention to exercise his option. To forestall the sale of Woodside and take advantage of an accelerated base for tax purposes, Catalano suggested to the Heagertys to secure a loan against Woodside from a lending institution, and lend him from the proceeds of the loan the amount of $550,000, in exchange for a deed of trust and a note which he would execute in favor of the Heagertys. The Heagertys agreed and borrowed $1,200,000 from Home Savings. (RT 598-600)

In 1989, following Dr. Heagerty's death, Catalano again expressed to Heagerty his intention to exercise his option. Hoffman, who was representing Heagerty in another matter, advised Heagerty that Catalano's intended exercise of his option was "fraud," and that Catalano and Sereni should be sued. (RT 6380641) Heagerty agreed. Hoffman filed the Heagerty v. Catalano and Sereni action (hereafter, Heagerty-Catalano) on April 10, 1989. In May 1990, the action was concluded in Heagerty's favor. Woodside was returned to Heagerty. In addition, the court awarded Heagerty damages in the amount of $152,923.00, plus attorney fees and costs in the amount of $378,989.

Catalano and Sereni subsequently filed for bankruptcy (hereafter, Catalano bankruptcy). The judgment was discharged in bankruptcy as to Catalano. (RT 478) As to Sereni, the judgment was not discharged, but Heagerty was able to collect $67,140 only from Sereni.

In October 1989, while Heagerty-Catalano was pending, Catalano filed a complaint against Heagerty for injunctive relief, declaratory relief, and damages based upon the $550,000 promissory note owed by Catalano to Heagerty. Heagerty filed a cross-complaint against Fidelity National Insurance Title Co. (hereafter, Heagerty-Fidelity) for Fidelity's failure to defend under the title insurance policy it had issued on the deed of trust securing the $550,000 promissory note. The court dismissed Catalano's complaint.

In December 1990, Hoffman filed for Heagerty a case in federal court against Home Savings (hereafter, Catalano-Home Savings). The purpose of the lawsuit was to recover damages from Home Savings under a lender's liability theory, forestall the foreclosure on Woodside, and give Heagerty time to sell the property. For representing Heagerty in this action, Hoffman charged Heagerty, on a contingency basis, attorney fees equal to one-third of what might be recovered in the litigation, in addition to a non-refundable retainer up front in the amount of $50,000, plus actual costs. Heagerty lost this case. The court granted summary judgment to Home Savings. Heagerty appealed, and lost again.

On May 2, 1991, while Catalano-Home Savings was pending, Heagerty sold Woodside for $2,150,000. Of this amount, Heagerty paid Home Savings $1,200,000.

Hoffman subsequently placed Heagerty under the protection of chapter 11 of the Bankruptcy Code, charging Heagerty $11,380.50 for attorney fees. (Exh. 15)

CONTENTIONS

Hoffman contends:

1. There was insufficient evidence to support the judgment and no substantial evidence to support the order denying Hoffman's motion for judgment notwithstanding the verdict. (AOB 10)

2. The trial court abused its discretion and committed prejudicial error in allowing William Gwire to testify as an expert witness. (AOB 31)

3. The court abused its discretion in awarding Heagerty prejudgment interest and unreasonable attorney and expert fees. (AOB 41)

4. The trial court did not have jurisdiction to enter a judgment against Kazubowski as a partner of the law firm because the law firm was sued under its common name, and Kazubowski was only named and served as an individual cross-defendant. Moreover, Kazubowski received a nonsuit on the cross-complaint. (AOB 46)

5. There was insufficient evidence to support the judgment denying Hoffman's complaint.

DISCUSSION
Sufficiency of Evidence

Hoffman contends there was insufficient evidence to support the judgment and no substantial evidence to support the order denying Hoffman's motion for judgment notwithstanding the verdict. (AOB 10) The contention is without merit.

In arguing this contention, Hoffman claims:

1. The statute of limitations was not tolled because there was no continuous representation regarding the specific subject matter in which the alleged wrongful act or omission occurred.

2. Hoffman did not breach its fiduciary duty to Heagerty.

3. Heagerty has failed to prove damages.

The rule is settled that whenever the issue on appeal is sufficiency of evidence, our power as an appellate court "begins and ends with a determination as to whether there is any substantial evidence, contradicted or uncontradicted, which will support the conclusion reached by the [trier of fact]." (Crawford v. Southern Pacific Co. (1935) 3 Cal.2d 427, 429.) In determining the presence of substantial evidence, "[a]ll of the evidence most favorable to the respondent must be accepted as true, and that unfavorable discarded as not having sufficient verity, to be accepted by the trier of fact. If the evidence so viewed is sufficient as a matter of law, the judgment must be affirmed." (Estate of Teel (1944) 25 Cal.2d 520, 527.)

We cannot, on appeal, reweigh the evidence. (Estate of Teel, supra, 25 Cal.2d at p. 527.) "It is the province of the jury to resolve conflicts in the evidence and to determine the credibility of witnesses." (Fredette v. City of Long Beach (1986) 187 Cal.App.3d 122, 127.) "When two or more inferences can be reasonably deduced from the facts, the reviewing court is without power to substitute its deductions for those of the trial court." (Crawford v. Southern Pacific Co., supra, 3 Cal.2d at p. 429.)

However, "[s]ubstantial evidence 'is not synonymous with "any" evidence. To constitute sufficient substantiality to support the verdict, the evidence must be "reasonable in nature, credible, and of solid value;" it must actually be 'substantial' proof of the essentials which the law requires in a particular case.'" [Citation.]" (Osborn v. Irwin Memorial Blood Bank (1992) 5 Cal.App.4th 234, 284.)

Statute of Limitations

Hoffman represented Heagerty from October 28, 1988 until November 11, 1993. On July 8, 1994, which was within one year from the end of that representation, Hoffman sued Heagerty for attorney fees in the amount of $270,781.60, representing the unpaid balance of the $1,013,610 total attorney fees Hoffman had charged Heagerty. (CT 1; RT 178) On September 8, 1994, which was likewise within one year of the termination of Hoffman's representation of Heagerty, Heagerty answered Hoffman's complaint, and cross-complained against Hoffman for restitution of the unconscionable fees she had paid Hoffman.

Code of Civil Procedure section 340.6 provides, in pertinent part: "(a) An action against an attorney for a wrongful act or omission, other than for actual fraud, arising in the performance of professional services shall be commenced within one year after the plaintiff discovers, or through the use of reasonable diligence should have discovered, the facts constituting the wrongful act or omission, or four years from the date of the wrongful act or omission, whichever occurs first. In no event shall the time for commencement of legal action exceed four years except that the period shall be tolled during the time that any of the following exist: [¶] (1) The plaintiff has not sustained actual injury; [¶] (2) The attorney continues to represent the plaintiff regarding the <u>specific subject matter</u> in which the alleged wrongful act or omission occurred; [¶] (3) The attorney willfully conceals the facts constituting the wrongful act or omission when such facts are known to the attorney, except that this subdivision shall toll only the four-year limitation; and [¶] (4) The plaintiff is under a legal or physical disability which restricts the plaintiff's ability to commence legal action. [¶] (b) In an action based upon an instrument in writing, the effective date of which depends upon some act or event of the future, the period of limitations provided for by this section shall commence to run upon the occurrence of such act or event." (Emphasis added.)

Hoffman relies on the "specific subject matter" language in subdivision (a)(2), arguing that Heagerty-Catalano, Heagerty-Fidelity, Heagerty-Home Savings, and the Catalano bankruptcy were four different specific subject matters, with four different and separate periods of representation, and that all such periods had expired longer than one year at the time Heagerty filed her cross-complaint in the present action. We are not persuaded.

Heagerty's expert witness, William Gwire, testified that the Catalano bankruptcy, Heagerty-Fidelity, and Heagerty Home-Savings litigation were all spawned by the original case, Heagerty-Catalano, where Hoffman, in representation of Heagerty, sued Catalano to collect on Catalano's $550,000 note to Heagerty. The trial court agreed, and so do we.

There is clearly a common thread running through and connecting all the four matters subject of Hoffman's billings. That common thread was Woodside. Although the causes of action and issues involved in those four matters might have varied, the specific subject matter to which each cause of action related was the same: Woodside. To protect Heagerty's interest in Woodside and prevent Catalano from exercising his option to sell Woodside, which would have divested Heagerty of her interest in Woodside, Heagerty secured a $1,200,000 loan from Home Savings, mortgaging Woodside as security for the loan. Heagerty then loaned Catalano $550,000, in exchange for which, Catalano gave Heagerty his $550,000 note. Catalano's note implicated Heagerty's interest in Woodside in that Heagerty needed to collect on that note to pay Home Savings and prevent Home Savings from foreclosing on the mortgage. Thus, when Catalano did not pay the note, Heagerty sued to protect and preserve her interest in Woodside.

Heagerty-Fidelity arose from Fidelity's failure to defend Heagerty in the action which Catalano had filed against Heagerty for injunctive relief, declaratory relief, and damages, based upon the $550,000 note. As in Heagerty-Catalano, Heagerty-Fidelity was filed to protect and preserve Heagerty's interest in Woodside.

Heagerty-Home Savings was a close variation of the same Woodside theme. The underlying purpose of that action was, by Hoffman's own evidence, to recover damages under a lender's liability theory, forestall the foreclosure on Woodside, and give Heagerty time to sell the property.

The Catalano bankruptcy was simply an extension of Heagerty-Catalano. It was a post-judgment matter that implicated Heagerty's ability to collect on the note and pay the Woodside mortgage.

Because Heagerty's interest in Woodside was the underlying subject and concern in all the four matters subject of Hoffman's charges and billings for attorney fees, Hoffman's representation of Heagerty must be viewed as one connected and continuous representation on the Woodside subject matter. As stated in Gurkewitz v. Haberman (1982) 137 Cal.App.3d 328, 333: "The tolling provision in Code of Civil Procedure section 340.6, subdivision (a)(2) is substantially similar to the 'continuous representation' rule created by the New York courts. The New York rule in attorney malpractice cases was derived from concepts delineated in medical malpractice decisions. The explanation for this policy is stated as follows: 'We believe that the rule is equally relevant to the conduct of litigation by attorneys. The resemblance between the continuous treatment of a condition of a patient by a physician and the continuous representation of a client in a lawsuit by an attorney is more than superficial. In both instances the relationship between the parties is marked by trust and confidence; in both there is presented an aspect of the relationship not sporadic but developing; and in both the recipient of the service is necessarily at a disadvantage to question the reason for the tactics employed or the manner in which the tactics are executed.' [Citation.] [¶] We hold that, so long as there are unsettled matters tangential to a case, and the attorney assists the client with these matters, he is acting as his representative."

We conclude Hoffman's representation of Heagerty, as reflected in her billings to her for services rendered up to November 11, 1995, relates to the same specific subject matter of Woodside, and is not barred by the statute of limitations.

Breach of Fiduciary Duty

We also find substantial evidence to support the trial court's finding that Hoffman breached its fiduciary duty to Heagerty.

"It is settled that an attorney-client relationship is of the very highest fiduciary character and always requires utmost fidelity and fair dealing on the part of the attorney. [Citations.]" (Matter of Priamos (Review Dept. of the State Bar of California, 1998) 98 Daily Journal D.A.R. 1327; Beery v. State Bar (1987) 43 Cal.3d 802, 813.) "The relation between attorney and client is a fiduciary relation of the very highest character, and binds the attorney to most conscientious fidelity— uberrima fides. [Citations.]" (Zador Corp. v. C.K. Kwan (1995) 31 Cal.App.4th 1285, 1293.) Pursuant to this duty of fidelity, "[a] [lawyer] shall not enter into an agreement for, charge or collect an illegal or unconscionable fee." (Rules of Professional Conduct, rule 4-200.)

Here, Gwire testified that Hoffman had failed to evaluate the risks of the litigation and had failed to examine other possible remedies available to Heagerty that would have saved Heagerty the litigation costs she was charged for. Gwire told the jury, thus: "It's my opinion that Ms. Hoffman in the first few months of her presentation of Mrs. Heagerty failed to apprise the client of the risks of the litigation, failed to evaluate the risks of the litigation, failed to examine any other possible remedies that would have saved Mrs. Heagerty from plunging into the seriousness of litigation, failed to analyze a great many factors that most lawyers take a look at when they decide to take the serious step of filing a lawsuit, particularly when you file a lawsuit against another attorney, and particularly against another attorney like Robert Catalano. The dangers of filing such a lawsuit. [¶] I didn't see any evidence of any evaluation of those dangers. I didn't see any analysis of what the litigation was going to cost. I saw no analysis of whether Mrs. Heagerty could really afford the litigation. In fact, I didn't see any analysis of whether there was any budget prepared for what this litigation was going to cost after the lawsuit was filed, and mind you, that I think there was a great deal that could be done in those first few weeks when Mrs. Heagerty came to Ms. Hoffman for advice about what to do. The direction of the dispute could have been steered into something that could have been resolved in Mrs. Heagerty's favor. But the decision was made to file the lawsuit. [¶] And in the first couple of months after the lawsuit was filed there was still a tremendous opportunity, great opportunity to extricate Mrs. Heagerty from the litigation. That first filing should have achieved the purpose, and instead, what I saw was what I described before, which is the fomenting of the litigation, kind of stirring the pot kind of activity on the part of Ms. Hoffman, what I felt were unreasonable demands made of the other side, the rejection of very reasonable settlement offers from the other side to try to resolve the matter, pushing the matter to the point where the attorneys' fees that were starting to be incurred in the case were starting to take over the case. As the fees mounted into the 30, 40, 50, $80,000 level on both sides. [¶] There was an unwillingness to stop the litigation. Both sides now were looking to get their legal fees paid. And the litigation took on a life of its own. In my opinion that whole plunge, that whole step into litigation was never properly thought through by Ms. Hoffman. . . . [¶] That's—that's where the conduct fell below the standard of care. In my opinion a reasonable litigator would have examined all of those factors and come to the conclusion that there were ways to protect Mrs. Heagerty that didn't involve litigation." (RT 210-212)

Concluding that Hoffman's conduct constituted breach of fiduciary duty, Gwire continued: "Well, the fiduciary duty—and I don't know whether it's been explained in this case or not—but fiduciary duty is the highest duty that the law accords individuals. It's the duty that we as partners have to our firms. The duty that the lawyer has to their clients. The highest duty known in law, and it basically means that you have the fiduciary as the lawyer to put your interests below that of the client. The client comes first, no matter what. Even if it means that you're going to be compensated greatly. If the—if it—it makes more sense to go the other way, you need to put your interests below that of the client. [¶] So when we talk about a breach of fiduciary duty we're talking about the failure of the attorney to put his or her interests below that of the client's. In the case of entering into something like litigation, particularly litigation like you're talking about here that was endless, that was potentially a black hole, you have to get the informed consent of your client. It's like going in for an operation to a hospital. The doctor sits down and tells you all of the risks, and usually they have you sign a form called Informed Consent. The law requires the attorney to get informed consent from the client. And that means spelling out all the risks of litigation, all of the dangers and merits of the case. [¶] In this case I saw nothing to indicate that that informed consent was ever received. I saw nothing to indicate that the information was ever actually imparted to Mrs. Heagerty. [¶] And I do want to add this, the files that I went through contained a great many handwritten notes by Ms. Hoffman and her associate, Ms. Falk, whose extensive documentation about what was going on in those first few months—I saw nothing indicating that that had ever been discussed. I saw no writing that a budget had ever been prepared where you sit down and say, okay, let's take a look at what this might cost. Nothing like that. [¶] I also reviewed the bills on a line-item basis. I went through every bill that had been presented to Mrs. Heagerty. There was nothing ever in any of the descriptions in the bills to indicate that there had been any analysis of the case." (RT 214-215)

 Gwire's testimony of itself provided substantial evidence to support the trial court's finding of breach of fiduciary duty. Pursuant to Evidence Code section 411, the testimony of even one witness is enough to support a judgment.

Proof of Damages

Hoffman claims the total value of the judgment in Heagerty's favor in Heagerty-Catalano was $3,036,912, particularized as follows: quieting of title to Woodside, $2,500,000; damages, $182,923; attorney fees, $325,000; costs, $28,989. (AOB 23)

The claim is specious. The fact is, of that judgment Heagerty received $615,891.12 only from the proceeds of the sale of Woodside. (RT 488-489) Of this amount, $550,000 could be considered as representing Catalano's note which, by reason of the deed of trust executed by Catalano, Heagerty could have recovered from the proceeds of the Woodside sale even without the Heagerty-Catalano action. Therefore, not counting the value of Catalano's note, Heagerty's net gain from the Heagerty-Catalano action was only $65,891.12. To this may be added the $67,140 which Heagerty recovered in the Sereni bankruptcy matter and the $31,927 she recovered in the Fidelity litigation. However, these recoveries were far exceeded by the attorney fees and costs Hoffman charged Heagerty in these matters. The fees and costs in the Fidelity litigation alone was $287,763.10. The additional fees and costs for the Sereni bankruptcy and collection were $36,655.53.

Stated differently, adding together the $65,891.12 net gain from the Heagerty-Catalano litigation, the $31,927 from the Fidelity litigation, and the $67,140 from the Sereni collection, Heagerty received a net recovery of $164,958.12. For this net recovery, however, Hoffman charged Heagerty for attorney fees the sum of $1,053,833.30. Heagerty's loss was therefore $888,875.18. From this amount may be deducted the unpaid balance of $270,781.60 subject of this collection action. That leaves Heagerty a final loss of $618,053.58.

On these facts, the award of $295,660.32 damages to Heagerty is clearly supported by substantial evidence.

Gwire's Testimony

Hoffman contends the trial court abused its discretion and committed prejudicial error in allowing Gwire to testify as an expert witness. (AOB 31) We disagree.

"Generally, it is for the trial court to determine the competency and qualification of a witness to state an opinion, and upon appeal its ruling will not be disturbed in the absence of a manifest showing of abuse of discretion. [Citation.]" (People v. Haeussler (1953) 41 Cal.2d 252, 261.)

Here, Gwire is a licensed attorney. He had been in practice for 23 years. His practice included real estate and business litigation. He also had experience in real estate transactional practice. Since 1989, he has been focusing his practice in the area of professional responsibility, particularly in "representing clients involved in disputes against their lawyers," while at the same time "doing numbers, real estate litigation." (RT 185, 186) Gwire presently heads a five-lawyer office that "go[es] after lawyers for overcharging, for malpractice, for ethics violations, and that's probably anywhere from about half to two-thirds of the practice. And the other third I do primarily—is primarily business and real estate litigation still." (RT 186) Gwire belonged to the special committee on professional responsibility of the State Bar of California. In addition, he had served as an arbitrator for the State Bar of California in fee disputes for three or four years, in addition to being an arbitrator for the local bar association for fee disputes. (RT 188) A substantial part of Gwire's malpractice cases "involve[d] real estate in the underlying transaction." (RT 189) Gwire had qualified and testified before as an expert. He had "testified in superior court, in federal court, and in arbitrations." (RT 189)

On these facts, we conclude the trial court did not abuse its discretion in qualifying Gwire and allowing him to testify as an expert.

Hoffman's reliance on Huffman v. Lindquist (1951) 37 Cal.2d 465, is misplaced. Huffman was a medical malpractice case. Unlike Gwire here, the proffered expert witness in that case was an elderly physician who had not actively practiced medicine for years.

Prejudgment Interest, Attorney Fees, Expert Fees

Hoffman contends the trial court abused its discretion in awarding Heagerty prejudgment interest and unreasonable attorney and expert fees. (AOB 41) The contention is without merit.

Hoffman claims Heagerty was not entitled to prejudgment interest, and the trial court erred in awarding her prejudgment interest in the amount of $53,243.16, because Heagerty did not have a cause of action in contract in her cross-complaint, and the damages awarded her were for the tort cause of action of breach of fiduciary duty on her cross-complaint. (AOB 42) We are not persuaded.

Civil Code section 3287, subdivision (b), states: "Every person who is entitled under any judgment to receive damages based upon a cause of action in contract where the claim was unliquidated, may also recover interest thereon from a date prior to the entry of judgment as the court may, in its discretion, fix, but in no event earlier than the date the action was filed."

Here, Hoffman sued Heagerty on Heagerty's written contract for attorney fees. Heagerty cross-complained, alleging malpractice, breach of fiduciary duty, and fraud. In claiming breach of fiduciary duty, Heagerty alleged that the attorney fees Hoffman charged and collected from her, based on their written attorney fee contract, was unconscionable. Hoffman lost. Had he won, a prejudgment interest award in his favor would have been permissible. The fact that he lost did not make the prejudgment interest award to Heagerty invalid. The very contract that Hoffman sought to enforce was the same contract that Heagerty attacked in her cross-complaint. That contract carried a provision for attorney fees.

In Chesapeake Industries, Inc. v. Togova Enterprises, Inc. (1983) 149 Cal.App.3d 901, 906, the court stated: "[I]njured parties should be compensated for the loss of the use of their money during the period between the assertion of a claim and the rendition of judgment. [Citations.]" We agree with Heagerty that simple justice demands that Hoffman, having had the use of Heagerty's $295,666.32 for over three years, should be liable for reasonable interest thereon, since to do otherwise would make a mockery of the statutory intent. (RT 24)

As to the reasonableness of Heagerty's attorney fee award, it has been held: "It is well established that the determination of what constitutes reasonable attorney fees is committed to the discretion of the trial court, whose decision cannot be reversed in the absence of an abuse of discretion. [Citations.] The value of legal services performed in a case is a matter in which the trial court has its own expertise. [Citation.] The trial court may make its own determination of the value of the services contrary to, or without the necessity for, expert testimony. [Citations.] The trial court makes its determination after consideration of a number of factors, including the nature of the litigation, its difficulty, the amount involved, the skill required in its handling, the skill employed, the attention given, the success or failure, and other circumstances in the case. [Citation.]" (Melnyk v. Robledo (1976) 64 Cal.App.3d 618, 623-624.)

Here, the cost bill was verified. (CT 360) Heagerty's counsel also submitted a declaration setting forth his qualifications as trial counsel, and detailing the services, time and fees incurred. (CT 354-358) Such evidence constituted substantial evidence to support the trial court's award of attorney fees.

As to the expert fees, Gwire charged $175 for consultation and $250 per hour for testimony. By denying Hoffman's motion to tax costs, the trial court implicitly found Gwire's fee reasonable. Hoffman has presented no convincing argument to show that Gwire's rate was unreasonable.

We conclude the trial court did not abuse its discretion in awarding Heagerty prejudgment interest, attorney fees, and expert fees.

Judgment Against Kazubowski

Hoffman contends the trial court did not have jurisdiction to enter a judgment against Kazubowski as a partner of the law firm because the law firm was sued under its common name and Kazubowski was only named and served as an individual cross-defendant, and received a nonsuit on the cross-complaint. (AOB 46) We disagree.

In her cross-complaint, Heagerty named Hoffman & Kazubowski, Diana Hoffman, and John Kazubowski as cross-defendants. The record reflects that the answer and cross-complaint were served by mail on Hoffman & Kazubowski, through its attorney, Diana Hoffman, on August 25, 1994. (CT 16) Diana Hoffman and Kazubowski were served personally on September 22, 1994. (CT 22-23) The cross-complaint alleges that Hoffman & Kazubowski is a co-partnership.

VII. Lawyer's Fiduciary Duty to Client

On July 11, 1995, Hoffman responded to the cross-complaint with a general denial on behalf of cross-defendants "Hoffman, et. al." (CT 45)

After Heagerty had presented her case on her cross complaint, Kazubowski moved for a nonsuit on the basis that Heagerty had presented no evidence of malpractice, breach of fiduciary duty, or fraud against Kazubowski in his individual capacity. Kazubowski's nonsuit motion did not challenge Heagerty's cross-complaint on the ground of lack of service. Heagerty's counsel conceded the nonsuit, but only with respect to Kazubowski liability in his individual capacity, not with respect to his liability as a partner of the law firm. At the hearing on the motion, the following representations were made:

"MR. BRIDGMAN: Yes, Your Honor. I would agree there's no evidence of fraud on the part of Mr. Kazubowski and that there is no evidence of breach of fiduciary breach of obligation.

"THE COURT: Would you stip to a non-suit on those two points?

"MR. BRIDGMAN: As to Mr. Kazubowski only, Your Honor.

"THE COURT: Yeah.

"MR. BRIDGMAN: <u>But as to the negligence count, it would seem to me there's evidence of plenty in here that Mr. Kazubowski and Ms. Hoffman were law partners and therefor his responsibility as a partner is the same as hers.</u>

"MR. KAZUBOWSKI: <u>We're not objecting to that. We're just asking that I be dismissed as an individual because I'm named as an individual.</u>

"MR. BRIDGMAN: The reason I want him in here, Your Honor, and I apologize to you, Mr. Kazubowski, <u>as a partner he's jointly liable to his partner</u>. The reason I'm in here is there's been a lot of talk about the collectibility and I want as many pockets as I can find.

"THE COURT: This is a partnership, right? Not a professional corporation, it's a partnership.

"MS. HOFFMAN: Correct.

"THE COURT: All right. So, I would think he's on the hook for everything else." (RT 1263) (Emphasis added.)

Clearly, the court had jurisdiction to enter judgment against Kazubowski in his capacity as a partner of Hoffman & Kazubowski. The nonsuit applied only to Kazubowski in his individual capacity.

Kazubowski's reliance on Fazzi v. Peters (1968) 68 Cal.2d 590, is misplaced. Fazzi held that judgment may not be entered upon a partner who had been served but not been made a party to the action against the partnership. Here, however, Kazubowski was not only served; he was also a party to the action. Indeed, in the colloquy quoted above, when counsel for Heagerty told the court that he would stipulate to the nonsuit, but only as to the negligence count, because "it would seem to me there's evidence of plenty in here that Mr. Kazubowski and Ms. Hoffman were law partners and therefor his responsibility as a partner is the same as hers," Kazubowski represented to the court: "We're not objecting to that. We're just asking that I be dismissed as an individual because I'm named as an individual." (RT 1263)

Therefore, in addition to there being evidence in the record that Kazubowski is a party to the action as a partner in Hoffman & Kazubowski, Kazubowski is also estopped from denying his open representations to the court.

Judgment on Hoffman's Complaint

Hoffman contends there was insufficient evidence to grant Heagerty judgment on Hoffman's complaint. (AOB 48) This contention is contradicted by our determination that the trial court's findings on the issues of statute of limitations, breach of fiduciary duty, and damages are supported by substantial evidence, and is, for that reason, rejected.

DISPOSITION

The judgment is affirmed.

VIII.
People v. Castaneda
(Unpublished)

Castaneda illustrates the difference between trial by jury, which is the system used in the United States, a common law country, and trial by judge alone, which is the system used in the Philippines, a civil law jurisdiction. In a jury trial, it is important that the jurors, who are lay people not very well versed in the law, be correctly instructed in the law by the judge. They need to know the law because the guilt or innocence of the accused turns on what the law is. Many of the issues brought on appeal challenge the correctness of the court's instructions. If the judge erroneously instructs the jury on the law, the error is reversible. The reversal may result in a new trial, where a different jury may be constituted, if the prosecution decides to try the defendant anew.

Also, the court has to be careful about the kind of evidence it will admit for the jury to consider. Some evidence may be more prejudicial than probative. The court needs to make sure that evidence that is substantially more prejudicial than probative is excluded. Balancing the probative value of the evidence against its potential for prejudice is no easy task for the trial court. Many errors of judgment in this balancing task result in reversal.

In the Philippines, the rules of evidence are not as demanding. This is because the judge who decides what evidence to admit and what to exclude is the same judge who decides the guilt or innocence of the accused. This is not to say that the judge can just admit any evidence he likes. The rules of evidence prescribe what evidence is admissible and what evidence is not. It is not unusual for a Philippine judge, however, who is confronted with evidence lying in the gray area of admissibility and nonadmissibility, to simply rule that "the evidence is admitted for what it may be worth." The American judge cannot make that kind of ruling.

In a criminal case appeal, challenges to the sufficiency of the evidence are, as in a civil case appeal, reviewed under the substantial evidence standard of review. However, the substantial evidence standard of review for criminal cases is formulated a little differently from the substantial evidence standard of review for civil cases. In civil cases, the power of the appellate court "begins and ends with a determination as to whether there is any substantial evidence, contradicted or uncontradicted, which will support the conclusion reached by the [trier of fact]." (*Crawford v. Southern Pacific Co.* (1935) 3 Cal.2d 427, 429.) This means that every evidence favorable to the appellee, including contradicted evidence, must be accepted as true. If the totality of the uncontradicted and the contradicted evidence is sufficient to support the judgment, the judgment must be affirmed. In criminal cases, on the other hand, the inquiry to satisfy the deferential substantial evidence standard of review is not whether the evidence proves the guilt of the accused beyond a reasonable doubt, but whether substantial evidence supports the conclusion of the trier of fact that guilt has been proved beyond a reasonable doubt. (*People v. Johnson* (1980) 26 Cal.3d 557, 576.)

The opinion in *People v. Castaneda* follows:

Paul Castaneda was charged by information with murder (Pen. Code, § 187; count 1),[8] attempted robbery (§§ 211, 664; count 2), possession of a firearm by a felon (§ 12021, subd. (a); count 3), and assault with a deadly weapon (§ 245, subd. (a)(1); count 4). As enhancements, the information alleged a prior prison term (§ 667.5); as to count 1, a special circumstance of attempted robbery (§ 190.2, subd. (a)(17)); as to counts 1 and 2, personal use of a firearm (§§ 1203.06, subd. (a)(1), 12022.5) and arming a principal with a firearm (§ 12022, subd. (a)(1)).

Defendant pleaded not guilty and denied the enhancing allegations.

By reason of the agreement that the matter would be tried as voluntary manslaughter and defendant's maximum prison term exposure would be 18 years, defendant waived jury trial.

Court trial ensued. The court found defendant guilty of voluntary manslaughter. The court also found true the enhancing allegations that a principal was armed with a firearm and that defendant had served a prior prison term. The allegation that defendant personally used a firearm was found not true.

---

[8] Further statutory references in this case are to the Penal Code unless otherwise stated.

The court sentenced defendant to the upper term of 11 years for voluntary manslaughter. As enhancements, the court added one year for the finding that a principal was armed with a firearm, and another year for the finding of a prior prison term. Defendant's total prison term was 13 years.

We affirm.

FACTS

Jose Cruz Gonzales (victim) was shot dead in Salinas on October 25, 1991. No one witnessed the actual shooting. However, two sisters, Carmen and Veronica Rodriguez, witnessed the attack on victim, heard the gunshot, and saw some of the persons involved. In a photo lineup the following day, and also in a second photo lineup two days later, Carmen positively identified defendant and Ernesto Garcia as two of the participants. Veronica also positively identified defendant and Garcia in the photo lineup the day after the incident. A third witness, Eddie Reyes, also heard the gunshot, but could not clearly identify the participants. However, he stated during a pretrial photo lineup that defendant and Garcia were "possibly" two of the participants.

A more detailed statement of the facts is included in the discussion, infra, of defendant's challenge to the sufficiency of the evidence.

CONTENTIONS

On appeal, defendant contends:

1. There was insufficient evidence to show that defendant participated in the attack on victim.

2. The trial court prejudicially erred in permitting the prosecutor to use irrelevant and unduly prejudicial association evidence.

DISCUSSION

Sufficiency of Evidence

Defendant's contention that the evidence was insufficient to support the voluntary manslaughter conviction is without merit.

On appeal, the standard of review is not whether the evidence proves guilt beyond a reasonable doubt, but whether substantial evidence supports the conclusion of the trier of fact that guilt has been proved beyond a reasonable doubt. (People v. Johnson (1980) 26 Cal.3d 557,

576.) As stated in Johnson, "'[t]he appellate court must determine whether a reasonable trier of fact could have found the prosecution sustained its burden of proving the defendant guilty beyond a reasonable doubt.'" (Ibid.)

Also, "[i]n determining whether a reasonable trier of fact could have found defendant guilty beyond a reasonable doubt, the appellate court 'must view the evidence in a light most favorable to respondent and presume in support of the judgment the existence of every fact the trier could reasonably deduce from the evidence.' [Citations.]" (People v. Johnson, supra, 26 Cal.3d at pp. 576-577.) "Evidence, to be 'substantial' must be 'of ponderable legal significance . . . reasonable in nature, credible, and of solid value.' [Citations.]" (Id. at p. 576.)

Here, the sisters Carmen and Veronica witnessed the attack and heard the gunshot. Carmen testified that she and Veronica were inside their apartment watching television when she heard somebody outside screaming her father's name. Carmen ran to the door and opened it. Carmen saw victim, a family friend who was known to her as "Gaucho," and another man looking up and facing her. Carmen was able to see the two men clearly because the area was lighted. The other man was pushing victim towards an area under the stairs of apartment number 1.

Carmen also saw three other "men running on the side of the apartment" toward where victim and the other man were. Carmen closed the door and ran to the window where Veronica was. Carmen was not able to see anything from the window, but heard victim, whose voice she recognized, screaming. She also heard sounds "like if somebody was hitting him." Carmen heard victim asking to be left alone and other voices telling victim that if he did not give them money they were going to kill him.

Two of the men Carmen had seen had guns. While the men were fighting under the stairs of apartment number 1, Carmen heard a gun click three or four times and the men telling victim "it was going to be his last chance." Victim asked the men not to shoot him. Carmen saw one man with a gun leave, then looked back. She heard that man say: "'Come on, just leave him alone.'" After the man looked back, Carmen heard a gunshot. The men ran away.

The following day, Detective Kimm showed Carmen a photographic lineup. Kimm told Carmen that she did not have to identify anybody from the lineup and that the persons she saw the night before might not be in the pictures. Carmen identified defendant and Garcia as two of the men involved in the attack. Carmen was "positive" about her identification.

Two days later, Carmen was asked to look at more photographs at the police station. Carmen again positively identified defendant, Garcia, and Jaime Rodriguez.

A month later in November 1991, Carmen went to the jailhouse for an in-person lineup. Defendant was not in the lineup because he could not be found. Carmen did not positively identify anyone, but stated that Salvador Castaneda, who was defendant's brother, looked familiar. Roque Ugale, an investigator with the district attorney's office who conducted the in-person lineup, testified that Salvador Castaneda looked similar to defendant.

After this in-person lineup, Carmen's family moved out of Salinas. In July 1992, Carmen returned for another in-person lineup. Carmen testified that her memory at that time was no longer "as good as it was right after this happened." During this lineup, Carmen was not able to identify anybody.

At trial, Carmen positively identified defendant as one of the persons she saw during the attack on October 25, 1991.

The day after the shooting, Veronica was also shown a photo lineup. Veronica identified defendant and Garcia as two of the persons who were involved in the incident.

At the in-person lineup on November 21, 1991, Veronica positively identified Garcia. She also stated that Salvador Castaneda looked familiar.

At the July 1992 in-person lineup, Veronica was not able to identify anyone.

Reyes, who was occupying another unit in the same apartment complex, also heard the gunshot and saw "a couple of guys running" towards a car parked in the driveway of one of the apartments. Although Reyes could not identify clearly the persons he saw, he told Detective Roecker at a photographic lineup three days after the incident that defendant "was possibly one of the individuals who walked around the corner and got in the vehicle," and that "it was possible that [Garcia] was another individual involved in the incident."

We are persuaded that on these facts the trial count's conclusion that defendant was guilty of voluntary manslaughter beyond a reasonable doubt is supported by substantial evidence.

Association Evidence

We also find no merit to defendant's contention that the trial court abused its discretion in permitting the prosecution to introduce evidence of defendant's past association with Garcia.

Prior to trial, the prosecution moved in limine[9] to introduce evidence that on previous occasions a number of police officers had seen defendant in the company of Garcia. The prosecution argued that the evidence would tend to show the correctness of the eyewitnesses' identification of defendant and Garcia. Defendant objected on relevancy and Evidence Code section 352 grounds.[10]

The court ruled that the fact that defendant and Garcia had a long-term association was "obviously relevant" to "give credence and credibility to the identification." To avoid undue prejudice, however, the court also ruled that "the individual facts of where they associate" and "the other facts surrounding the contacts" were not admissible.

At trial, the parties stipulated to the following sanitized version[11] of the association evidence: (1) On June 24, 1990, Officer Gerhardstein contacted defendant. Defendant was driving a car and the passenger

---

[9] (Added) A motion *in limine* is a motion before the trial to address issues that might come up before the trial. The resolution of those issues before trial avoids delay in the trial, which can be wasteful and expensive, given that the jury is already assembled. Besides avoiding trial delay, in *limine motions* help insure that certain motions, the resolution of which could influence the thinking of the jury, are raised and heard outside the presence of the jury.

[10] (Added) California Evidence Code section 352 gives the court discretion to exclude evidence if the probative value of the evidence is substantially outweighed by the probability that its admission will necessitate undue consumption of time, or create substantial danger of undue prejudice, of confusing the issues, or of misleading the jury.

[11] (Added) Sanitizing evidence is common practice in jury trials. Some evidence may only be partly probative. The rest may be more prejudicial under Evidence Code section 352 than probative. To protect the jury from the prejudicial part of the evidence, the court may sanitize the evidence by admitting only the relevant and probative part and excluding the prejudicial part.

was Garcia. (2) On April 5, 1990, Officer Stewart contacted defendant at his residence. Garcia was present and living at the residence. (3) On June 14, 1990, Stewart contacted defendant again at his residence. As in the earlier contact, Garcia was present and appeared to be living at the residence. (4) On April 28, 1990, Officer McKean contacted defendant, who was with Garcia. (5) On December 24, 1989, Officer Gates contacted defendant, who was in the company of Garcia. (7) On June 1, 1990, Officer Wheelus located a studio-type photograph in which defendant and Garcia posed together.

The rule is settled that a trial court is vested with wide discretion in determining the relevancy of evidence. (People v. Green (1980) 27 Cal.3d 1, 19.) Further, "[i]t is for the trial court to determine whether the probative value is outweighed by the possible prejudicial effect and to admit or exclude it accordingly. [Citation.]" (People v. Archerd (1970) 3 Cal.3d 615, 638.) The trial court's determination cannot be disturbed on appeal in the absence of a clear showing of abuse of discretion. (People v. Price (1991) 1 Cal.4th 324, 433.)

A critical issue in this case was the issue of defendant's identity. At the photo lineups, Carmen and Veronica picked out defendant and Garcia as two of the persons they saw during the attack. Common sense suggests that if defendant and Garcia had been seen together a number of times in the past, the fact that the two persons who were picked out in the photo lineups turned out to be defendant and Garcia would tend to lend credence and reliability to the identification made by Carmen and Veronica. The evidence was therefore relevant. "'[R]elevant evidence' is all evidence 'including evidence relevant to the credibility of a witness or hearsay declarant, having any tendency in reason to prove or disprove any disputed fact that is of consequence to the determination of the action' [citation] . . . ." (People v. Green, supra, 27 Cal.3d at p. 19.)

Thus, it was held in People v. Contreras (1983) 144 Cal.App.3d 749, 756, that the defendant's membership in a gang was relevant to show identity. Likewise, in People v. Beyea (1974) 38 Cal.App.3d 176, 194, the court held that the defendant's membership in Hell's Angels was admissible to show identity.

Defendant's reliance on Evidence Code section 1101, subdivision (a), is misplaced. The association evidence in this case was not admitted to show criminal propensity. Indeed, the sanitized version made no reference whatsoever to any arrest or criminal record. Rather, the association evidence was admitted only to establish the reliability and correctness of Carmen's and Veronica's identification, and therefore their credibility as witnesses. Under Evidence Code section 1101, subdivision (c), "[n]othing in this section affects the admissibility of evidence offered to support or attack the credibility of a witness." Likewise, under subdivision (b), evidence of prior acts is admissible to show identity.

The recent case of People v. Ewoldt (1994) 7 Cal.4th 380, 413, cited by defendant in his letter brief, is inapposite. The issue in that case was the admissibility of evidence of defendant's prior uncharged misconduct to prove his misconduct on a specified occasion. The defendant contended that the evidence was inadmissible under Evidence Code section 1101, subdivision (a). The People countered that Evidence Code section 1101 is no longer in effect because of the adoption of article 1, section 28, subdivision (d), of the Constitution, which was the initiative measure enacted in 1982 as part of Proposition 8. The Supreme Court held that "even if the adoption of section 28(d) abrogated section 1101, the Legislature reenacted section 1101 in 1986 when it amended that statute by more than a two-thirds vote." (People v. Ewoldt, supra, 7 Cal.4th at p. 390.) The high court noted that pursuant to article 1, section 28, subdivision (d), of the Constitution, relevant evidence shall not be excluded in any criminal proceeding, "'[e]xcept as provided by statute hereafter enacted by a two-thirds vote of the membership in each house of the Legislature . . . .'" (Ibid.)

Here, we are not dealing with evidence of prior uncharged misconduct. The association evidence that was admitted was sanitized precisely to remove any appearance of misconduct. It was admitted only to show that if defendant and Garcia had been seen together in prior occasions, the witnesses' positive recognition of Garcia as one of the men involved in the attack lends greater credibility to their identification of defendant as one of the men with Garcia on that occasion. And because this was a court trial, there was no realistic danger of the court appreciating the association evidence for improper purposes or of getting the issues confused.

Nor do we find merit in defendant's contention that the association evidence was unduly prejudicial. "Prejudice," within the meaning of Evidence Code section 352, "is not the prejudice or damage to a defense that naturally flows from relevant, highly probative evidence. '[A]ll evidence which tends to prove guilt is prejudicial or damaging to the defendant's case. The stronger the evidence, the more it is "prejudicial." The "prejudice" referred to in Evidence Code section 352 applies to evidence which uniquely tends to evoke an emotional bias against the defendant as an individual and which has very little effect on the issues. In applying [Evidence Code] section 352, "prejudicial" is not synonymous with "damaging."' [Citation.]" (People v. Karis (1988) 46 Cal.3d 612, 638.)

Moreover, we have stated that absent a clear abuse of discretion the trial court's determination that a challenged evidence is more probative than prejudicial will not be disturbed on appeal. (People v. Terry (1970) 2 Cal.3d 362, 403.)

Here, the trial court weighed the probative value of the questioned evidence against the potential for prejudice and determined that the evidence needed to be sanitized to be admissible. The trial court informed the parties that while the probative value of the association evidence outweighed its prejudicial effect, "the individual facts of where they associate" and "the other facts surrounding the contacts" were not admissible. Pursuant to the court's ruling, the parties sanitized the evidence and stipulated that on various occasions in the past Salinas police officers had seen defendant in the company of Garcia. As so sanitized, we see nothing unduly prejudicial in the challenged evidence.

Finally, defendant claims that the admission of the questioned association evidence violated his right to federal due process. We disagree.

In Spencer v. Texas (1967) 385 U.S. 554, 563-564, the United States Supreme Court observed that "[c]ases in this Court have long proceeded on the premise that the Due Process Clause guarantees the fundamental elements of fairness in a criminal trial. [Citations.]" In the context of an evidence question, this means that the erroneous admission of evidence must render the defendant's trial "fundamentally unfair" in order to violate federal due process. (<u>Butcher</u> v. <u>Marquez</u> (9th Cir. 1985) 758 F.2d 373, 378.)

In this case, defendant has not shown how the admission of the sanitized association evidence had rendered his trial fundamentally unfair.

Therefore, the trial court did not abuse its discretion in admitting the challenged association evidence.

<u>DISPOSITION</u>

The judgment is affirmed.

IX.
People v. Lasoya
(Unpublished)

Lasoya provides another glimpse into how the jury system in the United States works. As mentioned, we have no juries in the Philippines. Ours is a civil law system where the judge determines both questions of fact and law. Under the jury system of trial, the jury determines issues of fact, and the judge decides questions of law. Because the jury is composed of lay persons who need to know the applicable law to be able to discharge their function properly, the court instructs the jury on the applicable law. Many cases are appealed because the defendant believes that the court did not instruct the jury on the law correctly. Instructional errors are reversible. Many matters that Philippine courts find cut and dried, such as evidence of a defendant's prior convictions, or the admission of identification evidence, or what constitutes a lesser included offense, are delicate and crucial issues under the jury system.

As a rule, the court instructs the jury on a point of law when requested by a party to do so. In some cases, however, the court is required to instruct the jury *sua sponte*; i.e., on its own without being requested to do so. On fundamental points of law, the court is required to instruct the jury *sua sponte*. Even on non-fundamental points of law, the court must instruct the jury where the evidence presented to the court demands instruction on the law to guide the jury in the appreciation of the evidence.

In the Philippines, as in California, evidence of past conduct, such as prior conviction, is not admissible to prove that the defendant committed the crime charged. However, there is some difference in the way that these jurisdictions view the importance of such evidence. In the Philippines, section 46 of the Rules of Court provides that "[e]vidence that one did or omitted to do a certain thing at one time is not admissible to prove that he did or omitted to do the same or a similar thing at another time; but it may be received to prove a specific intent or knowledge, identity, plan, system, scheme, habit, custom or usage, and the like." In California, Evidence Code section 1101 (a) also states that "evidence of a person's character or a trait of his or her character (whether in the form of an opinion, evidence of reputation, or evidence of specific instances of his or her conduct) is inadmissible when offered to prove his or her conduct on a specified occasion." However, subdivision (b) of the same section is emphatic that "[n]othing in this section prohibits the admission of evidence that a person committed a crime, civil wrong, or other act when relevant to prove some fact (such as motive, opportunity, intent, preparation, plan, knowledge, identity, absence of mistake or accident, or whether a defendant in a prosecution for an unlawful sexual act or attempted unlawful sexual act did not reasonably and in good faith believe that the victim consented) other than his or her disposition to commit such an act."

Thus, in both jurisdictions, a prior conviction is not admissible to prove that the accused committed the charged offense. Likewise, in both jurisdictions, a prior conviction is admissible to prove, for example, specific intent or plan. However, in the Philippines, nothing more is required for a prior conviction to be admissible to prove specific intent or plan. In California, on the other hand, it is not enough that the prior conviction will prove specific intent or plan. It is further required that the prior conviction, while tending to prove specific intent or plan, will not at the same time show that because the defendant had the specific intent or plan, he also had the disposition to commit the crime charged. Disposition evidence is inadmissible because it is more prejudicial than probative. Determining at what point evidence of prior conduct is just intent or plan evidence, and at what point it becomes disposition evidence, is difficult for a judge to do. Many such issues reach our court, the claim being that the trial court erred in weighing the probative value of the evidence against its dispositional value.

Some questions arise when a prior conviction is used to impeach the credibility of a defendant-witness. When a prior conviction is used for this purpose, there is danger that the jury, who is otherwise shielded from evidence of the defendant's prior conviction, may develop prejudice against the defendant by reason of the defendant's prior criminal record. The potential for prejudice is even greater when the prior conviction is for a crime similar to the crime of which the defendant is presently charged. In such a case, the court has to be particularly careful in weighing the probative value of the prior conviction for impeachment purposes against its potential for undue prejudice. This problem was also addressed in *Lasoya*.

In California, as in the rest of the United States, the identification of the defendant by a witness is a delicate issue. The identification procedure must not be unduly suggestive to be admissible. Any identification procedure that gives rise to a substantial likelihood of misidentification cannot be admitted because it violates the defendant's right to due process. The rule is pretty much the same in the Philippines.

Interestingly, American jurisprudence, while not binding, has persuasive effect on Philippine courts. The case of *Neil v. Biggers*, for instance, a U.S. Supreme Court decision which I cited *infra*, was also cited by the Philippine Supreme Court in *People v. Teehankee*, 249 SCRA 54 (Oct. 6, 1995), and again in *People v. Navales* (Aug. 8, 2000), to affirm the rule that the totality of circumstances provides the test to determine whether the corruption of the out-of-court identification contaminated the integrity of the in-court identification.

In *Lasoya*, a juror was removed by the court, upon motion of the prosecution, after the presentation of the evidence, but before the jury started its deliberation. Wrongful removal of a juror presents due process concerns. For example, the defendant could argue that the juror who was removed could have been a hold-out juror who could have prevented unanimity for conviction. In the American jury system, the vote of the jury must be unanimous to reach a verdict of either conviction or acquittal. If the jury cannot agree on a unanimous verdict, we have what is called a "hung jury," which is like saying that the issue of the defendant's guilt or innocence has been left hanging or unsettled. In such a case, the judge may declare a mistrial, which leaves the door open for a retrial with a different jury, if the prosecution chooses to do so. Otherwise, in the absence of a conviction and another prosecution, the defendant is free. So when a juror is removed, and the removal is raised as an issue in the appeal, the question for the appellate court is whether the removal of the juror was wrongful or for cause. If for cause, there is no due process infringement.

The opinion in *People v. Lasoya* follows:

Jesse Consuelo Lasoya was charged by amended information with murder (Pen. Code, § 187).[12] The information further alleged that defendant had suffered a prior serious felony conviction (§ 667, subd. (a)), served two prior prison terms (§ 667.5, subd. (b)), and was a habitual offender (§ 667.7, subd. (a)(1)).

After entering a not guilty plea, defendant waived jury trial on the priors.

The jury found defendant guilty of second degree murder.

At the bifurcated trial on the priors, the court found true the allegations of prior convictions and prior prison terms.

The court sentenced defendant to a total prison term of 23 years to life, as follows: 15 years to life for the murder; 1 year for the use enhancement; 5 years for the prior serious felony conviction; and 1 year for each of the 2 prior prison terms.

We remand for resentencing, and affirm in all other respects.

FACTS

In the afternoon of November 2, 1992, at a little past 3 p.m., Norman Machaud was driving on Del Monte Street in Salinas. He had two passengers: Elizabeth Flores, who was seated in the front passenger seat; and Manuel, his 14-year-old son, who was seated behind him in the back seat. Norman had just picked up Manuel from school, where Manuel was attending ninth grade.

Traffic on Del Monte Street was heavy in Norman's direction. As Norman entered that traffic, it came to a stop and remained so for about one-and-one-half to two minutes.

Norman testified that after he had stopped, he saw victim and defendant. Victim, who was about five or ten feet away from Norman, was wearing a white T-shirt and bleeding on his side. Norman saw victim look at his side and over his left shoulder. Victim appeared "a

---

[12] Further statutory references in this case are to the Penal Code unless otherwise stated.

little stunned," and kept walking forward. Victim had no weapon and took no aggressive action against defendant. Norman lost sight of victim after victim had walked five or ten feet away.

Defendant was about five or six feet away from victim, facing victim. Defendant watched victim walk away, then turned around and snickered. Defendant walked toward a car in a parking lot. Norman saw three people inside the car. Defendant entered the car. The car drove off heading eastbound on Del Monte, which was the direction victim had taken.

Manuel testified that while they were on Del Monte near the San Martin Market, something caught his attention. He observed two persons, one of whom appeared to be injured. The other, whom Manuel identified as defendant, was holding a big knife in his hand. The knife looked "[l]ike a butcher knife." Manuel estimated the blade length to be almost eight inches. Defendant was "all cool and everything," had "a little s[m]irk" or "a sneer" on his face, and was "[w]alking cool[ly]" toward the parking lot on Del Monte. Defendant "jumped" into the rear passenger seat of a white, four-door Oldsmobile. Three other people were already in the car. The car drove out of the parking lot and proceeded in the same direction toward which victim was walking. As the car passed by Manuel, Manuel wrote down the first two numbers or letters of the license plate because he "didn't want to let them get away." Manuel called the police when he got home. Manuel gave the numbers or letters he had written down to the police.

Flores corroborated the testimonies of Norman and Manuel. Flores testified that victim and defendant were face-to-face and close enough to touch each other, but that they parted "really fast" by turning away from each other. Victim was hurt; he had a hole in his side under his arm and was bleeding. Flores saw victim hold his hands to his side, take them away, and look at the blood on his hands. Victim looked "scared" and "astonished." Defendant was holding "a big knife" with blood on it.

Flores saw victim walk. Defendant also walked away opposite the direction victim had taken and toward the parking lot on Del Monte. Defendant had "[l]ike a smirk, a grin" on his face. Defendant got into the back seat of a white four-door car. There were already three or four other people inside the car. The car left the parking lot and followed the direction victim had taken. Flores saw the occupants of the car taunting victim and using "pointing gestures."

Officer Avery testified that he was flagged down by a man at Sunrise Street. When he got out of his car, he saw victim lying face down on the ground. Victim was "kind of gurgling" and had a large blood stain. Victim was still alive but unable to converse.

An ambulance took victim to the hospital where victim died about an hour later.

John Randolph Hain, a forensic pathologist, testified that he performed the autopsy on victim. The autopsy revealed a stab wound on the left side of victim's chest approximately two inches below the level of the nipples. The wound, which was about four inches deep, cut through the left lung, the sac surrounding the heart, and into the center of the heart. In Hain's opinion, the stab wound was the cause of victim's death. Hain also testified that the stab wound was consistent with a long-bladed knife, and not consistent with anything else other than a knife.

Testifying in his own defense, defendant said that at around 10 a.m. on November 2, 1992, he, victim, and other persons were at the house of Gayla Dorado. There, defendant and victim shared drugs and mixed up a speed ball. After lunch, defendant, victim, and a certain Ruben drove to Kilbreth and Del Monte to see three drug connections. They parked at a parking lot on Del Monte.

Defendant testified that victim walked over to a parking spot where some drug dealers were parked because victim wanted to get "some dope fronted." After defendant had lost sight of victim, defendant heard victim say "Jesse." When defendant turned, victim told him "I'm hit." Defendant went to victim with a wrench in his hand. Victim showed defendant where he had been stabbed. Defendant saw a spot of blood the size of an apple on victim's left side. Victim started to panic and ran in the direction opposite where their car was parked. Defendant did not follow victim because he had an injured knee. Defendant told victim to go back to the car. When victim did not do as asked, defendant walked away from victim and returned to their car.

When defendant got back to the car, Charlie and George were already in the car. Defendant and the persons in the car proceeded to Sunrise to pick up victim. When they got to Sunrise, they heard sirens. Ruben said he was not going to pick up victim because he (Ruben) "was under the influence and he had warrants and he had to go pick up his wife." Defendant did not think that victim was wounded "that bad." Defendant said he had known victim for about 17 or 18 years and considered victim a close friend. He said he had no reason to kill victim, and denied killing him.

CONTENTIONS

On appeal, defendant contends:

1. The admission over objection of evidence of defendant's prior convictions for assault with a deadly weapon to impeach him requires reversal.

2. The trial court's failure to instruct on involuntary manslaughter as a lesser included offense to murder was error requiring reversal.

3. The trial court's wrongful removal of a juror prior to deliberations requires reversal.

4. The trial court's denial of defendant's motion to exclude identifications of defendant was error requiring reversal.

5. Because the trial court erred in enhancing defendant's sentence twice for the same prior conviction, his sentence should be reduced by one year.

DISCUSSION
Prior Convictions

Defendant contends the admission over objection of evidence of his prior convictions for assault with a deadly weapon to impeach him requires reversal. We disagree.

In People v. Castro (1985) 38 Cal.3d 301, 306, the court, construing article I, section 28, subdivision (f), of the Constitution (hereafter, Proposition 8), held that, subject to the trial court's discretion under Evidence Code section 352, "subdivision (f) authorizes the use of any felony conviction which necessarily involves moral turpitude, even if the immoral trait is one other than dishonesty. On the other hand, subdivision (d), as well as due process, forbids the use of convictions of felonies which do not necessarily involve moral turpitude."

In this case, both of defendant's prior convictions were for assault with a deadly weapon. (§ 245, subd. (a)(1).) The first conviction (Nov. 30, 1984) was nine years old; the second (June 9, 1987), six years old. Defendant concedes that assault with a deadly weapon is a crime involving moral turpitude. (People v. Means (1986) 177 Cal.App.3d 138, 139.)

Defendant argues that evidence of his prior convictions was only marginally probative of his veracity or honesty. In support of this argument, defendant cites People v. Rist (1976) 16 Cal.3d 211, 222, which stated that "convictions which are assaultive in nature do not weigh as heavily in the balance favoring admissibility as those convictions which are based on dishonesty or some other lack of integrity." Defendant also cites People v. Rollo (1977) 20 Cal.3d 109, 118, which noted that "'"[a]cts of violence . . . generally have little or no direct bearing on honesty and veracity.'" [Citation.]"

In People v. Castro, supra, 38 Cal.3d at pages 306-308, the court, tracing the historical background of Proposition 8, observed that it was the "series of decisions delineating the boundaries of permissible discretion" (at p. 307) that led to the adoption of that initiative measure. Included in that "series of decisions" were the decisions defendant now relies on: People v. Rist, supra, 16 Cal.3d 211 and People v. Rollo, supra, 20 Cal.3d 109. The Castro court determined that "there seems to be little doubt that the drafters of section 28 wanted a change and that the voters legislated it." (38 Cal.3d at p. 308.) Because Rist and Rollo were among the cases the Proposition 8 voters had legislated against, those cases are now of questionable precedential value on the issue for which they are here cited.

Defendant also argues that his priors were remote enough in time to support their exclusion for impeachment purposes. Defendant cites in support of this argument People v. Beagle (1972) 6 Cal.3d 441 and People v. Antick (1975) 15 Cal.3d 79.

However, the observation in Beagle was that remoteness may be a basis for excluding otherwise relevant impeaching prior "'if it occurred long before and has been followed by a legally blameless life.'" (6 Cal.3d at p. 453, citation omitted.) Here, defendant concedes that he had not led a "legally blameless life" since his two prior convictions; in fact, he admits to spending "most of [that] time in jail." Beagle is therefore inapposite.

As to People v. Antick, supra, 15 Cal.3d 79, that case was included in the "series of decisions" that was deemed disapproved by Proposition 8. (People v. Castro, supra, 38 Cal.3d at pp. 307-308.) Therefore, like Rist and Rollo, Antick is also of little, if any, precedential value.

Defendant further argues that the priors should have been excluded because they "were substantially similar to the crime [defendant] was charged with." In making this argument, defendant quotes People v. Fries (1979) 24 Cal.3d 222, 230, which stated: "While the risk of undue prejudice is substantial when any prior conviction is used to impeach the credibility of a defendant-witness, it is far greater when the prior conviction is similar or identical to the crime charged. [Citations.]"

Fries was, however, among the decisions specifically mentioned in Castro as contributing to the backdrop of Proposition 8 and against which the voters reacted by adopting Proposition 8. (38 Cal.3d at p. 308.) Therefore, its precedential value is also highly suspect.

In any event, the similarity of the priors to the charged offense does not compel exclusion of the evidence. (People v. Dillingham (1986) 186 Cal.App.3d 688, 695.) The trial court has discretion to admit even an identical prior. (People v. Stewart (1985) 171 Cal.App.3d 59, 65.) The critical question is always whether that discretion has been abused.

The rule is well settled that on appeal the trial court's exercise of discretion will not be disturbed absent a clear showing of abuse. (People v. Terry (1970) 2 Cal.3d 362, 403.) Because the cases relied on by defendant (Rist, Rollo, Antick, and Fries) have been rejected by the Proposition 8 voters, defendant's reliance thereon is misplaced, or at least insufficient to overcome the presumption that the trial court soundly exercised its discretion.

However, we agree with defendant that the record fails to show that the trial court had engaged in a weighing process in reaching its conclusion.

After the defense and the prosecution had argued the issue of whether defendant's priors were more prejudicial than probative, the court stated: "We previously discussed these. I'll deny the motion with respect to both of them. [¶] If he testifies, obviously the underlying facts will not become [sic] into evidence, only the conviction of the charge itself. [¶] The underlying facts obviously would not come in unless there's a further order of the Court, depends upon what the testimony is."

The trial court's statement is short of the requirement articulated in People v. Farmer (1989) 47 Cal.3d 888, 906, that "[t]he weighing must be made explicit in the record. [Citations.]" (Emphasis added.)

In Farmer, the trial court had ruled as follows: "'I don't believe the tape is that emotional. You know, we get more emotional things presented to us through the media every day. It's a horrible thing, but I wouldn't in no way equate it to a photograph of a girl, for example, who has been brutalized and raped and murdered. It's nothing like that.'" (47 Cal.3d at pp. 906-907.)

On appeal, the court held that the statement did not "affirmatively" show that the trial court had engaged in a weighing process. Said the court: "The [trial] court's analysis is sufficient as far as it goes, but fails to mention the other side of the balance: the probative value, which might be so slight that even a modestly prejudicial piece of evidence should be excluded. Because the court did not make explicit its weighing process, the admission of the tape recording was error." (47 Cal.3d at p. 907.)

In People v. Green (1980) 27 Cal.3d 1, 25, the court explained that "the reason for the rule is to furnish the appellate courts with the record necessary for meaningful review of any ensuing claim of abuse of discretion; an additional reason is to ensure that the ruling on the motion 'be the product of a mature and careful reflection on the part of the judge,' i.e., to 'promote judicial deliberation before judicial action' [citation]."

We find the record in this case far more deficient than the record in Farmer. The record before us does not indicate why the trial court concluded that evidence of defendant's prior convictions was more probative than prejudicial. The reference to a "previous discussion" leads nowhere; our review of the record fails to disclose what was in that "previous discussion," or if that discussion was recorded at all. "Silence in the record does not allow the inference that the court understood and performed its duty; the court must affirmatively articulate the fact that it has weighed probative value against prejudice. [Citations.]" (People v. Farmer, supra, 47 Cal.3d at p. 906.)

Nevertheless, we will not reverse; the error was harmless. "To determine prejudice we must inquire whether the trial court would have reached a different result if it had weighed the relevant considerations and stated that fact on the record." (People v. Farmer, supra, 47 Cal.3d at p. 907.)

In Farmer, the court concluded that had the weighing been done and that fact stated in the record, the result would have been the same because the probative value of the questioned evidence on the crucial issue of the lucidity of the victim's mental faculties "outweighed any prejudice to defendant . . . ." (Id. at p. 907.)

Here, the priors were highly probative for impeachment purposes because defendant's defense was that he had nothing to do with victim's killing. Defendant's credibility was therefore a crucial issue. Consequently, evidence to impeach that credibility was highly probative.

On the other hand, the evidence's potential for prejudice was not as high because the court had indicated its intent to sanitize the evidence: "If he testifies, obviously the underlying facts will not become [sic] into evidence, only the conviction of the charge itself."

Therefore, had the trial court weighed those competing concerns and stated that fact on the record, it is not reasonably probable that the result would have been more favorable to defendant. (People v. Watson (1956) 46 Cal.2d 818, 836.)

Lesser Included Offense Instruction

Defendant contends that the trial court's failure to instruct sua sponte on involuntary manslaughter as a lesser included offense to murder was error requiring reversal. The contention is without merit.

The rule on lesser included offense instructions is: "The court has a duty to instruct sua sponte on lesser included offenses when the evidence raises a question as to whether all of the elements of the charged offense were present, but has no such duty when there is no evidence that the offense was less than that charged." (People v. Lewis (1990) 50 Cal.3d 262, 276.) "Put another way, there is no obligation to instruct on included offenses unless there is some evidence, not merely minimal or insubstantial evidence but evidence from which a jury could reasonably conclude, that the offense was less than that charged." (People v. Jones (1992) 2 Cal.App.4th 867, 870.)

In People v. Wickersham (1982) 32 Cal.3d 307, 326, the court stated that "'the duty to give instructions, sua sponte, on particular defenses and their relevance to the charged offense arises only if it appears that the defendant is relying on such a defense, or if there is substantial evidence supportive of such a defense and the defense is not inconsistent with the defendant's theory of the case. Indeed, this limitation on the duty of the trial court is necessary not only because it would be unduly burdensome to require more of trial judges, but also because of the potential prejudice to defendants if instructions were given on defenses inconsistent with the theory relied upon.' [Citation.]"

More recently, in People v. Berryman (1993) 6 Cal.4th 1048, 1081, the court stressed that "[a] court is not obligated to instruct sua sponte on involuntary manslaughter as a lesser included offense unless there is substantial evidence, i.e., evidence from which a rational trier of fact could find beyond a reasonable doubt [citation] that the defendant killed his victim 'in the commission of an unlawful act, not amounting to felony; or in the commission of a lawful act which might produce death, in an unlawful manner, or without due caution and circumspection' [citation]."

Here, defendant's defense was that he had no role whatsoever in victim's death. Defendant attributed victim's killing to, possibly, the work of drug dealers. Such a defense is totally inconsistent with involuntary manslaughter. Therefore, under Wickersham, the court was not required to instruct sua sponte on involuntary manslaughter as a lesser included offense.

Nor was such an instruction required under Berryman. There was no evidence that the killing occurred during the perpetration either of a misdemeanor or of a lawful act performed with criminal negligence. Granting arguendo that defendant had taken drugs, there is no showing that the taking of those drugs constituted commission of a lawful act which produced death "'in an unlawful manner, or without due caution and circumspection' [citation]." (6 Cal.4th at p. 1081.).

People v. Saille (1991) 54 Cal.3d 1103, is inapposite. Because defendant denied any role in the killing of victim, the question of whether defendant was voluntarily intoxicated and whether by reason of that voluntary intoxication he did not have the requisite mental state, is irrelevant.

Removal of Juror

Defendant contends that the trial court's removal of a juror prior to deliberations was wrongful and therefore requires reversal. We disagree.

Among the questions the trial court posed to all prospective jurors during voir dire on March 8, 1993 were the following: "Anybody ever had any connection at all as a witness or in any way any connection with any of the members of the Monterey County District Attorney's Office or investigators?"

"Anybody ever been to court, been a witness at all before, other than Mr. Ray?"

"Anybody else been a witness in court in any type of proceeding, come to court at all?"

"Anybody have any second thoughts, any reason you can think of that has come up now that you feel we should know about or maybe it would be best that you not serve on this particular case?"

In addition, certain prospective jurors who had responded to the court's questions (Jose Parra was not among them) were asked the following questions: "Ever been in court for any reason yourself? [¶] [] Never testified as a witness, never been involved in anything?"

"Ever been in the court for any reason other than jury duty as a party to any type of a case or a witness or anything like that?"

"Have you ever been to court for any reason? [¶] [] You've never had any contact with anyone from the DA's office?"

"Have you ever been in court yourself for any reason, witness, party to an action, anything?"

"In court for anything other than maybe your own divorce and things of that nature?"

"Ever been in court yourself for any reason?"

"Have you ever been in court yourself for other than jury duty?"

After other jurors were asked the foregoing questions, the court asked juror Jose Parra if he had anything to tell the court. Parra answered "No."

On March 9, 1993, following the presentation of evidence by both sides, the court talked to Parra outside the presence of the other jurors. The following colloquy transpired: "THE COURT: Mr. Parra, it's come to my attention that you might have a driving under the influence conviction, a fact that you're on probation for that, and a violation of that probation by driving on a suspended or revoked license in 1992, and warrants out for your arrest. There is a Jose Luis Parra, Junior?

"MR. PARRA: Yeah. I didn't know about no ticket or warrants for my arrest.

"THE COURT: You're Jose Luis Parra, Junior, and did you live at 415 California Street?

"MR. PARRA: I still live there.

"THE COURT: The records in the Municipal Court indicate you were on probation for a driving under the influence in about 1987, right around in that period of time?

"MR. PARRA: I have no idea.

"THE COURT: And that you were arrested on March 8th. You were stopped by a Salinas police officer on Sunday, March 8th, 1992 at 10:40 for running a red light and driving on a suspended or revoked license, and you were given an appearance date of March 30th of 1992. And in the Municipal Court at 8:15, that you failed to appear on that particular occasion and a warrant was issued for your arrest?

"MR. PARRA: Oh, yeah, I had a court date in Monterey, Monterey City.

"THE COURT: Actually it would have been a court date here in this courthouse at 240 Church Street, was what the citation indicated. So and there's warrants out for your arrest now for both the driving under the influence charge and the violation of that probation for driving on—I'm just telling you.

"MR. PARRA: Okay, cause I was in Star Lodge. It's an alcohol rehab, and I was coming back from there and I still have—I still am clean.

"THE COURT: I don't know. All I know is that there's—all I know is there's warrants out for your arrest for those things that took place and the warrants issued since April of 92.

". . . . .

"THE COURT: Is there some reason you didn't mention these things when I asked you yesterday whether or not you've been in court for any reason?"

"MR. PARRA: No. Well, just the traffic tickets when I was younger, but I didn't think there would be a warrant for my arrest because I know I've always appeared. . . ."

On March 10, 1993, outside the presence of the jury, the prosecutor moved that Parra be removed for cause and that an alternate be substituted in his place, pursuant to section 1089. The prosecutor argued that Parra had failed to disclose his appearances in court, his arrests, and his familiarity with the scene. The prosecutor also stated that Parra could be biased against the prosecution because his probation violations and new cases would be prosecuted by the district attorney's office.

Over defense objection, the trial court granted the prosecution's motion, stating: "[T]he fact of the matter is that it's not a situation where he's been in court for a drunk driving charge and it's completed. [¶] You know, we get a number of people on jury duty who have had misdemeanor convictions before. There's actually warrants out for his arrest. Those warrants were at the request of the District Attorney's Office. They have prosecuted him and there's a pending prosecution against him at this time. There's no doubt in my mind that had that be [sic] brought up during the course of the questioning and there was actual pending violations of probation, even if they were pending without warrants, that he would have been excused for cause, and the District Attorney would have exercised a peremptory in any rate. [¶] So under all of those circumstances, I think his answers—I think he did fail to give us the answers when he should have given them, was well aware that he should have given them, and that it would be—and there is good cause for excusing him at this point."

We find that, on these facts, Parra's removal was not an abuse of discretion.

Section 1089 provides, in relevant part: "If at any time, whether before or after the final submission of the case to the jury, a juror . . . upon other good cause shown to the court is found to be unable to perform his duty, . . . the court may order him to be discharged and draw the name of an alternate, who shall then take his place in the jury box, and be subject to the same rules and regulations as though he had been selected as one of the original jurors."

In People v. Price (1991) 1 Cal.4th 324, 400, it was stated: "When the trial court discovers during trial that a juror misrepresented or concealed material information on voir dire tending to show bias, the trial court may discharge the juror if, after examination of the juror, the record discloses reasonable grounds for inferring bias as a 'demonstrable reality,' even though the juror continues to deny bias. [Citations.]"

The discharge of a juror for cause is a matter within the sound discretion of the trial court; it is seldom a ground for reversal on appeal. (People v. Morris (1991) 53 Cal.3d 152, 183.) "An appellate court reviews a trial court's finding of good cause under the deferential abuse-of-discretion standard. [Citations.]" (People v. Price, supra, 1 Cal.4th at p. 400.)

Here, the information concealed by Parra during voir dire relating to his convictions, probation violations, and arrest warrants, was material. That information reasonably permitted the inference that Parra was biased against the prosecution, despite his protestations to the contrary. Concealing that information made the inference even stronger. "Concealment by a potential juror constitutes implied bias justifying disqualification. [Citations.]" (People v. Morris, supra, 53 Cal.3d at pp. 183-184.) As the trial court observed, had such information been disclosed during voir dire, Parra would have been excused for cause, or, at any rate, would have been peremptorily challenged by the prosecution.

Identification Evidence

Defendant contends that the trial court's denial of his motion to suppress evidence of all identifications of him by the three eyewitnesses was error requiring reversal. We disagree.

Before trial, defendant moved to suppress the identifications made by witnesses Norman, Manuel, and Flores during the photographic lineup, the live lineup, and in court.

The evidence at the suppression hearing shows that while Norman, Manuel, and Flores were on Del Monte Street near the San Martin Market, something caught Manuel's attention. Manuel saw two people, one of whom appeared to be injured. The second person, whom Manuel identified as defendant, had a knife. Manuel described defendant to the police as about "five six, five five" feet tall, "170, 165" pounds, black hair, dark and thick mustache, and wearing a gray T-shirt or sweater and gray pants.

Norman testified that as he made the right turn from Kilbreth onto Del Monte, he had to stop for a couple of minutes because traffic in his direction was heavy and had stopped. Norman saw two people about three feet apart from each other. One of the two had a knife in his hand. Norman subsequently identified defendant as the person with the knife. Norman described defendant to the police as about five ten to six feet tall, weighing about 170 or 180 pounds, wearing a gray and black long-sleeved sweater, a mustache, and a short and clean haircut.

Flores testified that while their car was stopped she saw two men standing together and they "separated real quick." One of the men, whom she identified as defendant, was holding a knife. Flores described defendant to the police as "a Hispanic male with short hair combed back with a mustache," "about five seven, five nine," weighing "145, 160," wearing dark pants and a sweater.

That night, the police showed photographic lineups to the eyewitnesses at their homes. The lineup consisted of individual pictures of six men, all of whom had mustaches.

Manuel identified defendant's picture as that of the man with the knife. Although Manuel noticed the sweater worn by defendant in the picture, he said it was not the sweater that made him recognize defendant.

Manuel said that he had taken a good look of defendant on the street and that at the photo line up he was "looking at the mustache mostly."

When Norman was shown the photographic lineup, he picked out numbers two and six. At that time, Norman was not positive because the pictures were small and "it [was a] little bit hard to distinguish." Moreover, he realized that "[t]he picture is always a little bit, little deceiving."

When Flores was shown the photographic lineup, she pointed to picture number two, but did not positively identify anyone.

The following day, Norman went to the live lineup at the jail. Norman said he "knew what [he] was looking for, but [he] just needed a real person to look at." Norman identified defendant. Norman said the photo lineup helped him "make [his] determination between the two that [he] was looking at" because defendant was the one person who was present in both lineups. However, Norman emphasized that he was able to identify defendant in the lineup "based on the face." He said defendant's face was "not a hard face to forget when you see it in person."

Manuel went to the live lineup a few days later. Manuel identified defendant based on his memory of what he had seen on Del Monte Street. Manuel said he did not pick out defendant because of the photograph he had earlier seen. He said he picked out defendant because he "got a good picture" of him on November 2.

Flores testified that when she identified defendant in the live lineup, she was "pretty sure" of her selection. Her selection at the live lineup was the same as her selection in the photo lineup. Flores said that when she went to the live lineup, she had "kind of this picture in [her] mind" from the day the incident occurred on the streets. She further said that she did not remember the photo lineup well when she viewed the live lineup because she "was going more by what [she] saw that day than anything else."

In court, Norman, Manuel, and Flores positively identified defendant.

Norman identified defendant in court because he remembered defendant's face from the street. Norman said that as soon as he turned the corner and came to a complete stop, he noticed the victim on the sidewalk. He was able to see defendant and the victim clearly because he stopped for about one-and-a-half to two minutes and he was only about fifteen to twenty feet from where the victim and defendant were standing. There was nothing blocking Norman's view of defendant. Norman said he looked at defendant's face "[l]ong enough to get a positive I.D." At the time Norman testified in court, he still remembered what the man with the knife looked like, and he identified that man as defendant.

Manuel testified that even as he was testifying in court, he still had a good memory of what he had seen on the street, independent of viewing any lineup.

Flores testified that she identified defendant in court not because she had seen him at the live lineup but because she remembered defendant from the street. She said that when she observed defendant on November 2, 1992, there was nothing between her and defendant. She had a clear view of defendant and had a clear view of his face. She still remembered the way defendant smirked.

On these facts, we reject for lack of merit defendant's contention that the photographic lineup was impermissibly suggestive. To be impermissibly suggestive, the identification procedure must give rise "to a very substantial likelihood of irreparable misidentification." (Simmons v. United States (1968) 390 U.S. 377, 384.) "It is the likelihood of misidentification which violates a defendant's right to due process . . . ." (Neil v. Biggers (1972) 409 U.S. 188, 198.)

Furthermore, the trial court's finding that the out-of-court identification was not excessively suggestive must be upheld if supported by substantial evidence. (People v. Gomez (1976) 63 Cal.App.3d 328, 335, 336.) Conflicting factual versions must be resolved in favor of the finding of the trial court. (Id. at p. 336.)

On appeal, "[t]he burden is on the defendant to demonstrate unfairness in the manner the [out-of-court identification] was conducted, i.e., to demonstrate that the circumstances were unduly suggestive. [Citation.] Appellant must show unfairness as a demonstrable reality, not just speculation. [Citation.]" (In re Carlos M. (1990) 220 Cal.App.3d 372, 386.)

Here, Norman picked out two photographs from the lineup but could not determine which of them was the picture of the person he saw on the street because the pictures resembled each other very closely and were too small to permit a positive identification. Moreover, he felt that there was always something deceiving in pictures. Norman wanted to be sure by looking at the persons live. Flores could not identify defendant positively from the photo lineup. Although she had selected defendant's picture in the photo lineup, she said she could not be positive until she had seen the person live.

If the pictures were too small and two of them resembled each other so closely that Norman found positive identification impossible, and if Norman and Flores could not make a positive identification by just looking at the pictures, then the lineup could not have been impermissibly suggestive.

Nor was the live lineup unfairly suggestive. Both at the photo lineup and the live lineup, the three eyewitnesses were separately told by the police that the person they saw on November 2 might or might not be in the lineups, and that if they were not positive they did not have to make any identification. Although Norman said he was aided in his determination by the fact that defendant was the only person in the live lineup who was also in the photo lineup, he stressed that he based his identification of defendant on his memory of what occurred on November 2.

In <u>Neil</u> v. <u>Biggers, supra,</u> 409 U.S. at pages 199-200, the court stated that in evaluating the likelihood of misidentification, the court is to consider such factors as "the opportunity of the witness to view the criminal at the time of the crime, the witness' degree of attention, the accuracy of the witness' prior description of the criminal, the level of certainty demonstrated by the witness at the confrontation, and the length of the time between the crime and the confrontation."

Here, the witnesses observed defendant for approximately two minutes. Manuel had a particular reason to remember defendant's face clearly because even as he was watching what was happening he had already determined out of a sense of civic duty to report the incident to the authorities; he even wrote down the first two numbers or letters of the Oldsmobile's license plate. Norman and Flores also realized that something wrong was happening, and thus had reason to observe defendant carefully. They remembered clearly defendant's "smirk." All the three eyewitnesses saw the blood on victim's side and the knife in defendant's hand. Only the width of the road separated them from defendant, and their view of defendant was unobstructed. Within hours, they gave their description of defendant to the police, and their description matched each other's in virtually every essential respect.

On these facts, we conclude that the likelihood of misidentification under the Neil factors was not "very substantial."

Be that as it may, the "[o]bservation of a suspect through an unfairly suggestive procedure does not always bar identification testimony at the trial. Such testimony is nevertheless admissible if the prosecution establishes 'by clear and convincing evidence that the in-court identification [is] based upon observations of the suspect other than the lineup identification.' [Citations.]" (People v. Bisogni (1971) 4 Cal.3d 582, 587.) Even if the pretrial confrontation was illegal, the admission of an in-court identification which has a source of origin independent of such illegal confrontation is not error. (People v. Martin (1970) 2 Cal.3d 822, 831.)

Here, the record discloses that the in-court identifications of defendant by Norman, Manuel, and Flores were based on what they observed of defendant on November 2, independently of the photo and live lineups. Consequently, such in-court identifications are admissible evidence regardless of the issue of the validity of the out-of-court lineups.

Sentence Enhancement

Defendant contends that pursuant to People v. Jones (1993) 5 Cal.4th 1142, one of the one-year enhancements imposed pursuant to section 667.5, subdivision (b), should be stricken. Respondent interposes no objection, noting that for the reasons stated in Jones, "it appears that the one-year enhancement for the 1987 prior offense of assault with a deadly weapon under Penal Code section 667.5, subdivision (b) should be stricken."

The record shows that in the amended information filed February 18, 1993, it was alleged that defendant had previously been convicted of the serious felony of assault with a deadly weapon, with great bodily injury, within the meaning of section 667, subdivision (a). The amended information further alleged that for the same conviction defendant served a prison term within the meaning of section 667.5, subdivision (b).

Finding both allegations to be true, the trial court enhanced defendant's sentence by five years for the serious felony conviction pursuant to section 667, subdivision (a), and by another year for the prison term resulting from such conviction.

In People v. Jones, supra, 5 Cal.4th at page 1144, the court determined that in approving Proposition 8 the electorate did not intend a prison sentence to be enhanced both for a prior conviction and for the prison term resulting from that conviction. The court therefore remanded the case to the trial court with directions to strike the additional one-year enhancement under section 667.5, subdivision (c).

We must do the same here. We find Jones indistinguishable in all pertinent respects.

Reasonable Doubt Instruction

Defendant has filed a supplemental brief raising the constitutionality of CALJIC No. 2.90, based upon Cage v. Louisiana (1990) 498 U.S. 39 and Sandoval v. California (No. 92-9049, cert. granted Sept. 28, 1993). The United States Supreme Court has now upheld this instruction. (Victor v. Nebraska (1994) ___ U.S. ___ [114 S.Ct. 1239].)

DISPOSITION

The one-year enhancement under section 667.5, subdivision (b), for the prison term that resulted from the serious felony conviction for which a five-year enhancement under section 667, subdivision (a), was also imposed, is stricken. This cause is remanded with instructions to resentence defendant accordingly, and to send a corrected copy of the abstract of judgment to the Department of Corrections. In all other respects, the judgment is affirmed.

X.
People v. Olson
(Unpublished)

Olson is another case involving jury issues. In *Olson*, the court instructed the jury that they should conduct themselves during their deliberations in accordance with the instructions of the court, and that if any juror should disobey the court's instructions, it is the duty of the other jurors to make such misconduct known to the court. The defendant challenged the validity of this instruction, arguing that it violates the doctrine of jury nullification, which gives to the jury the power to acquit, regardless of the evidence of guilt. We rejected the jury nullification argument, and held that jury nullification is not the law in California.

In the Philippines, the intentional killing of a human being is either homicide or murder. It is murder if the killing is committed with treachery or other qualifying circumstances. In the absence of those qualifying circumstances, the killing is the lesser offense of homicide. In the United States, homicide is the generic term used for all kinds of unlawful killing. It is murder if the killing is committed with malice aforethought. Murder, in turn, is divided into murder of the first degree and murder of the second degree, depending on the circumstances surrounding the commission of the crime. In California, if the murder is committed by lying in wait, or with torture, or with any of the special circumstances described in section 189 of the Penal Code, the murder is of the first degree. All other kinds of murder are of the second degree. The unlawful killing of a human being without malice is manslaughter. In California, there are three kinds of manslaughter: voluntary manslaughter; involuntary manslaughter; and vehicular manslaughter. Manslaughter is voluntary if it is committed upon a sudden quarrel or heat of passion. It is involuntary if the killing happens in the commission of an act not amounting to a felony, or in the commission of a lawful act that might produce death in an unlawful manner, or if the killing was done without due caution or circumspection. Vehicle manslaughter is manslaughter resulting from the driving of a vehicle.

Olson also addressed the cruel and/or unusual punishment issue raised by the defendant. The defendant argued that the penalty he received for the second degree murder conviction was only 15 years to life. However, the total sentence he was to serve reached 40 years to life because of the additional penalty of 25 years to life for the firearm use. The defendant claimed that the additional penalty of 25 years to life for the firearm use was out of proportion to the murder penalty itself, and thus cruel and/or unusual. We rejected this argument.

The opinion in *People v. Olson* follows:

Defendant Harry Lee Olson was charged by information with murder (Pen. Code, § 187).[13] The information further alleged that defendant used a firearm in the commission of the offense (§ 12022.5, subd. (a)(1)), and that he personally and intentionally used a firearm causing great bodily injury or death (§ 12022.53, subd. (b)-(d)). (CT 92-94) Defendant pleaded not guilty and denied the special allegations. (CT 96) The jury found defendant guilty of second degree murder, and also found true the firearm allegations. (CT 279-283) The trial court sentenced defendant to a total prison term of 40 years to life, as follows: 15 years to life for the second degree murder conviction, plus a consecutive term of 25 years to life for the personal and intentional use of a firearm causing great bodily injury or death. (CT 302-304)

We affirm.

FACTS

Defendant and John Justin were friends and roommates in an apartment they shared on Sheridan Avenue in San Jose. Defendant considered Justin, a cocaine dealer, his best friend, and helped Justin in his cocaine business. Justin owned a .357 magnum revolver. (RT 33, 38, 42-44, 47-48, 87-88)

On February 17, 1998, Justin, who was large and strong, had an ankle injury. Justin moved about in a wheelchair, using a cane to help himself get out of the wheelchair. On that date, Timothy Tachibana and his girlfriend, Karan Hatzenbeler, visited Justin at his apartment.

---

[13] Further statutory references in this case are to the Penal Code unless otherwise stated.

Tachibana and Hatzenbeler knew Justin. Tachibana bought cocaine from Justin once a week. (RT 41-42, 50-51, 60, 89-92)

Defendant was in the apartment at the time of the visit, baking a pie. Defendant asked Hatzenbeler if the pie he was baking was browning too fast. The two talked about baking, after which, Hatzenbeler went to the bathroom. (RT 51, 92-94)

Tachibana went with Justin to a bedroom where Justin kept his computer. (RT 52, 86-87, 92) Tachibana worked on Justin's computer, and remained in the room to continue working on the computer when Justin left the room later. (RT 52) After Justin had left the room, Tachibana heard him yell something like "I'm not kidding," and "you need to move out." (RT 53)

From the bathroom, Hatzenbeler heard Justin and defendant arguing. Justin was saying: "I'm not playing with you Skip [defendant's nickname], I'm not playing with you." (RT 94) Hatzenbeler also heard defendant say: "I'm tired of taking your shit, I'm tired of you telling me where I'm going to go." (RT 95)

The argument did not last long. (RT 53-54) Tachibana heard sounds that sounded like "pop, pop, pop." (RT 54, 95-96) Hatzenbeler heard the same sounds, and wondered if they were gunshots, but concluded they were not. (RT 95-96)

Tachibana went to the hallway. He saw Justin on his stomach stretched out on the floor. (RT 57-58, 96-97) Defendant was standing near Justin's shoulders with a gun, which was pointed at the floor. (RT 57) The gun looked like an old-fashioned revolver. Defendant was saying a prayer. (RT 58, 102) Defendant told Tachibana and Hatzenbeler to leave, saying: "You never saw me and I never saw you and your name will never come up." (RT 55-56, 102, 104) Tachibana and Hatzenbeler did not see blood or any other weapon. (RT 58, 99-100)

When they left, Tachibana and Hatzenbeler did not think that Justin had been shot because defendant was calm and the sounds they heard did not sound like gunshots. (RT 62) They thought that what they had seen was a practical joke. Tachibana knew that Justin had played jokes before. (RT 62, 105)

Later that evening, defendant called Tachibana, telling Tachibana there was nothing to worry, and that nothing had happened. (RT 63)

Tachibana called Justin for the next three days, but received no live answer. The answering machine gave the same message, which concerned Tachibana because Tachibana knew that Justin frequently changed his answering machine message. (RT 64, 106-107) Hatzenbeler called Justin once. When defendant answered the phone, Hatzenbeler hung up. (RT 106)

Several days later, Tachibana and Hatzenbeler went to the police station and reported what they knew. (RT 65-66)

On February 20, 1998 Palo Alto police officers went to Justin's apartment to check on his welfare. (RT 192-193) Defendant answered the door and invited the officers in. (RT 193) Defendant told the officers not to mind the mess because he was remodeling the apartment. The officers told defendant they were checking on Justin's welfare. Defendant replied he and Justin had an argument and that Justin had gone to the East Bay to visit his parents, and would be back later that night. (RT 195) The officers, sensing a strong odor of carpet deodorizer and noticing dark stains on the carpet and on the wall, looked around. (RT 194, 197-198)

Defendant asked: "Do you want me to cut the bullshit?" (RT 201) The officers said they did. (RT 201) Defendant told the officers that he and Justin had an argument and that Justin pulled a golf club. Defendant pushed Justin out of the wheelchair. As Justin fell down, a gun "popped out" from under the wheelchair's seat. Defendant grabbed the gun and shot Justin with it. (RT 201) The officers asked where Justin was. Defendant said: "Right there," pointing to a rolled-up carpet standing against the wall. (RT 202-203) The officers unrolled the carpet and found Justin's body; it was in a state of decomposition. The officers arrested defendant. (RT 203, 204) Defendant told the officers: "Yeah, I know, I did it, and I knew you guys would be coming." (RT 204)

Without being asked, defendant added: "Yeah, well, I did it, what can I say. I don't know what happened. We got in a fight, what can I say. He's a pretty big boy. He tried to hit me and I shot him. I've been sitting here for the last three days waiting for you guys. I wanted to pick up the phone and call, but I didn't know what to say. I just shot my best friend. When I killed him, I killed us both. I guess I was just waiting for you to come. Not only did I kill someone, but I did this to my best friend. I've been sitting here praying with him for the last three days just hoping you would come." (RT 205)

The autopsy revealed two gunshot wounds to the head, two gunshot wounds to the body, and one defensive wound to the hand. The hand wound and one head wound were different from the other wounds in that they were inflicted by a "snake shot," which was described as a shot fired from a cartridge containing not a single projectile, but several small BBs. The other wounds were inflicted by shots fired from a standard, single-projectile cartridge. (RT 220-224, 226-227, 230, 236) No toxicology work could be done on Justin's body because of the "deterioration of the tissues." (RT 236)

While in police custody, defendant waived his Miranda[14] rights. Defendant spoke to the police and even provided a videotaped reenactment of the shooting. (RT 266-267, 284; Augmented CT 1-88) In his confession to the police, defendant stated: "(Unintelligible) at this point er my roommate and I have been friends for many years but it's been strained the last couple of years and er there's been some things that have built up in the last couple of weeks and er we got in, in an argument pretty steadily and er I have been a little unstable in reference to mentally. Not too together recently because of some events that have been happening and er we just got in a big argument and er he's a pretty big guy and er I dunno. He came at me and er I took his gun away from him. He came at me with his gun. I dunno what he's gonna, figure he's gonna do with it and I had my close and I just turned around and shot him." (ACT 9-10)

Defendant elaborated that during the argument, when Justin reached for his gun, defendant "knocked him kinda over and it fell on the ground and then I grabbed my gun and I, you know, and er next thing I know I'd shot him. I was, my gun was empty. I went picked up his gun. Shot him with his own gun. So when you check the body there'll be like two or three shots from my gun and I had to go get his gun to finish it. And I, I don't know how many times I shot him but I, well I know my gun was empty." (ACT 11)

Explaining the cause of the fight, defendant went on: "[Tachibana and Hatzenbeler] came in and er they went in near the office and er he

---

14 *Miranda v. Arizona* (1966) 384 U.S. 436.

[Justin] came back out and said, 'Well, I need some money' and I said, 'Well, you're not getting from me.' 'Well, I'm gonna send them to go get the stuff I wanna use your money I don't wanna use my money.' 'Why in the fuck would I give you any money?' [Justin] said, 'Well, you still owe for rent.' I said, 'I'm not paying you any more, more money 'cos I'm moving out.' So him and I start arguing about it. I said, 'Hey, you're not gonna discuss this at a later time when you and I are by ourselves,' and he started yelling screaming. Next thing I know he reached for a gun and boom, boom. I knocked him down. He fell down on the floor. I reached over bed, got my gun and went boom, boom, boom, and he was down." (ACT 15)

Defendant said that after Tachibana and Hatzenbeler had left, Justin, who was moaning, tried to crawl out in an attempt to escape. Defendant picked up Justin's gun and shot Justin in the back of the head. (ACT 16, 18-24, 34-36, 43-44, 86-87) Defendant then put Justin's body on the carpet and rolled the carpet over it. (ACT 17)

Testifying in his defense, defendant stated that he and Justin were "best friends," and that he helped Justin in his drug business. (RT 293) On February 17, 1998, while being visited by Tachibana and Hatzenbeler, defendant and Justin had an argument. (RT 295-296) Defendant was in his bedroom watching television when Justin entered in his wheelchair. Justin asked defendant for money so that he could have Tachibana go and buy cocaine. (RT 297) Defendant refused to give the money. Justin became abusive, and yelled: "Give me the money." (RT 298) When defendant continued to refuse to give the money, Justin reached under the cushion of his wheelchair, where defendant knew Justin kept a gun, and pulled the gun out. (RT 299-301) Defendant lunged at Justin, striking Justin's left shoulder. (RT 300-301) The wheelchair spun. Defendant turned around, reached for his own gun, and "[came] back out shooting," firing three times. (RT 301) When Tachibana and Hatzenbeler came to where he was, he told them to leave. (RT 301-302) When defendant saw Justin crawling, he shot him one more time. (RT 302)

X. Jury Nullification

CONTENTIONS

Defendant contends:

1. The trial court erred in giving CALJIC No. 17.14.1 because that instruction impinged upon defendant's Sixth and Fourteenth Amendment rights to a unanimous jury and to have the jury free to use its power of nullification. (AOB 10)

2. The jury instructions on voluntary manslaughter created an improper presumption favoring a murder verdict. (AOB 27)

3. The definition of reasonable doubt given to the jury violated defendant's right to due process of law, requiring reversal per se. (AOB 34)

4. The sentence enhancement for firearm use constitutes cruel and/or unusual punishment.

*DI*SCUSSION
CALJIC No. *17.14.1*

Defendant contends the trial court erred in giving CALJIC No. 17.14.1 because that instruction impinged upon defendant's Sixth and Fourteenth Amendment rights to a unanimous jury and to have the jury free to use its power of nullification. We disagree.

The court instructed the jury on CALJIC No. 17.41.1, as follows: "The integrity of a trial requires that jurors at all times during their deliberations conduct themselves as required by these instructions. Accordingly, should it occur that any juror refuses to deliberate or expresses an intention to disregard the law or to decide the case based on penalty or punishment, or any other improper basis, it is the obligation of the other jurors to immediately advise the Court of the situation." (2 RT 483; II CT 234) Defendant argues that CALJIC No. 17.41.1 should not have been given because: (1) it impinged upon his right to a unanimous verdict by twelve independent jurors, each deciding the case for himself or herself free from improper pressures before voting individually and then determining if unanimity has been achieved; (2) it violates the doctrine of jury nullification, which is implicit in the Sixth Amendment; and (3) public policy considerations support defendant's position. The argument is not persuasive.

First, the doctrine of jury nullification is not the law in California. As stated in People v. Baca (1996) 48 Cal.App.4th 1703, 1707-1708: "While the notion of nullification has been embraced by some writers [citations], it has virtually no support in modern American precedent. The arguments of its adherents and its unavoidable flaws are fully reviewed in Judge Levanthal's thoughtful opinion for the District of Columbia Circuit in United States v. Dougherty (D.C. Cir. 1972) 473 F.2d 1113, 1130-1137. [¶] Juries have had the naked power to 'nullify' for over 300 years, since Bushell's Case (1670) 89 Eng.Rep. 2 [6 Howell's State Trials 999]. But while 'jurors may have the power to ignore the law . . . their duty is to apply the law as interpreted by the court [as] they should be so instructed.' [Citations.] [¶] The California cases, while recognizing the jury's 'undisputed power' to acquit regardless of the evidence of guilt, reject suggestions that the jury be informed of that power, much less invited to use it. [Citations.] Justice Mosk may have said it best, in People v. Dillon [(1983) 34 Cal.3d 441, 487-488, footnote 39]. In replying to Justice Kaus's position in favor of a nullification instruction, he said: '. . . it cannot seriously be urged that, when asked by the jurors, a trial judge must advise them: "I have instructed you on the law applicable to this case. Follow it or ignore it, as you choose." Such advice may achieve pragmatic justice in isolated instances, but we suggest the more likely result is anarchy.' [Citation.] [¶] We are offered a single modern precedent to the contrary, a trial court opinion by a federal judge in Tennessee. (U.S. v. Datcher (M.D.Tenn. 1993) 830 F.Supp. 411.) That case held that a defendant is entitled to have the jury informed of information 'that might lead to nullification.' [Citation.] Datcher has not been followed by other courts. It has, in fact, been rejected by the Sixth Circuit, of which the Middle District of Tennessee is a part. (U.S. v. Chesney (6th Cir. 1996) 86 F.3d 564, 574.) Certainly no California court has embraced it, and ours will not be the first."

Since Baca, at least two other California decisions (People v. Sanchez (1997) 58 Cal.App.4th 1435, and People v. Nichols (1997) 54 Cal.App.4th 21) have also rejected Datcher and the jury nullification doctrine.

Datcher is also inconsistent with Shannon v. United States (1994) 512 U.S. 573, 579, which stated: "It is well established that when a jury has no sentencing function, it should be admonished to 'reach its verdict without regard to what sentence might be imposed.' [Citation.] The principle that juries are not to consider the consequences of their verdicts is a reflection of the basic division of labor in our legal system between judge and jury. The jury's function is to find the facts and to decide whether, on those facts, the defendant is guilty of the crime charged. The judge, by contrast, imposes sentence on the defendant after the jury has arrived at a guilty verdict. Information regarding the consequences of a verdict is therefore irrelevant to the jury's task. Moreover, providing jurors sentencing information invites them to ponder matters that are not within their province, distracts them from their factfinding responsibilities, and creates a strong possibility of confusion. [Citations.]" (Footnotes omitted.)

As to the portion of CALJIC No. 17.41.1 instructing the jury that they should immediately advise the court of the situation "should it occur that any juror refuses to deliberate or expresses an intention to disregard the law or to decide the case based on penalty or punishment or any other improper basis," that instruction no more than instructs the jurors what their obligation is when any juror engages in juror misconduct. Because jurors must apply the law, as instructed by the court, it is misconduct for a juror to refuse to obey the court's instruction. Misconduct by a juror taints the integrity of the judicial process, and should be prevented whenever possible, and rectified when committed. Yet, because the jurors deliberate by themselves, they alone would know when jury misconduct is committed by any of them. It is thus essential that jurors report to the court when any of them engages in jury misconduct. Consequently, an instruction informing the jurors of this duty and exhorting them to report any jury misconduct so that the same may be corrected, and the integrity of the judicial process preserved, is not only proper, but necessary.

Defendant argues that CALJIC No. 17.41.1 compromises the jury's privacy and inhibits jury deliberations. The fear is unfounded. There is no showing that the jury's privacy in this case was in fact compromised, or their deliberations inhibited. Defendant bears the burden of showing that the challenged instruction in fact prejudiced him.

Defendant's public policy argument also fails. Any claim of jury privacy must be balanced against the need to protect the judicial process from jury misconduct. We do not think the instruction in question has disturbed that balance. Certainly, defendant has made no attempt to show that the jury's right to secrecy in this case outweighs the court's need to be informed of any jury misconduct or of refusal by any juror to follow the court's instructions.

We conclude the trial court did not err in giving CALJIC No. 17.41.1.

Voluntary Manslaughter Instruction

Defendant contends the jury instructions on voluntary manslaughter created an improper presumption favoring a murder verdict. (AOB 27) The contention is without merit.

Defendant claims that CALJIC Nos. 8.42 and 8.43 articulate the concept that a manslaughter verdict requires a reduction of the homicide from murder. (AOB 27) Defendant complains that CALJIC No. 8.42 begins with the words "[t]o reduce an intentional felonious homicide from the offense of murder to manslaughter upon the ground of sudden quarrel or heat or passion," and that CALIC No. 8.43 similarly leads with the words "[t]o reduce a killing upon sudden quarrel or heat of passion from murder to manslaughter . . . ." Defendant goes on to point out that similar language appears repeatedly throughout the two instructions. Defendant argues that the frequent references to the same concept "creates in the minds of the jurors the construct that they should return a murder verdict unless the defense has convinced them that the homicide should be reduced to manslaughter." (AOB 27) Such a construct, defendant claims, "is an impermissible intrusion into the deliberative process and it sets up a presumption that a homicide is murder rather than manslaughter, an improper presumption, rather than permitting the jury to begin deliberations on a clean slate with all levels of crime submitted to the jury deemed worthy of even-handed consideration." (AOB 27)

The argument ignores the rule that jury instructions should be read together and not in isolation from each other. "It is well established in California that the correctness of jury instructions is to be determined from the entire charge of the court, not from a consideration of parts of an instruction or from a particular instruction. [Citations.]" (People v. Burgener (1986) 41 Cal.3d 505, 538.) On appeal, the issue is whether the jury understood the instructions in an erroneous way, given the entirety of the instructions and all other relevant circumstances. (People v. Kelly (1992) 1 Cal.4th 495, 525-526.)

CALJIC No. 8.42 reads in pertinent part: "To reduce an intentional felonious homicide from the offense of murder to manslaughter upon the ground of sudden quarrel or heat of passion, the provocation must be of the character and degree as naturally would excite and arouse the passion, and the assailant must act under the influence of that sudden quarrel or heat of passion. . . . [¶] If there was provocation, . . . but of a nature not normally sufficient to arouse passion, or if sufficient time elapsed between the provocation and the fatal blow for passion to subside and reason to return, and if an unlawful killing of a human being followed the provocation and had all the elements of murder, as I have defined it, the mere fact of slight or remote provocation will not reduce the offense to manslaughter." (CT 205-206)

CALJIC No. 8.43 likewise reads in pertinent part: "To reduce a killing upon a sudden quarrel or heat of passion from murder to manslaughter the killing must have occurred while the slayer was acting under the direct and immediate influence of the quarrel or heat of passion. Where the influence of the sudden quarrel or heat of passion has ceased to obscure the mind of the accused, and sufficient time has elapsed for angry passion to end and for reason to control his conduct, it will no longer reduce an intentional killing to manslaughter." (CT 207)

However, before giving CALJIC Nos. 8.42 and 8.43, the court instructed the jury to consider the instructions as a whole. The court also instructed the jury on CALJIC Nos. 8.50 and 17.10. CALJIC No. 8.50 states: "The distinction between murder and manslaughter is that murder requires malice while manslaughter does not. [¶] When the act causing the death, though unlawful, is done in the heat of passion or is excited by a sudden quarrel that amounts to adequate provocation, or in the actual but unreasonable belief in the necessity to defend against imminent peril to life or great bodily injury, the offense is manslaughter. In that case, even if an intent to kill exists, the law is that malice, which is an essential element of murder, is absent. [¶] To establish that a killing is murder and not manslaughter, the burden is on the People to prove beyond a reasonable doubt each of the elements of murder and that the act which caused the death was not done in the heat of passion or upon a sudden quarrel or in the actual, even though unreasonable, belief in the necessity to defend against imminent peril to life or great bodily injury." (CT 204) (Emphasis added.)

CALJIC No. 17.10 was modified, and given as follows: "If you are not satisfied beyond a reasonable doubt that the defendant is guilty of the crime charged, you may nevertheless convict him of any lesser crime, if you are convinced beyond a reasonable doubt that the defendant is guilty of the lesser crime. [¶] The crime of 2nd [degree] murder is lesser to that of 1st [degree] murder. [¶] The crime of voluntary [manslaughter] is lesser to that of 2nd [degree] murder. [¶] Thus, you are to determine whether the defendant is guilty or not guilty of the crime charged in count[] 1 or of any lesser crimes. In doing so, you have discretion to choose the order in which you evaluate each crime and consider the evidence pertaining to it. You may find it productive to consider and reach a tentative conclusion on all charges and lesser crimes before reaching any final verdicts. However, the court cannot accept a guilty verdict on a lesser crime unless you have unanimously found the defendant not guilty of the greater crime." (CT 223-224) (Emphasis added.)

Reading the instructions as a whole, defendant's claim that the instructions "surely create[] in the minds of the jurors the construct that they should return a murder verdict unless the defense has convinced them that the homicide should be reduced to manslaughter," (AOB 27) cannot be sustained. The claim is baseless because the court also told the jury that "the burden is on the People to prove beyond a reasonable doubt each of the elements of murder and that the act which caused the death was not done in the heat of passion or upon a sudden quarrel or in the actual, even though unreasonable, belief in the necessity to defend against imminent peril to life or great bodily injury," (CT 204) and that in determining whether defendant was guilty or not of the crimes charged the jury had discretion to choose the order in which it was to evaluate each crime and consider the evidence pertaining to it. The presumption is that the jury understood and followed the court's instructions. (People v. Danielson (1992) 3 Cal.4th 691, 722.)

Defendant's reliance on People v. Owens (1994) 27 Cal.App.4th 1155, and People v. Kurtzman (1988) 46 Cal.3d 322, is misplaced. Those cases involved different instructions and different propositions. Owens addressed CALJIC No. 10.46.2, and Kurtzman addressed CALJIC No. 8.75.

We conclude the trial court did not err in giving CALJIC Nos. 8.42 and 8.43.

New Reasonable Doubt Instruction

Defendant contends the reasonable doubt instruction given in this case lowered the prosecutor's burden of proof below the requirements of constitutional due process. (AOB 41) We already resolved this issue in People v. Hurtado (1996) 47 Cal.App.4th 805, 815-816, and People v. Tran (1996) 47 Cal.App.4th 253, 262-263, where we concluded that instructing the jury in the new language of CALJIC No. 2.90 is not error.

Cruel and Unusual Punishment

Defendant contends the sentence enhancement for firearm use constitutes cruel and/or unusual punishment. The issue is waived. In any event, it is without merit.

Defendant did not object to his sentence on cruel and/or unusual punishment grounds at the time it was imposed. That failure waived the objection. As stated in People v. Scott (1994) 9 Cal.4th 331, 356: "[W]e hold that complaints about the manner in which the trial court exercises its sentencing discretion and articulates its supporting reasons cannot be raised for the first time on appeal. We disapprove any contrary view or holdings expressed by the Courts of Appeal."

Objections on cruel and/or unusual punishment grounds are covered by this rule. Thus, in People v. Kelly (1997) 52 Cal.App.4th 568, 583, the court held that defendant's failure to raise below the issue of cruel and unusual punishment waived the issue on appeal. To the same effect was the earlier decision in People v. DeJesus (1995) 38 Cal.App.4th 1, 27.

Regardless, the section 12022.53 does not provide for a cruel and/or unusual punishment. In People v. Martinez (1999) 76 Cal.App.4th 489, 493-495, the court rejected a similar cruel-and-unusual-penalty argument by stating: "The trial court imposed a low term of five years for attempted murder (187, subd. (a), 664, subd. (a)) plus an enhancement of twenty-five years to life, pursuant to section 12022.53. Section 12022.53, also known as the '10-20- life' law, was enacted in 1997 to substantially increase the penalties for using a firearm in the commission of designated felonies. The Legislature found 'that substantially longer prison sentences must be imposed on felons who use firearms in the commission of their crimes, in order to protect our citizens and deter violent crime.' (Stats. 1997, ch. 503, 1.) Among the designated felonies is appellant's crime, attempted murder. . . . [¶] The statute provides increasing prison terms (10 years, 20 years, and 25 years to life) for increasingly serious circumstances of firearm use. Under subdivision (b), if the defendant 'personally used a firearm' (which can mean merely displaying an unloaded or inoperable firearm, People v. Masbruch (1996) 13 Cal.4th 1001, 1006-1007), the mandatory additional consecutive punishment is 10 years. Under subdivision (c), if the defendant 'intentionally and personally discharged a firearm,' the mandatory additional consecutive punishment is 20 years. Under subdivision (d), applicable to appellant, if the defendant 'intentionally and personally discharged a firearm and proximately caused great bodily injury, as defined in Section 12022.7, or death, to any person other than an accomplice,' the mandatory additional consecutive punishment is 25 years to life. The punishment is not subject to being stricken or reduced in the trial court's discretion. Subdivision (h) provides, 'Notwithstanding Section 1385 or any other provision of law, the court shall not strike an allegation under this section or a finding bringing a person within the provisions of this section.' [¶] Appellant contends that section 12022.53, either on its face or as applied to him, constitutes cruel or unusual punishment under either the United States or California Constitution. [Citation.] In Hamelin v. Michigan (1991) 501 U.S. 957, a majority of the court held that a state mandatory sentence of life without possibility of parole for possession of substantial amounts of cocaine did not constitute cruel and unusual punishment under the federal Constitution. Two justices were of the view that in cases not involving the death penalty, the Eighth Amendment provides for no judicial review whether the length of a legislatively mandated sentence is excessively disproportionate to the crime [citation]; the three concurring justices agreed that the length of a legislatively mandated sentence could be held unconstitutional, but only in cases of 'extreme sentences that are "grossly disproportionate" to the crime.' [Citations.] " Under the California Constitution, a sentence may be cruel or unusual if it is 'so disproportionate to the crime for which it is inflicted that it shocks the conscience and offends fundamental notions of human dignity.' [Citation.] " The main technique of analysis under California law is to consider the nature both of the offense and of the offender. (People v. Dillon (1983) 34 Cal.3d 441, 479.) The nature of the offense is viewed both in the abstract and in the totality of circumstances surrounding its actual commission; the nature of the offender focuses on the particular person before the court, the inquiry being whether the punishment is grossly disproportionate to the defendant's individual culpability, as shown by such factors as age, prior criminality, personal characteristics, and state of mind. [Citations.] [¶] The judicial inquiry commences with great deference to the Legislature. Fixing the penalty for crimes is the province of the Legislature, which is in the best position to evaluate the gravity of different crimes and to make judgments among different penological approaches. [Citations.] Only in the rarest of cases could a court declare that the length of a sentence mandated by the Legislature is unconstitutionally excessive. [Citations.] This is not such a case. [¶] Appellant, focusing only on subdivision (d), contends '[t]he statute is constitutionally defective because it does not recognize significant gradations of culpability depending on the severity of the current offense, and does not take into consideration mitigating factors.' This is not a fair description of the statute. Section 12022.53 as a whole represents a careful gradation by the Legislature of the consequences of gun use in the commission of serious crimes. The section is limited, in the first place, to convictions of certain very serious felonies. The statute then sets forth three gradations of punishment based on increasingly serious types and consequences of firearm use in the commission of the designated felonies: 10 years if the defendant merely used a firearm, 20 years if the defendant personally and intentionally discharged it, and 25 years to life if the defendant's intentional discharge of the firearm proximately caused great bodily injury. Furthermore, the provision in question is an enhancement to the base term for the underlying conviction; a trial court retains flexibility as to fixing the underlying base term for attempted murder. [Citation.] . . . Thus, contrary to appellant's contention, the statute does recognize different gradations of culpability. [Citations.] Appellant contends that within the confines of subdivision (d), significant variations in the degree of great bodily injury are conceivable, which the statute gives no discretion to consider. This does not render the statute unconstitutionally excessive. Lines must be drawn somewhere, and the Legislature has reasonably drawn the line at great bodily injury. The fact that subdivision (d) leaves no additional room for trial court discretion based on different gradations of great bodily injury does not render the punishment cruel or unusual. [Citations.]"

We agree with the analysis set forth in Martinez, and conclude with the Martinez court that the sentence enhancement provided by section 12022.53 does not constitute cruel and/or unusual punishment.

As to the actual sentence imposed in this case, we do not find it cruel and/or unusual under the test set forth in Dillon, which calls for an examination of the nature both of the offense and of the offender. (Dillon, supra, 34 Cal.3d at p. 479.) First, defendant concedes that "viewed in the abstract, appellant's crime is among the most serious in our society." (AOB 73) That concession takes care of the nature-of-the-offense prong of the Dillon test.

As to the nature of the offender, defendant admitted to helping Justin in his drug business, and kept his own gun loaded and close at hand, suggesting readiness for use whenever needed. Defendant also picked up Justin's gun and used it to fire more shots at Justin after defendant had exhausted the rounds in his own gun, demonstrating clear intent and determination to kill Justin with a gun. Justin was already down wounded and helpless when defendant picked up Justin's gun and finished off Justin with it.

The fact that defendant has no prior criminal record is of little consequence. Defendant admitted to helping Justin in Justin's drug business, itself an uncharged offense. Moreover, lack of a significant prior criminal record is not determinative on the issue of cruel and/or unusual punishment. (Martinez, supra, 76 Cal.App.4th at p. 497.)

Defendant's comparison of California's firearm enhancement statute to the firearm enhancement statutes of other jurisdictions may be a matter of legislative interest, but is of little help to this court. California is not controlled by the laws of other states. How California views gun death is a matter it must decide for itself. The fact that it treats gun death differently and harsher does not of itself constitute a violation of the cruel and unusual clause of the Constitution.

DISPOSITION

The judgment is affirmed.

XI.
People v. Ireland
(Published at 33 Cal.App.4th 680)

Ireland was published because it addressed a new challenge to the constitutionality of California's new drunk driving law. Prior to the present California law on drunk driving, the test to determine whether a person was driving drunk was the amount of alcohol in his blood. The new law adds a new test to that determination. The new test is the amount of alcohol concentration in the driver's breath. A driver may thus be tested for drunkenness based on the amount of alcohol concentration in his blood or in the amount of alcohol concentration in his breath.

Breath testing for measuring alcohol concentration in the blood was challenged because of conversion problems. Before the new test, California's drunk driving law provided that a person was drunk, and could not drive a vehicle, if the amount of alcohol concentration in his blood was 0.08 percent or more, by weight. Direct blood test determined the person's level of alcohol concentration in the blood. The new test provides for a different basis of measurement. The breath analyzer does not measure the amount of alcohol concentration in a person's blood, but in his breath. Blood is liquid, but breath is vapor. How much concentration of alcohol in a person's breath is equivalent to 0.08 percent concentration in his blood? Science has not yet provided an exact answer. So if science has not settled the question, then, the argument goes, breath testing is not a scientifically reliable basis for determining whether a person is drunk for purposes of the drunk driving law.

The other argument is the equal protection clause of the constitution, which provides that persons similarly situated should be equally treated. The equal protection argument is that if it cannot be exactly determined whether the blood alcohol concentration in a person's breath is the exact equivalent of 0.08 alcohol concentration in his blood, then two persons equally drunk can have different alcohol concentration readings, depending on what test was used, and receive unequal treatment under the law. In *Ireland*, we upheld the validity of the new law.

Apart from the issue of the constitutionality of the new test, the Filipino reader may find interesting the discussion on policy issues that led to the enactment of California's drunk driving laws.

Ireland was subsequently cited by the California Supreme Court in *Hubbart v. Superior Court* (1999) 19 Cal.4th 1138, and by the other courts of appeal in *People v. Goslar* (1999) 70 Cal.App.4th 270; *Kerollis v. Department of Motor Vehicles* (1999) 75 Cal.App.4th 1299; *People v. Acevedo* (2001) 93 Cal.App.4th 757; *Hamilton v. Gourley* (2002) 103 Cal.App.4th 351; and *People v. Wilson* (2003), docket no. A102208.

The opinion in *People v. Ireland* follows:

Defendant Randy A. Ireland was charged by complaint in municipal court with misdemeanor offenses of driving under the influence of alcohol (Veh. Code, § 23152, subd. (a)),[15] and driving with .08 percent or more, by weight, of alcohol in his blood (§ 23152, subd. (b)).

The jury found defendant guilty on the section 23152, subdivision (b) count, but hung on the section 23152, subdivision (a) count. The trial court declared a mistrial on the subdivision (a) count, then later dismissed that count conditioned "upon ratification of verdict."

Defendant appealed to the appellate department of the superior court, which affirmed the judgment. More than a year later, the appellate department recalled the remittitur and certified the appeal to us. We accepted the transfer of the appeal because of the importance of the issues raised.

During the pendency of the appeal with this court, defendant requested that judicial notice be taken of certain scientific literature and legislative histories. Respondent interposed no objection. We decided to consider that request together with the consideration of the merits of this appeal. We now resolve to take judicial notice of the legislative histories submitted. As to the scientific literature, we take judicial notice only to the existence of the writings; the truth of the scientific claims written about cannot be judicially noticed, but must be proved, since

---

[15] Further statutory references in this case are to the Vehicle Code unless otherwise stated.

some of those claims are currently the subject of controversy. (Evid. Code, § 452.)

We affirm the judgment.

FACTS

On October 19, 1991, at 11:30 p.m., Capitola City Police Officer Philip Wowak stopped a van which he had observed speeding and following too closely. As Wowak approached the van, defendant driver rolled down the window. The officer smelled the odor of alcohol coming from the vehicle. He noticed, among other symptoms, that defendant's speech was slurred, his eyes were very bloodshot, and his movements were very slow and deliberate when retrieving his wallet and driver's license. Wowak conducted field sobriety tests, which defendant failed. Defendant told Wowak he had consumed one beer earlier that evening. Wowak arrested defendant for driving under the influence.

Wowak advised defendant that he had the choice of a blood, breath, or urine test. Defendant chose the breath test. Wowak, who had been trained in administering breath tests, administered the breath test to defendant at 12:01 a.m. and 12:02 a.m. The results showed alcohol concentrations of 0.11 percent and 0.10 percent.

Wowak advised defendant he could choose another test at no charge. Defendant declined to do so, saying "this is all he wanted to do."

The People presented as its expert witness Juan Bergado, a criminalist with the Department of Justice. Bergado reviewed the accuracy logs of the Intoxilyzer 5000 machine which was used for defendant's breath test, and concluded that the instrument was operating properly on the date of defendant's test.

Bergado explained that the 2100:1 breath-to-blood conversion ratio is determined from correlation studies wherein blood samples drawn from an individual's arm are compared to breath samples taken from that individual. He further explained that the 2100:1 ratio represents the parts of alcohol found in the breath compared to the parts of alcohol found in the blood drawn from the arm.

Testifying in his defense, defendant testified that he had a beer at a relative's home at about 6 p.m. At about 7 p.m., he, together with some relatives and friends, went to a restaurant for dinner. The dinner took two hours, during which time defendant consumed two beers. At 9:00 or 9:15 p.m., defendant went to another bar where he and his relatives and friends stayed for a half-hour or 40 minutes. They then went to a third bar (Castaways) where defendant consumed one beer. Approximately one hour later, defendant left for home.

Defendant's expert witness, William Gigiere, explained the basis of the 2100:1 alcohol-in-breath to alcohol-in-blood ratio. He testified that alcohol is first absorbed into the artery, then gets distributed throughout the body. The neurological effects of alcohol are the result of the alcohol coming in contact with the brain, which is the control center of the body. Alcohol reaches the veins after peak absorption. At peak absorption, the arterial value of alcohol is equal to its venous value "from a practical standpoint." Prior to peak absorption, the amount of alcohol in the artery (reflected by the breath test) will be greater than the amount of alcohol in the veins (reflected by the blood test). Consequently, the 2100:1 statutory partition ratio will be overstated during the absorptive phase and understated during the post-absorptive phase.

Gigiere testified that he had tested defendant on November 24, 1991, to determine defendant's partition ratio. Defendant's partition ratio during the absorption phase was 1329:1. During the post-absorptive stage, defendant's breath alcohol result was slightly lower than his venous blood alcohol result.

On cross-examination, Gigiere stated he could not say what defendant's partition ratio was at the time of defendant's arrest. Gigiere acknowledged that a person's partition ratio is germane to the time of the test.

CONTENTIONS

In this appeal, defendant contends:

1. The Legislature did not create a new substantive offense of driving with an excessive breath-alcohol content.

2. The Legislature did not intend to exclude evidence of the variability of blood:breath partition ratios.

3. Due process and the right to confront adverse witnesses entitle the accused to present evidence of the variability between blood and breath test results.

4. Unless defendants are allowed to challenge the blood:breath partition ratio, the statute creates an unconstitutional mandatory presumption.

5. To interpret the statute as creating a new offense of "excessive breath-alcohol" would violate equal protection because similarly-situated individuals would be held to different standards of conduct based on the arbitrary factor of which test was given.

DISCUSSION
Creation of New Substantive Offense

Defendant contends the Legislature did not create a new substantive offense of driving with an excessive breath-alcohol content. The contention is without merit.

The critical issue is not whether the 1991 amendment to section 23152, subdivision (b) (hereafter, 1991 amendment), creates a new substantive offense of driving with an excessive breath-alcohol content, but whether the Legislature has the power to prohibit any person with a certain amount of alcohol concentration in his or her breath from driving a motor vehicle. It is immaterial whether the prohibition is viewed as a new offense or as an alternative definition of an existing offense.

As amended in 1991, section 23152, subdivision (b), reads in pertinent part: "It is unlawful for any person who has 0.08 percent or more, by weight, of alcohol in his or her blood to drive a vehicle. [¶] For purposes of this subdivision, percent, by weight, of alcohol in a person's blood shall be based upon grams of alcohol per 100 milliliters of blood or grams of alcohol per 210 liters of breath." (See Stats. 1991, ch. 708, § 1.)

California's earliest law on drunk driving was a 1913 statute which provided: "No intoxicated person shall operate or drive a motor vehicle or other vehicle upon any public highway within this state." (Stats. 1913, ch. 326, § 17, p. 646; Burg v. Municipal Court (1983) 35 Cal.3d 257, 262.)

In 1969, the Legislature, recognizing the need for a more precise understanding of the offense of "driving under the influence," created a presumption that the driver is under the influence if he or she had .10 percent or more by weight of alcohol in his or her blood. (Burg v. Municipal Court, supra, 35 Cal.3d at p. 263; cf. Stats. 1969, ch. 231, § 1, p. 565.)

Reliance on this presumption subsequently proved inadequate. The Legislature realized that the ultimate question was still "defined in terms of the defendant's subjective behavior and condition: 'Was the defendant under the influence at the time he drove?'" (Burg v. Municipal Court, supra, 35 Cal.3d at p. 263.) In Burg, the court observed that "[c]elerity and certainty of punishment were frustrated by the ambiguity of the legal criteria; no matter what his blood-alcohol level, a defendant could escape conviction merely by raising a doubt as to his intoxication. [Citations.]" (Ibid.)

The magnitude of the problem was described by the court in Burg: "Nearly half of the traffic deaths in California between 1976-1980 involved drinking drivers. [Citation.] Nearly one quarter of all traffic accidents resulting in injury involved the use of alcohol. [Citation.] Traffic deaths in the United States exceed 50,000 annually, and approximately one-half of those fatalities are alcohol-related. [Citations.] [¶] The drunk driver cuts a wide swath of death, pain, grief, and untold physical and emotional injury across the roads of California and the nation. The monstrous proportions of the problem have often been lamented in graphic terms by this court and the United States Supreme Court. [Citations.] As observed in Breithaupt v. Abram (1957) 352 U.S. 432, '[t]he increasing slaughter on our highways, most of which should be avoidable, now reaches the astounding figures only heard of on the battlefield.' [Citation.] Indeed, in the years 1976 to 1980 there were many more injuries to California residents in alcohol-related traffic accidents than were suffered by the entire Union Army during the Civil War, and more were killed than in the bloodiest year of the Vietnam War. [Citation.] Given this setting, our observation that '[d]runken drivers are extremely dangerous people' [citation] seems almost to understate the horrific risk posed by those who drink and drive." (35 Cal.3d at pp. 261-262.)

In 1981, the Legislature fortified the drunk driving laws by amending subdivision (b) to section 23152. That new subdivision stated: "It is unlawful for any person who has 0.10 percent or more, by weight, of alcohol in his or her blood to drive a vehicle upon a highway or upon other than a highway in areas which are open to the general public. [¶] For purposes of this subdivision, percent, by weight, of alcohol shall be based upon grams of alcohol per 100 milliliters of blood." (See Stats. 1981, ch. 940, § 33.)

In Burg v. Municipal Court, supra, 35 Cal.3d at page 265, the court held that section 23152, subdivision (b), established a new and separate offense. More significantly, the court held that under the subdivision (b) scheme, it was no longer necessary to prove that the defendant was in fact under the influence; it was enough to prove that the defendant's blood-alcohol level was 0.10 percent or more.

The 1981 addition of subdivision (b) did not end the Legislature's quest for answers to the continuing "slaughter on our highways." In 1989, the Legislature further toughened its laws by lowering the blood-alcohol level requirement from .10 percent to .08 percent. (Stats. 1989, ch. 1114, § 27.)

However, because the proscribed driving was still based on the amount of alcohol present in the person's blood, it was necessary, in the case of defendants who elected urine or breath tests, to convert the alcohol readings in those tests to their corresponding blood-alcohol readings. The conversion was done by using the guidelines set forth in title 17, California Code of Regulations section 1220.4, subdivision (f): "A breath alcohol concentration shall be converted to an equivalent blood alcohol concentration by a calculation based on the relationship: the amount of alcohol in 2,100 milliliters of alveolar breath is equivalent to the amount of alcohol in 1 milliliter of blood."

The conversion requirement produced attacks on the reliability of the partition ratio. As noted in People v. Lepine (1989) 215 Cal.App.3d 91, 94: "[T]he ratio of 2,100 to 1 is not constant and varies from individual to individual and from time to time. . . . [¶] [V]ariations in partition ratios are the function of whether the individual is still absorbing the alcohol at the time the sample was taken, the temperature of the lungs, the speed of exhalation, the depth of exhalation, the amount of humidity in the air, the amount of mucus in the lungs and the individual's hematocrit, i.e., the ratio of blood cells to total blood volume."

The need for the prosecution to prove that breath-test readings met the .08 percent requirement when converted to blood-alcohol readings did not promote the legislative scheme. The Assembly Committee on Public Safety, the Senate Rules Committee, and the Senate Committee on Judiciary all decried that the challenges to the accuracy of the partition ratio had resulted in "expensive and time consuming evidentiary hearings and undermine[d] successful enforcement of driving under the influence laws." (Hearing notes of Assem. Com. on Public Safety (May 15, 1990) AB 4318.)

In 1990, Assembly Bill No. 4318 (hereafter, AB 4318) was introduced to "[e]liminate the need for conversion of a breath quantity to a blood concentration of alcohol by statutorily defining driving under the influence of alcohol in terms of the concentration of alcohol found in the breath when breath analysis is used." (Assem. Com. on Public Safety, May 15, 1990 hearing.) The committee explained that "[t]he complexities of the existing conversion or partition ratio result in a significant number of cases being challenged on the accuracy and applicability of the partition ratio." (Ibid.)

The Legislature's dissatisfaction with the conversion requirement led the Assembly Committee on Public Safety to focus its hearings on the specific issue of: "Should the offense of driving under the influence of alcohol be statutorily defined in terms of the concentration of alcohol found in the breath when breath analysis is used?" (Assem. Com. on Public Safety, May 15, 1990 hearing.)

The hearing notes of the Assembly Committee on Public Safety disclose that in addressing this issue, the committee considered the opinions of experts on the subject. Among the opinions expressly noted were those of M. F. Mason, Ph.D., Professor of Forensic Medicine and Toxicology, and K. M. Dubowski, Ph.D., Professor of Medicine and Director of Toxicology Laboratories, who had recommended that "'the conversion of a breath quantity to a blood concentration of ethanol, for forensic purposes, should be abandoned and the offense of driving while under the influence of alcohol should be statutorily defined in terms of the concentration of ethanol found in the breath in jurisdictions employing breath analysis. [Citation.]'"

At the Assembly third reading, the digest of AB 4318 stated that the bill would "[e]liminate the need for conversion of a breath quantity to a blood concentration of alcohol by statutorily defining driving under the influence of alcohol in terms of the concentration of alcohol found in the breath when breath analysis is used."

In the Senate, two committees conducted hearings on AB 4318. Both the Senate Rules Committee (Aug. 7, 1990) and the Senate Committee on the Judiciary (1989-1990 Reg. Sess.) recognized that AB 4318 "would statutorily define the offense of driving under the influence of alcohol in terms of the concentration of alcohol found in the breath when breath analysis is used." Both committees also observed that AB 4318 "would eliminate the need for conversion of a breath quantity to a blood concentration of alcohol by statutorily defining driving under the influence of alcohol in terms of the concentration of alcohol found in the breath when the breath analysis is used."

AB 4318 was not the first California legislative attempt to define driving under the influence in terms of the alcohol concentration in a person's breath. A precursor, Senate Bill No. 1119 (Stats. 1989, ch. 1114; hereafter, SB 1119), had earlier provided that chemical tests could alternatively be based on grams of alcohol per 210 liters of breath. However, SB 1119 had an effective date of January 1992. The Legislature did not want to wait until 1992 to put the new scheme into effect. AB 4319 was accordingly introduced to advance the operative date of the change.

As stated by the Assembly Committee on Public Safety: "Last year the Legislature approved and the Governor signed Senate Bill 1119 (Seymour) which, effective January 1992, eliminates the DUI partition ratio, an unnecessarily complicated method of converting units of alcohol per liter of breath into the current standard of .08% blood alcohol per milliliter of blood. AB 4318 simply speeds up the effective date to January 1, 1991, in an effort to provide relief to our beleaguered DUI trial process. [¶] [] SB 1119 set the standard for breath alcohol content at grams of alcohol per 210 liters breath or grams of alcohol per 100 milliliters of blood. AB 4318 merely speeds up the effective date of this clarifying language. [¶] AB 4318 provides a necessary tool in our ongoing battle against drunk drivers."

The intent of AB 4318 to eliminate conversion and, instead, alternatively define driving under the influence "in terms of the concentration of alcohol found in the breath when breath analysis is used," is thus abundantly clear; it is, in fact, explicit. In People v. Bransford (1994) 8 Cal.4th 885, 890, the Supreme Court stated that there is only one reasonable manner in which to read the 1991 amendment, and that is that "the Legislature intended the statute to criminalize the act of driving either with the specified blood-alcohol level or with the specified breath-alcohol level."

Consequently, the trial court did not err in holding that evidence of the inaccuracy of the 2100:1 partition ratio, when applied to defendant under the section 23152, subdivision (b) count, was irrelevant.

Apart from being irrelevant in the sense of being unnecessary under the current legislative scheme, the proffered evidence is also irrelevant in another respect. Defendant's post-arrest breath test, which showed alcohol concentrations of .11 percent and .10 percent, was taken approximately six hours after consumption of the first beer, three hours after consumption of the second and third beers, and one to one-and-a-half hours after consumption of the third beer. The test was therefore taken after most of the alcohol, if not all, had been fully absorbed into defendant's bloodstream. Gigiere had testified that, in the case of beer, alcohol absorption reaches its peak from "30 to 180 minutes, 73 minutes average on a [sic] empty stomach. Food would make it longer."

On the other hand, the breath test performed by Gigiere on November 24, showing defendant's partition ratio at 1329:1, was conducted 20 minutes after the measured consumption of alcohol under controlled conditions. It is evident that defendant's physiological condition at the time Gigiere administered his breath test is not comparable to defendant's physiological condition at the time Wowak administered the post-arrest breath test. Because, as Gigiere testified, a person's partition ratio is "germane to the moment that you test," defendant's partition ratio at the time of Gigiere's test was irrelevant to establish defendant's partition ratio at the time of his arrest.

Due Process

Defendant contends next that to prevent him from adducing evidence of the variability between blood- and breath-alcohol measurements is to prevent him from challenging the accuracy of the breath test, and that would be a violation of his state and federal rights to due process and to confront adverse witnesses. We disagree.

In arguing due process, defendant cites a number of reasons why breath tests are inaccurate predictors of true alcohol content, among them: "the phase of alcohol absorption, body temperature, the condensation effect, the physiology of human lungs, breathing technique, the blood hematocrit, and residual mouth alcohol." Defendant claims that "[c]ertainly, due process must afford the accused the right to adduce evidence that his or her own blood:breath partition ratio is significantly lower than the assumed 1:2100, particularly if it, combined with other evidence, establishes that his or her alcohol content was below .08 percent."

The flaw in this argument is the assumption that the 1991 amendment requires the alcohol content in the breath to be quantitatively equivalent to the .08 percent alcohol content in the blood. As discussed, there is no such requirement. The statutory scheme under the 1991 amendment is for the blood-alcohol ratio to apply when blood test is used, and for the breath-alcohol ratio to apply when breath test is used, regardless of their conversion values.

When the Legislature enacted the 1991 amendment, it was aware of the "complexities" of converting breath-alcohol values to blood-alcohol values. Indeed, it was precisely because of those complexities that the Legislature decided to eliminate the conversion requirement, accepting as sufficient for defining legislative policy a prohibition on driving based on the presence in a person's breath of a certain amount of alcohol.

The Legislature's power to regulate driving is beyond constitutional challenge. "[T]he area of driving is particularly appropriate for extensive legislative regulation, and that the state's traditionally broad police power authority to enact any measure which reasonably relates to public health or safety operates with full force in this domain." (Hernandez v. Department of Motor Vehicles (1981) 30 Cal.3d 70, 74.) "Surely, the regulation of drinking drivers in a state that experienced 338,344 arrests for 'drunk driving' in 1982 is well within the legitimate police power of the Legislature." (Burg v. Municipal Court, supra 35 Cal.3d at p. 267, fn. omitted.)

The fact that the current state of scientific knowledge has not settled the ongoing scientific debate as to the best method of measuring inebriation does not preclude the Legislature from regulating driving based on conflicting scientific theories. It has been held that "where scientific opinions conflict on a particular point, the Legislature is free to adopt the opinion it chooses, and the court will not substitute its judgment for that of the Legislature. [Citation.]" (State v. Brayman (Wash. 1988) 751 P.2d 294, 300.) Courts "cannot[] arbitrate scientific disputes." (People v. Lepine, supra, 215 Cal.App.3d at p. 100.)

Although the reliability of breath tests has been questioned by some experts, other experts have endorsed such tests as the more reliable measure of the amount of alcohol affecting the brain. As discussed by a New Jersey court in State v. Downie (N.J. 1990) 569 A.2d 242, 250: "In light of the scientific and legislative evidence, we find unpersuasive the argument that blood should be the sure and ultimate measure of inebriation. Blood, itself is not monolithic. Venous blood differs from the arterial blood, which actually takes alcohol to the brain. Venous blood may be far less accurate as an indication of the amount of alcohol affecting the brain than breath in the absorptive phase. Given the fact that the legislature desired to bar driving while intoxicated, it appears logical that the blood contemplated was the arterial blood, which takes alcohol to the brain. Because arterial blood is practically unobtainable, then breath, not venous blood, is the most consistently accurate reflection of the concentration of alcohol affecting the brain. Thus, the legislative and judicial reference to 'blood' is not an intended concession that blood tests are the preferred method for ascertaining inebriation." (Footnote omitted.)

Indeed, the experts cited in the hearing notes of California's Assembly Public Safety Committee, Senate Rules Committee, and Senate Judiciary Committee, recommended that blood tests as a method of measuring inebriation be abandoned in favor of breath tests. However, instead of abandoning the blood test in favor of the breath test, the

Legislature decided to adopt both tests and to allow their use on an alternative basis.

Whether the course chosen by the Legislature is sound is not for the courts to review. "The wisdom of the legislation is not at issue in analyzing its constitutionality, and neither the availability of less drastic remedial alternatives nor the legislative failure to solve all related ills at once will invalidate a statute. [Citations.]" (Hale v. Morgan (1978) 22 Cal.3d 388, 398.)

In Burg v. Municipal Court, supra, 35 Cal.3d at page 269, the court held that the 1981 version of section 23152, subdivision (b), met the due process requirement of being "definite enough to provide (1) a standard of conduct for those whose activities are proscribed and (2) a standard for police enforcement and for ascertainment of guilt." Because the 1991 amendment is similar to the 1981 version for purposes of due process analysis, we must likewise reject defendant's present due process challenge.

There is, however, a kind of due process challenge that was not foreclosed by Burg. Defendant is not precluded from questioning the reliability of the instrument used or the procedure followed. (People v. Bransford, supra, 8 Cal.4th at p. 893.)

In this case, however, the People presented evidence to show that the breath analyzer used was operating properly, that Wowak was qualified to administer the test, and that Wowak followed prescribed procedures. Defendant interposed no challenge to this evidence. Defendant cannot therefore complain that his due process rights were violated in this respect.

Mandatory Presumption

Defendant contends that unless defendants are permitted to challenge the blood:breath partition ratio, the 1991 amendment creates an irrebuttable, conclusive presumption that breath-alcohol levels are accurate and necessarily translate into blood-alcohol levels at a ratio of 1:2100. Defendant argues that under the trial court's interpretation of the 1991 amendment, the trier of fact must presume an element of the offense, specifically blood-alcohol level in excess of .08 percent, from the evidentiary fact of a breath-alcohol level in excess of .08 percent.

The Supreme Court recently settled this question in People v. Bransford, supra, 8 Cal.4th 885. There it held that the 1991 amendment "did not presume that the driver was intoxicated or 'under the influence'; instead, it defined the substantive offense of driving with a specified concentration of alcohol in the body. Thus, it did not create an irrebuttable conclusive presumption." (At pp. 892-893.)

Equal Protection

Defendant contends that to interpret the 1991 amendment as creating a new offense of "excessive breath-alcohol" would violate equal protection because similarly-situated individuals would be held to different standards of conduct based on the arbitrary factor of which test was given. The contention is without merit.

The essence of equal protection is that "persons similarly situated with respect to the legitimate purpose of the law receive like treatment." (Purdy & Fitzpatrick v. State of California (1969) 71 Cal.2d 566, 578.) "The first prerequisite to a meritorious claim under the equal protection clause is a showing that the state has adopted a classification that affects two or more similarly situated groups in an unequal manner. [Citation.]" (In re Eric J. (1979) 25 Cal.3d 522, 530, fn. omitted.)

Under the 1991 amendment, the persons similarly situated are drinking drivers. The amendment does not treat any member of that group differently. Any member of the group has the same right as any other member to elect a breath test or a blood test.

To demonstrate unequal protection, defendant asks us to consider two identical persons, twins, each with a true blood-alcohol concentration of .07 percent and a true breath-alcohol content of .09 percent. Defendant argues that hypothetically if one twin took a breath test and the other a blood test, the twin taking the blood test would go home while the twin taking the breath test would go to jail.

The argument is inappropriate. "The rule is well established . . . that one will not be heard to attack a statute on grounds that are not shown to be applicable to himself and that a court will not consider every conceivable situation which might arise under the language of the statute and will not consider the question of constitutionality with reference to hypothetical situations. [Citations.]" (In re Cregler (1961) 56 Cal.2d 308, 313.)

Moreover, so long as persons in the same group are not discriminated against in the choice of tests to take, there is no denial of equal protection. "'The unlawful administration by state officers of a state statute fair on its face, resulting in its unequal application to those who are entitled to be treated alike, is not a denial of equal protection unless there is shown to be present in it an element of intentional or purposeful discrimination.'" (Murgia v. Municipal Court (1975) 15 Cal.3d 286, 297, citation omitted.)

As stated in People v. Enriquez (1977) 19 Cal.3d 221, 229: "The equal protection clause does not assure defendant of the same treatment as all other felons; it assures him only . . . that he will receive like treatment with all other persons similarly situated." "[I]t is not a denial of equal protection that one guilty person is prosecuted while others equally guilty are not. [Citations.]" (People v. Tallagua (1985) 174 Cal.App.3d 145, 150.)

We conclude the 1991 amendment does not violate the state and federal equal protection clauses.

DISPOSITION

The judgment is affirmed.

XII.
People v. Stevens
(Published at 34 Cal.App.4th 56)

Cell phones are very popular in the Philippines, so much so that because they are used very extensively for texting messages, the country prides itself in being called the "Texting Capital of the World." *Stevens* illustrates potential pitfalls when cell phones are used for unlawful purposes. Although *Stevens* was decided before the advent of cell phones, the technology involved in that case, cordless phones, works on similar technology as cell phones, which is transmitting messages through air waves, as opposed to technology used by traditional phones, which transmits messages through cable lines.

Stevens was published because it addressed for the first time the issue of whether California's law prohibiting the interception of cordless telephone conversations was preempted by the Communications Act of 1934 and the federal eavesdropping and wiretapping statutes.

The preemption issue is probably of little, if any, significance in the Philippines. In the United States, federal law preempts state law. It should be noted, however, that the power of the federal government to enact laws is not unlimited. It can legislate only on matters directly entrusted to it by the states under the United States Constitution. Powers not expressly conferred, or not necessarily implied from the powers conferred, are reserved to the states. On matters reserved by the states for their own jurisdiction, the federal government cannot encroach. In the Philippines, we have no preemption issues of constitutional concern. If there is conflict between an act of the legislature and a provincial or city ordinance, the question is not one of preemption, but simply of the nullity of the local ordinance. This is because, unlike the states of the United States which gave up some powers to the federation but retained the rest to themselves, the provinces of the Philippines are mere creatures of the legislature, and, as such, possess no more powers than what the legislature gives them. So if a province acts beyond the powers given to it by the legislature, or contrary to an act of the legislature, it exceeds it powers, and the ordinance is void.

The opinion in *People v. Stevens* follows:

FACTS

After defendant's van was stopped by Officer Duscio, defendant consented to a search of the vehicle. Duscio found inside the vehicle electronic equipment, 24 audio cassettes with names of women handwritten on them, a scanner, and a tape recorder.

Asked about the audio tapes, defendant told Duscio that his hobby was "to listen to people." Subsequent police investigation revealed that the tapes were recordings of conversations made by the women on cordless telephones. The identities of some of the other parties to the conversations were later determined.

The scanner in defendant's vehicle allowed defendant to listen in on the radio frequencies of the cordless telephones.

DISCUSSION

We reject, for lack of merit, defendant's contention that the activity proscribed by section 632.6, subdivision (a) (intercepting cordless telephone communications),[16] is preempted by federal law.

In arguing preemption, defendant cites to the Communications Act of 1934 (47 U.S.C. § 151 et. seq.) (hereafter, Communications Act), which created the Federal Communications Commission (hereafter, FCC) and the federal eavesdropping and wiretapping statutes (18 U.S.C. §§ 2510-2521).

The test to determine whether a state statute is preempted by federal law was set forth by the United States Supreme Court in Florida Avocado Growers v. Paul (1963) 373 U.S. 132, 146-147, and restated in Head v. New Mexico Board (1963) 374 U.S. 424, 430. In Head, the court stated: "In areas of the law not inherently requiring national

---

[16] Section 632.6, subdivision (a), provides in relevant part: "Every person who, maliciously and without the consent of all parties to the communication, intercepts, receives, or assists in intercepting or receiving a communication transmitted between cordless telephones . . . , between any cordless telephone and a landline telephone, or between a cordless telephone and a cellular telephone shall be punished by a fine not exceeding two thousand five hundred dollars ($2,500), by imprisonment in the county jail not exceeding one year, or in the state prison, or by both that fine and imprisonment."

uniformity, our decisions are clear in requiring that state statutes, otherwise valid, must be upheld unless there is found 'such actual conflict between the two schemes of regulation that both cannot stand in the same area, [or] evidence of congressional design to preempt the field.' [Citation.]" (374 U.S. at p. 430.) There is intent to preempt where the purpose is to "displace all state regulations." (Florida Avocado Growers v. Paul, supra, 373 U.S. at pp. 147-148, fn. omitted.)

We examine the Communications Act first: "For the purpose of regulating interstate and foreign commerce in communication by wire and radio so as to make available, so far as possible, to all the people of the United States a rapid, efficient, Nation-wide, and world-wide wire and radio communication service with adequate facilities at reasonable charges, for the purpose of the national defense, for the purpose of promoting safety of life and property through the use of wire and radio communication, and for the purpose of securing a more effective execution of this policy by centralizing authority heretofore granted by law to several agencies and by granting additional authority with respect to interstate and foreign commerce in wire and radio communication, there is created a commission to be known as the 'Federal Communications Commission,' which shall be constituted as hereinafter provided, and which shall execute and enforce the provisions of this chapter." (47 U.S.C. § 151; emphasis added.)

Pursuant to this purpose clause, 47 United States Code section 152 provides in relevant part: "(a) The provisions of this chapter shall apply to all interstate and foreign communication by wire or radio and all interstate and foreign transmission of energy by radio, which originates and/or is received within the United States . . . . [¶] (b) . . . [N]othing in this chapter shall be construed to apply or to give the Commission jurisdiction with respect to (1) charges, classifications, practices, services, facilities, or regulations for or in connection with intrastate communication service by wire or radio of any carrier . . . ." (Emphasis added.)

As should be noted, the express purpose of 47 United States Code sections 151 and 152 is to regulate interstate and foreign communications. By express language, intrastate communication is excluded.

Other provisions of the Communications Act reflect that purpose. Thus, 47 United States Code section 556, entitled "Coordination of Federal, State, and local authority," states in relevant part: "(a) <u>Nothing</u> in this subchapter shall be construed to affect any authority of any State, political subdivision, or agency thereof, or franchising authority, regarding matters of <u>public health</u>, <u>safety</u>, and <u>welfare</u>, to the extent consistent with the express provisions of this subchapter." (Emphasis added.)

So also, 47 United States Code section 227(e)(1), which provides: "Except for the standards prescribed under subsection (d) of this section and subject to paragraph (2) of this subsection, <u>nothing</u> in this section or in the regulations prescribed under this section shall preempt any State law that imposes <u>more restrictive intrastate requirements or regulations on, or which prohibits</u> —[¶] (A) the use of telephone facsimile machines or other electronic devices to send unsolicited advertisements; [¶] (B) the use of automatic telephone dialing systems; [¶] (C) the use of artificial or prerecorded voice messages; or [¶] (D) the making of telephone solicitations." (Emphasis added.)

Although it may be argued that 47 United States Code section 227 does not specifically mention cordless telephones, the point is that the Communications Act invariably excludes intrastate communications from its coverage whenever the need to make the exclusion clear comes up.

We are not the first to read the Communications Act in this fashion. In <u>Pine Tree Tel. & Tel.</u> v. <u>Public Util. Com'n</u> (Me. 1993) 631 A.2d 57, 62, the Supreme Judicial Court of Maine held that while the Communications Act gave the FCC authority to regulate "'interstate and foreign commerce in wire and radio communication,'" it denied "the FCC jurisdiction 'with respect to . . . intrastate communications service,'" and that the "[a]uthority to regulate intrastate services remained with the several states."

In <u>Sherdon</u> v. <u>Dann</u> (Neb. 1975) 229 N.W.2d 531, 535, the Supreme Court of Nebraska held that while "[i]t is undisputed that Congress granted to the Federal Communications Commission the sole and exclusive jurisdiction over interstate and foreign telephone service . . . , [i]t is also undisputed that the Federal Communications

Act reserves to the states jurisdiction over intrastate telephone and telegraph communications."

In Radio Telephone Commun., Inc. v. Southeastern Tel. Co. (Fla. 1964) 170 So.2d 577, 580, the Supreme Court of Florida held that "'wire, mobile, or point-to-point radio telephone exchange service, or any combination thereof' . . . are essentially intra-state in nature, even though the radio portion of such services might 'spill over' into an adjoining state, since a radio signal cannot recognize nor stop at a state line; and it is clear that Congress intended to reserve to the several states the right to regulate such intra-state services . . . ."

Because intrastate communication is outside the purpose and scope of the Communications Act, defendant's argument that 47 United States Code was intended to blanket the communications field, including intrastate communications, cannot stand.

We now examine the federal eavesdropping and wiretapping statutes (18 U.S.C. §§ 2510-2521).

Defendant does not seriously challenge the proposition that 18 United States Code sections 2510-2521 do not preempt section 632.6, subdivision (a). Indeed, in his reply brief, defendant states that "the federal law which preempts state regulation of cordless phone radio transmission is not Title III [of the Omnibus Crime Control and Safe Streets Act of 1968], but the Federal Communications Act and its ancillary regulations."

Two decisions of the California Supreme Court (Halpin v. Superior Court (1972) 6 Cal.3d 885 and People v. Conklin (1974) 12 Cal.3d 259) have already held that the Omnibus Crime Control and Safe Streets Act (18 U.S.C. §§ 2510-2521) (hereafter, Omnibus Act) does not preempt state wiretapping legislation that is not more permissive than the federal scheme.

In Halpin, where the issue was the admissibility of the electronically monitored and tape-recorded conversation between Halpin and his wife inside a jail facility, the court stated that while Congress intended in the Omnibus Act "to enact comprehensive national legislation, against which all then existing federal and state legislation was to be measured," it "[a]t the same time . . . left room for the states to supplement the law in certain areas, provided the regulations are not more permissive. [Citation.]" (6 Cal.3d at pp. 898-899, fn. omitted.)

Halpin was reiterated in Conklín, where the issue was whether section 631, subdivision (a), which forbids wiretapping except by law enforcement officers or with the consent of all the parties, was preempted by federal law. In finding no preemption, Conklin stated that while both the federal and the state statutes regulate the same area, they differ in their schemes. "[T]he scheme of the federal act is based on the type of communication, that is, whether it is wire or oral; the state act, by contrast, on the type of surveillance, that is, whether it is wiretapping or eavesdropping. [Citation.]" (12 Cal.3d at p. 263.)

Conklin further stated that "[t]he respective powers of the federal and state governments to regulate the field of communications flow from different sources. Federal power finds its origin in the commerce clause [citations], even where the communications are entirely intrastate [citation]. [Citation.] State power is essentially the police power which is among those powers 'reserved to the States respectively, or to the people.' [Citation.]" (12 Cal.3d at pp. 262-263.)

Notably, the communications that were intercepted in Halpin and Conklin were conventional wire telephone communications. Here, on the other hand, the conversations that defendant intercepted were cordless telephone conversations. In a cordless telephone system, communication from the handset to the base unit is transmitted not by wire but by radio signals.

Senate Report No. 99-541, on the Electronic Communications Privacy Act of 1986 (Pub.L. No. 99-508, hereafter, ECPA) which amends title III of the Omnibus Act, described a cordless telephone, viz.: "A cordless telephone consists of a handset and a base unit wired to a landline and a household/business electrical current. A communication is transmitted from the handset to the base unit by AM or FM radio signals. From the base unit the communication is transmitted over wire, the same as a regular telephone call. The radio portions of these telephone calls can be intercepted with relative ease using standard AM radios." (1986 U.S. Code Cong. & Admin. News, p. 3563.)

Because the instant case involves the interception of the radio portion of a cordless telephone communication, the question is whether the preemption analysis employed in Halpin and Conklin should be applied to this case. We think it should be.

In Conklin, the court analyzed the preemption issue by propounding the question: "[D]id Congress intend to occupy the entire field and thereby intend to exclude state regulation on the same subject matter even where the federal and state laws are not in conflict with each other?" (12 Cal.3d at p. 265.) In concluding there was no such intention, Conklin stated: "Our conclusion . . . that Congress in enacting title III did not intend to occupy the entire field is supported by two indications of its intent. The first is a statement of congressional findings expressing the need for federal legislation and its purpose [citations]; the second is a report referred to in Halpin, which was submitted by the Senate Committee on the Judiciary [citation]." (Id. at pp. 266-267.)

Nothing in the ECPA manifests a change of intent on Congress's part. To the contrary, the ECPA was enacted precisely to reinforce that intent. Noting that the "tremendous advances in telecommunications and computer technologies" have made existing law "'hopelessly out of date,'" and that "[e]lectronic hardware making it possible for overzealous law enforcement agencies, industrial spies and private parties to intercept the personal or proprietary communications of others are readily available in the American market today," the same Senate Report explained that the purpose of the ECPA amendment was "to update and clarify Federal privacy protections and standards in light of dramatic changes in new computer and telecommunications technologies." (1986 U.S. Code Cong. & Admin. News, pp. 3556, 3557, 3555.)

However, although the ECPA was enacted to bring privacy protections up to date with dramatic changes in communications technology, Congress excluded cordless telephones from the definitions of "wire communication" and "electronic communication." (18 USCA §§ 2510(1), 2510(12).) The exclusion was explained in Senate Report No. 99-541, thusly: "Because communications made on some cordless telephones can be intercepted easily with readily available technologies, such as an AM radio, it would be inappropriate to make the interception of such a communication a criminal offense. The wire portion of a cordless communication remains fully covered, however." (1986 U.S. Code Cong. & Admin. News, p. 3566.)

Clearly, if Congress was not willing or ready to regulate cordless telephones, we cannot ascribe to that body an intent to preempt the field.

Recently (Oct. 25, 1994), Congress enacted the Communications Assistance for Law Enforcement Act (hereafter, CALEA) to amend the ECPA. One of the significant amendments introduced by the CALEA was the inclusion of cordless telephones in the ECPA's definitions of "wire communication" and "electronic communication." (Pub.L. No. 103-414 (Oct. 25, 1994) 1994 U.S. Code Cong. & Admin. News, No. 9, pp. 4290-4291, §§ 202(a)(1), 202(a)(2).)

Congress's decision to include cordless telephones in the coverage of the ECPA was dictated by privacy concerns. Thus, House Report No. 103-827, in recommending the passage of the CALEA, stated: "In the eight years since the enactment of ECPA, society's patterns of using electronic communications technology have changed dramatically. Millions of people now have electronic mail addresses. Business, nonprofit organizations and political groups conduct their work over the Internet. Individuals maintain a wide range of relationships on-line. Transactional records documenting these activities and associations are generated by service providers. For those who increasingly use these services, this transactional data reveals a great deal about their private lives, all of it compiled in one place. [¶] In addition, while the portion of cordless telephone communications occurring between the handset and base unit was excluded from ECPA's privacy protections, the 1991 Privacy and Technology Task Force found that '[t]he cordless phone, far from being a novelty item used only at "poolside," has become ubiquitous . . . . More and more communications are being carried out by people [using cordless phones] in private, in their homes and offices, with an expectation that such calls are just like any other phone call.'" (1994 U.S. Code Cong. & Admin. News, No. 9A, p. 3497.)

Under the ECPA, as amended by the CALEA, the penalty for intentionally intercepting cordless telephone communications is a fine of up to $500. (18 U.S.C.A. § 2511(4)(b)(ii); 1994 U.S. Code Cong. & Admin. News, No. 9A, p. 3510.) Section 632.6, subdivision (a), on the other hand, punishes such unlawful interceptions "by a fine not exceeding two thousand five hundred dollars ($2,500), by imprisonment in the county jail not exceeding one year, or in the state prison, or by both that fine and imprisonment." California's legislative scheme is thus not more permissive than the federal scheme.

Because under the ECPA, as amended by the CALEA, cordless telephones are considered a form of wire and electronic communication, and because the ECPA and the CALEA were enacted to serve the same purpose that the outdated title III of the Omnibus Act was intended to serve, we conclude the Halpin and Conklin preemption analysis applies with equal force to this case.

DISPOSITION

The judgment is affirmed.

XIII.
People v. Lattimore
(Unpublished)

Lattimore is a right-to-counsel case. It explores the extent of a defendant's right to counsel under the U.S. Constitution. The Philippine Constitution also provides for the right of the accused to counsel. However, the situations in which such right may be implicated have not been extensively litigated in the Philippines. In *Lattimore*, which was a criminal case, the accused's right to represent herself, without aid of counsel, was sustained because she made the choice to represent herself knowingly, voluntarily, and unequivocally, despite the court's admonition about the perils of making such a choice. In the Philippines, the accused, upon motion, may be allowed in all criminal prosecutions to self-representation, but only when it sufficiently appears to the court that he can properly protect his rights without the assistance of counsel (Rule 115, Rules of Criminal Procedure). In California, as in the rest of the United States, the ability to protect one's rights without the assistance of counsel is not a requirement to defeat the defendant's right to self-representation. All that is required is a knowing and voluntary choice after being advised by the court of the pitfalls of self-representation, of his right to be represented by counsel, and of the fact that in the presentation of his defense and the conduct of the proceedings the court will not bend or soften the rules to make things easier for him. He will be expected to perform at the same level as the lawyers—no quarters asked, and none given.

The opinion in *People v. Lattimore* follows:

Defendant Yvonne M. Lattimore was charged by amended information with three counts of presenting a fraudulent insurance claim (Pen. Code, § 550;[17] counts 1-3), two counts of grand theft (§ 487, subd. (a); counts 4-5), two counts of forgery (§ 470; counts 8, 11), two counts of forgery of an official seal (§ 472; counts 9, 12), two counts of passing a forged check (§ 4754a; counts 10, 13), one count of obtaining aid through false representations (Welf. & Inst. Code, § 10980, subd.

---

[17] Further statutory references in this case are to the Penal Code unless otherwise stated.

(c)(2); count 7), and one count of perjury (§ 118; count 7). (CT 362-369) Defendant pleaded not guilty on all counts and waived her right to counsel. (CT 370)

Upon motion by the prosecution, the court dismissed counts 9, 10, 12, and 13. (CT 525, 541)

The jury found defendant guilty on all the remaining counts. (CT 542-552)

The trial court placed defendant on probation for three years. (CT 591)

We affirm.

FACTS

Because the sole issue raised by defendant in this appeal is her claim that she was not properly advised of her right to counsel, we state only the facts relevant to that issue.

The initial complaint in this case was filed with the Monterey County municipal court as case no. MS 991163A. The record reflects that at the felony arraignment on May 26, 1999, the following transpired:

"THE COURT: There's been a complaint filed against you alleging some sort of fraud, grand theft, and apparently it's filed as a felony. [¶] Are you going to be hiring your own attorney in this matter?

"THE DEFENDANT: I'm going to represent myself, Your Honor. And I would like to state for the record I haven't seen a copy of the complaint; no police report; anything. I don't even know what the nature of the . . .

"THE COURT: The problem is sometimes when we give these documents to people a lot of people aren't responsible enough, and we tell them to give these to their attorney and the attorney comes in and says I haven't got a copy of it. [¶] But have you filled out the eligibility form? Do you work?

"THE DEFENDANT: I'm going to represent myself.

"THE COURT: And you understand that if you don't have money for an attorney, we'll appoint an attorney to represent you?

"THE DEFENDANT: Yes, I do. I understand.

"THE COURT: And you understand it's my advice, strong advice, that it's not wise to represent yourself, because you don't know all the legal implications, and you're held to the same standards of law as a lawyer? Do you understand that?

"THE DEFENDANT: Yes, I do.

"THE COURT: Having all that in mind—and at the time of pretrial we'll have a form for you to fill out to show that you know this and you wish to waive your right to an attorney. But that's what you wish to do; is that correct?

"THE DEFENDANT: That's correct.

"THE COURT: All right. Flag this for that file to have a Faretta waiver in that file for her to sign at the time of pretrial. [¶] Here's a copy of the complaint. . . . The defendant, record reflect, is representing herself." (ART 5/26/99, 2-3)

Case no. MS 991163A was apparently dismissed, and a new complaint was filed as case number MS990461A. (CT 24-25) Defendant was arraigned on the new complaint on July 6, 1999. The following colloquy is recorded:

"THE COURT: Ms. Lattimore, looks like we have a new complaint here. Ms. Lattimore, are you going to apply for an attorney or hire your own or represent yourself?

"THE DEFENDANT: I'm going to represent myself, Your Honor.

"THE COURT: All right. I think the court did allow you to represent yourself last time around; is that correct?

"THE DEFENDANT: That's correct.

"THE COURT: We won't bother going through all that again. Court will permit the defendant to represent herself in this matter, the court having previously found her capable or doing so. Do you wish to enter plea of not guilty at this time?

"THE DEFENDANT: Not guilty. . . .

"[Deputy District Attorney]: She provided a Faretta waiver as well, Your Honor." (RT 6/6/99, 1)

On August 19, 1999, defendant appeared for arraignment at the superior court. The following transpired:

"THE COURT: Recall the Lattimore case. [¶] Ms Lattimore, this is the time for your arraignment. [¶] I want to make sure you understand the constitutional right you have. [¶] You have an absolute right to a speedy and public trial. [¶] And you have the right to the assistance or help of an attorney at all stages of the proceedings. [¶] You have the right to be confronted by the witnesses against you, that is, to see, and hear, and have your attorney question the witnesses called to testify against you. [¶] You have the right to the process of the court to compel the attendance of any witnesses on your own behalf. [¶] You have the right to present evidence on your own behalf in defense to this charge. [¶] You have the right to the privilege against self-incrimination. [¶] Do you understand these rights?

"THE DEFENDANT: Yes, I do." (RT 8/19/99, 253-254)

The court admonished defendant of the seriousness of the charges against her and warned her of potential consequences of self-representation. The colloquy continued:

"THE COURT: . . . You're facing some serious charges here. You understand the charges that have been filed against you.

"THE DEFENDANT: Yes, I do.

"THE COURT: And you understand Count 1, unlawful acts related to claims, a violation of [section] 550? [¶] Each one of these carried a maximum of three years in State Prison, they could run consecutive, so you're looking at approximately five to six years in State prison. You understand that?

"THE DEFENDANT: I understand that.

"THE COURT: Count 2 is Penal Code section 550, unlawful acts related to claims. [¶] Count 3 is the same, 550. [¶] Count 4 is grand theft of personal property, [section] 487. [¶] is grand theft, 487. [¶] Count 6 is fraud, welfare fraud, [section] 10980(c)(2) of the Welfare and Institutions Code. [¶] Count 7 is perjury, [section] 118. [¶] Count 8 is forgery, [section] 470. [¶] Count 9 is [section] 472, forgery of an official seal. [¶] Count 10 is [section 475(a), forged checks. [¶] Count 11 is forgery of checks, 470. [¶] Count 12 is 472, forged and counterfeited documents. [¶] And count 13 is passing forced documents, [section] 4759a).

"THE DEFENDANT: I understand.

"THE COURT: Now—and you understand that the other judges have told you, tried to convince you that you ought to have an attorney. But you don't want an attorney, and that is an informed decision you're making; is that correct?

"THE DEFENDANT: That's correct.

"THE COURT: And you also understand that you're going to have to obey the same rules of evidence, and things that an attorney has to do; is that correct?

"THE DEFENDANT: That's correct.

"THE COURT: So, it's your informed decision you do not wish to have an attorney represent you?

"THE DEFENDANT: That's correct.

"THE COURT: You wish to represent yourself?

"THE DEFENDANT: That's correct." (RT 254-256)

Defendant went on to represent herself throughout the whole trial and sentencing proceedings.

DISCUSSION

Defendant's only contention in this appeal is that she was not properly advised of her right to counsel, including her right to court-appointed counsel, and that the error in failing to so advise her was prejudicial per se. (AOB 8) We disagree.

In <u>Faretta</u> v. <u>California</u> (1975) 422 U.S. 806, 834-835, the United States Supreme Court recognized a defendant's constitutional right to self-representation, stating: "It is undeniable that in most criminal prosecutions defendants could better defend with counsel's guidance than by their own unskilled efforts. But where the defendant will not voluntarily accept representation by counsel, the potential advantage of a lawyer's training and experience can be realized, if at all, only imperfectly. To force a lawyer on a defendant can only lead him to believe that the law contrives against him. Moreover, it is not inconceivable that in some rare instances, the defendant might in fact present his case more effectively by conducting his own defense. Personal liberties are not rooted in the law of averages. The right to defend is personal. The defendant, and not his lawyer or the State, will bear the personal consequences of a conviction. It is the defendant, therefore, who must be free personally to decide whether in his particular case counsel is to his advantage. And although he may conduct his own defense ultimately to his own detriment, his choice must be honored out of 'that respect for the individual which is the lifeblood of the law.' [Citation.] [¶] When an accused manages his own defense, he relinquishes, as a purely factual matter, many of the traditional benefits associated with the right to counsel. For this reason, in order to represent himself, the accused must 'knowingly and intelligently' forgo those relinquished benefits. [Citations.] Although a defendant need not himself have the skill and experience of a lawyer in order competently and intelligently to choose self-representation, he should be made aware of the dangers and disadvantages of self-representation, so that the record will establish that 'he knows what he is doing and his choice is made with eyes open.' [Citation.]"

The issue was also discussed by the California Supreme Court in People v. Marshall (1997) 15 Cal.4th 1, 20-21: "A defendant in a criminal case possesses two constitutional rights with respect to representation that are mutually exclusive. A defendant has the right to be represented by counsel at all critical stages of a criminal prosecution. [Citations.] At the same time, the United States Supreme Court has held that because the Sixth Amendment grants to the accused personally the right to present a defense, a defendant possesses the right to represent himself or herself. [Citation.] [¶] The United States Supreme Court has concluded in numerous cases and a variety of contexts that the federal Constitution requires assiduous protection of the right to counsel. The right to counsel is self-executing; the defendant need make no request for counsel in order to be entitled to legal representation. [Citation.] The right to counsel persists unless the defendant affirmatively waives that right. [Citation.] Courts must indulge every reasonable inference against waiver of the right to counsel. [Citation.] [¶] The high court has not extended the same kind of protection to the right of self-representation. In Faretta itself the court noted that a trial court may appoint advisory counsel for a pro se defendant even over objection [citation], and advisory counsel's unsolicited intervention at trial does not necessarily violate the defendant's right to present his or her own defense. [Citation.] The high court also warned that the right of self-representation is not a license to abuse the dignity of the courtroom, but a right that can be lost through deliberate, serious misconduct. [Citation.] Furthermore, unlike the right to be represented by counsel, the right of self-representation is not self-executing. In Faretta, 422 U.S. 806, the court held that a knowing, voluntary, and unequivocal assertion of the right of self-representation, made weeks before trial by a competent, literate defendant, should have been recognized (id. at pp. 835-836); subsequent decisions of lower courts have required expressly that the defendant make a timely and unequivocal assertion of the right of self-representation. [Citations.] As one court observed: '[T]he right of self-representation is waived unless defendants articulately and unmistakably demand to proceed pro se.' [Citation.]"

Accordingly, "in order to protect the fundamental constitutional right to counsel, one of the trial court's tasks when confronted with a motion for self-representation is to determine whether the defendant truly desires to represent himself or herself. [Citations.] The court faced with a motion for self-representation should evaluate not only whether the defendant has stated the motion clearly, but also the defendant's conduct and other words. Because the court should draw every reasonable inference against waiver of the right to counsel, the defendant's conduct or words reflecting ambivalence about self-representation may support the court's decision to deny the defendant's motion. A motion for self-representation made in passing anger or frustration, an ambivalent motion, or one made for the purpose of delay or to frustrate the orderly administration of justice may be denied." (Id. at p. 23.)

Here, defendant insisted on representing herself despite repeated attempts by both the municipal court and the superior court to dissuade from waiving her right to counsel. The colloquies reproduced above clearly demonstrate that defendant knowingly and voluntarily waived her right to counsel, and that defendant made that choice "with eyes open."

As a federal constitutional issue, there is no question that the right to counsel admonition given in this case by both the municipal court and the superior court passes constitutional muster. That is because the federal rule is that a waiver of the right to counsel once validly given continues throughout the duration of the proceedings unless it is withdrawn. As stated in Arnold v. United States (9th Cir. 1969) 414 F.2d 1056, 1059: "While it is true that the Sixth Amendment right to counsel applies at all critical stages of the prosecution, including the sentencing stage, it does not follow that once the assistance of counsel in court has been competently waived, a new waiver must be obtained at every subsequent court appearance by the defendant. A competent election by the defendant to represent himself and to decline the assistance of counsel once made before the court carries forward through all further proceedings in that case unless appointment of counsel for subsequent proceedings is expressly requested by the defendant or there are circumstances which suggest that the waiver was limited to a particular stage of the proceedings."

In United States v. Springer (9th Cir. 1959) 51 F.3d 861, the waiver of the right to counsel was made at the first trial, which ended in a mistrial. At the retrial of the same matter, the defendant claimed that he should have been advised again of his right to counsel and "recanvassed" to determine if he was waiving that right. The court rejected the claim, stating: "The retrial was obviously a continuation of the criminal prosecution, and the waiver was obviously intended to stand absent an attempt to withdraw it. The matter of representation was in Springer's hands alone. After his earnest and insistent request, he had been granted the right to represent himself. If he found himself wavering in his resolve so to do, he or his advisory counsel could have so informed the court. He did not waiver. His waiver of counsel stood." (Id. at p. 865.)

In California, however, the rule is quite different. Sections 859 and 987 require that a defendant who was advised of his or her right to counsel at the preliminary hearing arraignment in the municipal court be advised again of his or her right to counsel at the arraignment in the superior court. In pertinent part, section 859, which outlines the procedure for preliminary examination at the municipal court, provides: "The magistrate shall . . . inform the defendant that he or she has the right to have the assistance of counsel, ask the defendant if he or she desires the assistance of counsel, and allow the defendant reasonable time to send for counsel. . . . If the defendant desires and is unable to employ counsel, the court shall assign counsel to defend him or her . . . ." (Emphasis added.)

Likewise, section 987, subdivision (a), which prescribes the procedure for arraignment in the superior court, provides: "In a noncapital case, if the defendant appears for arraignment without counsel, he or she shall be informed by the court that it is his or her right to have counsel before being arraigned, and shall be asked if he or she desires the assistance of counsel. If he or she desires and is unable to employ counsel the court shall assign counsel to defend him or her." (Emphasis added.)

In People v. Sohrab (1997) 59 Cal.App.4th 89, the court held that under sections 859 and 987, a defendant's waiver of his or right to counsel in the municipal court does not automatically carry forward into the superior court. The superior court must also advise the defendant of his or her right to counsel. The court explained: "Although the case law is sparse on this issue, the California Supreme Court has clearly indicated that where the prosecution charges a defendant with a felony by filing a complaint in the municipal court, the defendant's waiver of the right to counsel in the municipal court does not continue in effect in superior court. In People v. McKenzie, the People conceded this point on the basis of sections 859 and 987. [Citation.] In People v. Crandell, the Supreme Court cited McKenzie for the proposition that '[i]n a felony case, neither an appointment of counsel nor a waiver of counsel in municipal court carries over into superior court.' [Citation.] . . . [¶] Furthermore, section 859 provides that the magistrate in the inferior court where the complaint has been filed must inform the defendant of his right to counsel at the arraignment on the complaint. [Citation.] When the information is filed in superior court, the defendant must again be arraigned in superior court on that document. [Citation.] . . . [¶] Here, it is clear the court violated section 987, subdivision (a) when it failed to inform appellant of his right to counsel when he appeared without counsel in superior court to be arraigned on the information. This is true even if the same judge sat as a municipal court judge and a superior court judge in the same case. The statutes do not provide an exception in these circumstances. [¶] . . . Thus, the underlying logic of the Supreme Court's pronouncement appears to be that the defendant is entitled to two separate advisements on his right to counsel, one when he is arraigned on the complaint in municipal court, and another when he is arraigned on the information in superior court. It appears this is the basis for the Supreme Court's holding that a waiver of counsel in municipal court does not carry over into superior court." (Id. at pp. 95-97.)

However, both under section 859 and section 987, if the case is noncapital, as is this case, the duty of the court to appoint counsel for the defendant arises only "[i]f the defendant desires and is unable to employ counsel."

Here, defendant was advised twice in the municipal court and once in the superior court that she had a right to the assistance of counsel. At the first arraignment, the court advised defendant that it would appoint counsel for her at no cost to her, even though defendant had told the court she did not want to be represented by counsel. In each of the three instances, the court admonished defendant of the seriousness of the charges against her and the high risks she was taking by insisting on self-representation. But in all of those instances, defendant was adamant in turning down the court's suggestion of counsel representation, and in insisting on representing herself.

Therefore, because defendant expressed no desire to be represented by counsel and insisted on representing herself, the court was under no duty to appoint counsel for defendant. It follows that advising defendant of her right to a court-appointed counsel if she could not afford counsel of her own was meaningless.

Citing In re Fresquez (1967) 67 Cal.2d 626, 629, defendant complains that "[t]he admonishments given to [her] were clearly insufficient," the "most serious omission" being "the failure to inform her that she had the right to court-appointed counsel." (AOB 10)

The record does not support this claim. To the contrary, the record shows that at the first felony arraignment on May 26, 1999, the court advised defendant of her right to a court-appointed counsel, and that defendant insisted on representing herself. When defendant expressed to the court that she wanted to represent herself, the court admonished her: "[Y]ou understand that if you don't have money for an attorney, we'll appoint an attorney to represent you?" (ART 5/26/99, 2) Defendant told the court she understood that. The court went on: "And you understand it's my advice, strong advice, that it's not wise to represent yourself, because you don't know all the legal implications, and you're held to the same standards of law as a lawyer? Do you understand that?" (ART 5/26/99, 3) Defendant responded: "Yes, I do." (ART 5/26/99, 3)

Although the initial complaint that led to the first arraignment was apparently dismissed and later replaced with a new complaint, such dismissal did not obliterate the advice given by the court to defendant of her right to a court-appointed counsel. As stated in In re Fresquez: "The Penal Code contains no provision requiring that at the time of sentence the defendant again be informed of his right to counsel. A proper instruction given in the manner required by statute is normally adequate to insure the preservation of a defendant's constitutional rights. [Citation.] Generally when a defendant has waived his right to counsel the burden is on him to take some affirmative action to reinstate his right thereto. [Citations.]" (Id. at pp. 633-634.)

Here, after waiving her right to counsel at the initial arraignment on May 26, 1999, defendant took no affirmative action to reinstate such right. Instead, she reiterated that waiver at the July 6, 1999 municipal court arraignment, and again at the August 19, 1999 superior court arraignment. The record shows that when defendant waived her right to counsel at the initial arraignment on May 26, 1999, the court explained to defendant that the court would appoint her counsel free of charge if she did not have the money for an attorney. Defendant responded she understood. As of May 26, 1999, therefore, defendant knew that her constitutional right to counsel included the right to have counsel appointed for her by the court if she could not afford one, and that the waiver of her right to counsel included the waiver to have counsel appointed for her, free of charge, by the court. There is no evidence that defendant subsequently lost this understanding of what the right to counsel includes when she again waived that right at the second municipal court arraignment on July 6, 1999, and at the superior court arraignment on August 19, 1999.

People v. Sohrab, supra, 59 Cal.App.4th 89, 97-98, which defendant relies on, is distinguishable. In Sohrab, the superior court judge, who was the same judge who presided over the preliminary hearing in the municipal court, at which the defendant was advised of his right to counsel, utterly failed to advise the defendant again of his right to counsel when the defendant was arraigned on the information in the superior court. Indeed, the Sohrab court distinguished that case from People v. Wilder (1995) 35 Cal.App.4th 489, People v. McArthur (1992) 11 Cal.App.4th 619, and People v. Cervantes (1978) 87 Cal.App.3d 281, by noting that, unlike those cases, Sohrab "does not involve a mere technical failure to properly advise appellant of the dangers of self-representation. Instead, it involves the trial court's utter failure to advise appellant of his right to counsel and to take a waiver of that right in the superior court." (Sohrab, supra, 59 Cal.App.4th at p. 100.)

We conclude defendant had been properly advised of her right to counsel both by the municipal court and by the superior court.

In any event, assuming error, it was harmless. At the first arraignment in the municipal court on May 26, 1999, when the court asked defendant if she wanted a lawyer, defendant's reply was: "I'm going to represent myself." The court advised defendant that if she did not have money for an attorney, the court was going to appoint her one at no cost to her. Defendant told the court she understood that, but insisted on representing herself. The court then admonished defendant that "it's my advice, strong advice, that it's not wise to represent yourself, because you don't know all the legal implications, and you're held to the same standards of law as a lawyer[.]" Again, defendant said she understood, but insisted on representing herself.

At the second municipal court arraignment on July 6, 1999, the court asked defendant if she was going to apply for an attorney, or hire her own, or represent herself. Defendant replied she was going to represent herself.

Finally, at the superior court arraignment on August 19, 1999, the court advised defendant that she had the right to the assistance of an attorney "at all stages of the proceedings." The court cautioned defendant that she was "facing some serious charges here," and tried to convince defendant that she "ought to have an attorney" because "you're going to have to obey the same rules of evidence, and things that an attorney has to do." Defendant responded she understood all that, but that it was her "informed decision" not to have an attorney represent her. (RT 254-256)

Clearly, defendant would have insisted on representing herself even if the superior court had advised her that it would appoint counsel for her if she wanted to be represented by an attorney, but could not afford the services of one. The error was therefore harmless regardless of whether the standard applied is the Watson[18] standard of reasonable probability of a more favorable outcome absent the error, or the Chapman[19] standard of harmless error beyond a reasonable doubt.

DISPOSITION

The judgment is affirmed.

---

[18] *People v. Watson* (1956) 46 Cal.2d 818, 836.
[19] *Chapman v. California* (1967) 386 U.S. 18.

XIV.
People v. Mitchell
(Unpublished)

Mitchell is another right-to-counsel case. Here, however, the issue is narrowed to whether the court was obligated to advise the defendant anew of his right to counsel after the defendant had insisted on his right to defend himself, where, following the defendant's exercise of his right to self-representation, certain facts developed that were not present at the time the defendant asserted his right to self-representation.

This could be a novel issue in the Philippines. In the 23 years that I practiced law in the Philippines, ending in 1985, I did not encounter this kind of issue either in Philippine case law or in commentaries by Philippine text writers.

I stated above, in my commentary on the jury system, that the court decides questions of law, and the jury decides questions of fact. Sometimes, that proposition can be problematic. Some issues are gray. When the issue is in a gray area, determining whether it is a question of law or of fact can be difficult. *Mitchell* presents such an instance. In *Mitchell*, the trial court instructed the jury that certain alleged false statements in the defendant's application for a driving license were, if found true, material facts to consider in determining whether the defendant had committed perjury. The defendant claimed that this instruction was erroneous because the question of whether the alleged false statements were material or not was a question of fact, not of law. When the court instructed the jury that the alleged false statements were material matters, it was encroaching on the province of the jury. It was up to the jury to determine whether those alleged false statements were material or not to the crime of perjury. The difficulty of the issue is reflected in the fact that the courts are divided. In an earlier case, *Lem You*, the California Supreme Court held that the question was one of law. In *Jimenez*, our court questioned the continuing validity of that rule, but felt required to apply it. Later, in *Kobrin*, the California Supreme Court reversed *Lem You*, and held that the question is one of fact because it goes to the elements of the crime of perjury, the presence or existence of which was for the jury to determine. We applied *Kobrin* in *Mitchell*, and reversed the trial court on this instruction issue.

In reversing the trial court, it was not necessary for us to go into a harmless error analysis. This was because the error was structural and therefore inherently prejudicial. The error was structural because it violated the division of functions between the court and the jury. The court cannot encroach on the jury's exclusive province to determine the facts. Any such encroachment infringes on the constitution's allotment of powers between the court and the jury.

There is another thing that interested me in *Mitchell*. It is the unusual fact of Russell specializing in the theft, not just of any watch, but of Rolex watches. This factual rarity had no bearing on the legal issues involved, but I found it interesting to know that even robbery of watches can be so sub-specialized.

The opinion in *People v. Mitchell* follows:

Defendant Jess Roderick Mitchell was charged by information with robbery (Pen. Code, §§ 211, 212.5, former subd. (b) [now subd. (c)]; count 1),[20] attempted murder (§§ 664, 187; count 2), assault with a firearm (§ 245, subd. (a)(2); count 3), auto theft (Veh. Code, § 10851; count 4), possession of stolen property (§ 496; count 5), fraudulent use of an access card with intent to defraud (§ 484g; count 6), carrying a concealed weapon in a vehicle with a prior weapons violation (§ 12025, subd. (a); count 7), two counts of carrying a loaded firearm in a vehicle (§ 12031, subd. (a); counts 8 and 9), and perjury in applying for a driver's license (§ 118; count 10). The information further alleged that defendant was armed with a firearm.

Defendant waived his right to counsel and asked the court that he be allowed to represent himself. The court initially denied defendant's request, but then granted it.

Subsequently, codefendant Calvin Russell, who had earlier pleaded not guilty, changed his plea and entered a guilty plea. Russell then testified against defendant.

---

[20] Further statutory references in this case are to the Penal Code unless otherwise indicated.

The jury found defendant guilty as charged, and also found true the enhancing allegations.

The court sentenced defendant to a total term of 14 years in state prison, as follows: the upper term of 9 years for attempted second degree murder; consecutive one-third midterms of 1 year for robbery; and 8 months each for auto theft, possession of stolen property, and carrying a concealed weapon in a vehicle. Sentences for assault with a firearm and fraudulent use of access card were stayed pursuant to section 654. A one-year enhancement for the arming finding was imposed.

We affirm in part, reverse in part, and remand for resentencing.

FACTS
The June 9, 1992 Incident

Russell met defendant in Houston, Texas in 1991. Defendant had driven there in a van with several other people. Russell testified that defendant's purpose in going to Texas was to rob drug dealers, and that in one $80,000 drug dealer robbery, Russell had provided important information to defendant, although Russell did not actually go with defendant to commit the robbery.

Russell came to California in early 1992. After staying with his cousin-in-law for a couple of days, Russell moved into defendant's house in Milpitas.

Russell had been a "street hustler" in Texas since he was nine years old. Russell defined a "street hustler" as "a person that revenues or make [sic] money by the streets," mostly "in an unlawful manner." The numerous ways that a street hustler "revenues money" include "gambling, selling drugs, stealing cars and selling them, doing robberies, pimping 'hos and all of that."

One criminal activity Russell had concentrated on was "Rolex watch robbery." Asked why, Russell explained: "It's a fast way to make money quick. It's a lot less victims being involved. It's a lot less anybody getting hurt. It's just easy. It's easy to do because it's only one thing that we are after and one person basically possesses it. [¶] So in other words, it's different than going into a store to rob a grocery store where you got a gang of people working. When you do a Rolex robbery, you just get one item and you cash it in and get paid."

Russell also explained why the best time to commit a Rolex robbery was during the day: "[F]or one reason, it's kind of hard to do a Rolex robbery at night unless you specifically know a person owns a Rolex. And two, . . . I don't believe in doing crime at night. . . . [¶] [] From the street knowledge that I have learned . . . it's easier to do work in the daytime because the police ain't going to be just really looking for you . . . in the heat of the day and it's very unexpected to everybody because the person that owns the Rolex don't even know it's coming and the police really doesn't have no idea of that type of robbery." Also, it is best to commit a Rolex robbery "when the freeways are crowded with congested traffic," "[b]ecause that's where you find the Rolex watches in the traffic. People riding, they—some of them drive with their arms on the window like this or some have a hand on the steering wheel like this and they just easily visible from basically 20, 30 feet."

Russell testified that on the morning of June 9, 1992, he and defendant left defendant's house to commit a Rolex robbery. They drove a Ford Escort belonging to one of defendant's friends. They picked up a third companion, Eugene Jackson (hereafter, Eugene), in East Palo Alto. As they were driving on a freeway going to San Jose, they spotted Patrick Jackson (hereafter, Jackson) driving a 1981 Mercedes Benz, wearing what appeared to be a Rolex watch. They followed Jackson, who exited I-280 at Stevens Creek and proceeded to a CompUSA store. Eugene stepped out of the Ford Escort to ascertain whether Jackson's watch was a genuine Rolex. Eugene approached Jackson and asked him for the time. Jackson looked at his watch, and in so doing exposed it to Eugene. Eugene went back to the Ford Escort and told Russell and defendant that Jackson's watch was a genuine Rolex.

Russell's group followed Jackson to Hunter Properties in Cupertino. Russell and defendant got out of their car to approach Jackson. Eugene stayed in the car. Defendant asked Jackson to give him his watch. Jackson refused, and the two fought. Russell went to Jackson, put a gun in Jackson's face, and asked Jackson: "Do you want some of this." Jackson said no, and gave up his watch. Russell asked for Jackson's wallet. As Jackson was reaching for his wallet, Regina Morella walked out of the Hunter Properties building. Morella asked what was going on. Russell told Morella to mind her own business. When Morella "said something again," Russell shot her. Morella was hit and suffered serious injuries, but did not die.

The May 13, 1992 Incident

On May 13, 1992, Dr. Jay Hann, a hand surgeon, drove his 1982 Oldsmobile Toronado to the Veterans Administration Hospital in Palo Alto. Inside the trunk of the car were valuable micro surgical instruments.

Russell testified that on that day he and defendant drove Stacy Wade, defendant's niece, in a van to the hospital so that Stacy could visit her boyfriend. While Russell and defendant were in the hospital parking lot, they decided to steal a car. Russell looked for a car that was easiest to steal, and found Hann's Toronado. Using a screwdriver, Russell opened the Toronado's window. He then entered the car and started the engine. Russell asked defendant to drive the car because he (Russell) was "not familiar with the area," and did not know which way to go if he had "to run from the police." Defendant drove the Toronado, and Russell followed him in the van.

The September 8, 1992 Incident

On September 8, 1992, Reza Mirshafiei, who was in the business of buying and selling used cars, was driving a Lexus which he had purchased from a private party to resell. The seller had given him spare keys to the car; one key opened all doors. Mirshafiei testified that he had placed his briefcase inside the trunk of the car, and might have inadvertently left the key he used to open the trunk in the trunk lock. Inside the briefcase were Mirshafiei's checkbooks, company checks, credit cards, and business records.

Russell testified that on that day, while he and defendant were out looking for Rolex watches, he saw a Lexus with a key in the trunk lock. He told defendant, who was driving, what he saw. Russell and defendant followed the Lexus to an auto dealer's auction. Defendant went to the Lexus, opened the trunk, and took the briefcase.

Defendant suggested using the credit cards. Russell initially opposed the idea because using other people's credit cards was not one of his "hustles"; however, Russell eventually went along. Defendant,

Russell, and Stephanie Crouts drove to the Zenith Wire Wheel Company (hereafter Zenith). Russell and Crouts went inside the store and ordered wheels and tires for Russell's car. They paid for the items with one of the credit cards, but were told to pick up the merchandise later because the shop had to make an adapter for the rims.

James Craig, the owner of Zenith, was suspicious about Russell's appearance because it did not match the ethnicity suggested by the name on the credit card. Craig called a credit card security agency and the Campbell Police.

When defendant, Russell, and Crouts returned to Zenith later in the day, the police were waiting for them. The trio turned back, but were stopped by the police at Harrison Avenue. The police searched the van. Among the items found was a Glock 9mm semiautomatic handgun.

False Identity

Investigation by the police revealed that one person had applied for driver's licenses under two names: Jess Willard and Jess Mitchell. The fingerprints on the license applications matched the booking fingerprints of defendant. During his testimony, defendant admitted that the Willard application was also his, and that he submitted it to obtain a false driver's license. Defendant used the Jess Willard driver's license for identification when he purchased his handguns.

CONTENTIONS

Defendant contends:

1. The trial court erred in failing to revisit the Faretta[21] question when Russell pled guilty and agreed to testify for the prosecution.

2. The trial court committed reversible error in failing to warn defendant before he testified of his privilege against self-incrimination.

3. The trial court erred in admitting evidence that defendant had pled guilty, and by instructing that defendant was an accomplice as a matter of law, without also instructing that defendant's guilty plea was not independent evidence that he was guilty.

---

[21] Faretta v. California (1975) 422 U.S. 806.

4. The trial court erred in giving unmodified CALJIC No. 2.11.5, thereby minimizing an important aspect of the careful scrutiny to be given Russell's testimony.

5. The trial court erred in admitting evidence of a crime, unrelated to the current charges, which Russell claimed defendant had committed in Texas in 1991.

6. The trial court impermissibly restricted defendant's ability to impeach Russell regarding Russell's legal problems in Texas and their effect on his role as a witness for the prosecution in this case.

7. Count 6 must be reversed because the trial court failed to instruct on an essential element of the offense; if not reversed, the count 6 conviction must be reduced to a misdemeanor.

8. The trial court erred by instructing that certain statements were material as a matter of law in regard to the perjury charge in count 10.

9. Because the amount of the restitution fine is not supported by the record, the case must be remanded for a hearing on the issue, or the fine must be reduced to the statutory minimum.

DISCUSSION
No Error in Failure to Revisit Faretta Question

Defendant contends the trial court erred in failing to revisit the Faretta question when codefendant Russell pled guilty and agreed to testify for the prosecution. We disagree.

Approximately one month after defendant had elected to represent himself, Russell, who was represented by the public defender, pled guilty and agreed to testify for the prosecution. Defendant claims that Russell's decision to plead guilty and testify for the prosecution constituted a "drastic increase in the risks of self-representation for defendant," and hence the trial court "should have inquired of Mr. Mitchell whether he wanted to reconsider his decision to represent himself under these new and eminently more hazardous circumstances."

Defendant cites no authority for the proposition that increase in the risks of self-representation is a ground to revisit the Faretta question. We think the proposition is unacceptable. Were we to accept the proposition, the question would be revisited each time a pro se defendant would make a mistake that would substantially increase the probability of his or her conviction. As this could happen innumerable times over the entire course of a criminal proceeding, revisiting the question as often would impose on the court a requirement that serves no constitutional or useful purpose.

In People v. Poplawski (1994) 25 Cal.App.4th 881, 889, this court held that the Faretta election of self-representation is valid and binding on a defendant for the rest of the proceedings if made competently, knowingly, intelligently, and voluntarily. We stated that "the only valid reasons for revoking a defendant's pro se status are disruptive in-court conduct or substantial evidence of incompetency." (Ibid.) None of the excepted situations is present here.

Defendant relies on language in U.S. v. Fazzini (7th Cir. 1989) 871 F.2d 635, 643 (hereafter, Fazzini), which states: "Once the defendant has knowingly and intelligently waived his right to counsel, only a substantial change in circumstances will require the district court to inquire whether the defendant wishes to revoke his earlier waiver." Defendant argues that "[a] more substantial change in circumstances than that which befell Mr. Mitchell in this case is difficult to imagine." The reliance is misplaced.

First, Fazzini in fact rejected the "substantial change" argument in that case. Second, Fazzini is factually distinguishable. In Fazzini, the defendant disputed that he ever waived his right to counsel. Indeed, the Fazzini court noted that "the record shows that the defendant never clearly stated that he waived his right to counsel. Instead, on several occasions, the defendant insisted that he was being forced to proceed pro se by the court and would have preferred to have new counsel appointed." (871 F.2d at p. 642.) Nevertheless, stating that "it is not necessary that a defendant verbally waive his right to counsel," the Fazzini court found that the defendant's actions in that case had the "effect of depriving himself of appointed counsel" and "establish[ing] a knowing and intentional choice." (Ibid.) Because the defendant had implicitly waived his right to counsel, Fazzini held that the court was not required to inquire of the defendant if he wanted to be represented by counsel at sentencing. (Ibid.) It was in the context of rejecting the defendant's claim that "it is incumbent upon the judge to ensure that at each critical phase of the proceedings, the defendant is asked whether he wishes to continue without counsel," that the court stated that "[o]nce the defendant has knowingly and intelligently waived his right to counsel, only a substantial change in circumstances will require the district court to inquire whether the defendant wishes to revoke his earlier waiver." (Id. at p. 643.)

It is thus plain that the weight of the evidence against the defendant or the complexity of the issues is a not factor to consider in granting or denying a defendant's Faretta request of self-representation. All that is required is that the defendant "'knowingly and intelligently'" waive his or her right to counsel. (Faretta v. California, supra, 422 U.S. at p. 835.) As stated in Faretta: "We need make no assessment of how well or poorly Faretta had mastered the intricacies of the hearsay rule and the California code provisions that govern challenges of potential jurors on voir dire. For his technical knowledge, as such, was not relevant to an assessment of his knowing exercise of the right to defend himself." (Id. at p. 836, fn. omitted.)

We conclude the trial court did not err in failing to revisit the Faretta question after Russell's change of plea and agreement to testify for the prosecution.

No Failure to Warn Against Self-incrimination

Defendant contends the trial court committed reversible error in failing to warn him before he testified of his right against self-incrimination. The contention is without merit.

The transcript of the Faretta hearing reveals that the trial court repeatedly advised defendant in the strongest terms possible against self-representation, warning him that he would be up against an experienced prosecutor who would be determined to convict him. Further, the court specifically advised defendant that he had a right to remain silent and to not testify; that if he testified, he waived all immunity and his privilege against self-incrimination, and hence could be cross-examined, and anything he might say could be used against him.

The following colloquy demonstrates the sufficiency of the trial court's advice and warning: "THE COURT: Now, Mr. Mitchell, it's one thing to be an intelligent person and have verbal skills. The woods are full of those people. But to step into here, it would be like me, for example, putting the pads on you and say go up and play wide receivers for the 49er's, not knowing the play book, not having worked out, not being in shape and go out there over the middle, I want you to catch a pass. I want to tell you Lawrence Taylor is there waiting for you. This is what Mr. Hood [the prosecutor] is. He's Lawrence Taylor waiting over the middle for you to come across and catch the ball. His interest is to put your lights out, legally speaking. [¶] Now, if you want to jump into that mess, you can do it, it's your call. But you've never been down this path before. Watching it on television, talking to other people and saying to yourself, if I'm going to fall, I'm going to do it the hard way. I'm going to represent myself. I'm going to try to make every motion I can. I'm going to try to make a record for appellate purposes so that when it's appealed, it's reversed. That's kind of throwing in the towel. That's saying, I know I'm going to be convicted, but I hope it gets reversed two or three years later. That's a big gamble. . . . [¶] Now, have you had—in your college courses, have you taken classes, for example, in public speaking or business law or anything like that?

"DEFENDANT MITCHELL: No, sir. I was an electrical engineer.

"THE COURT: All right. Well, then, you should be familiar then with the term 'force is mass times acceleration.' And the force with which you get hit in this case is going to be a big mass at high speed. That's going to be the D.A.'s case with his experience. [¶] Now, I can't protect you on objections. I can't protect you when you ask a question, he objects, and you don't know how to ask a question. I can simply sustain it. I can't give you direction how to ask the question. That's one of the most difficult things for persons who represent themselves to do. How to ask a witness a question so that they can get the truth out of it and not testify as they want to. Coupled with the fact if you do testify, anything you say can or will be used against you. You don't have to be forced to testify. You have the right to remain silent."

Later in the Faretta hearing, after defendant had insisted on self-representation despite the court's advice to the contrary, the court called codefendant Russell and his counsel, and discussion about the potential consequences in the event defendant decided to testify ensued: "MS. BERNADINI [Russell's counsel]: Your Honor, you also might imagine what would happen if Mr. Mitchell wanted to testify. If Mr. Mitchell choose [sic] to testify and overlapping evidence is presented by the District Attorney, he can be cross-examined on a case which he is represented by Mr. Furst—

"THE COURT: Right.

"MS. BERNADINI: — where the evidence is the same.

"THE COURT: And I'm sure Mr. Furst would say to him, I advise you not to testify and refuse to answer those questions. Once he takes the stand and says anything to anybody on direct, he waives all immunity and waives his privilege against self-incrimination. [¶] [] Mr. Mitchell, let me ask you one or two questions. Do you intend to go forward with your case in municipal court, attempted murder charge, and represent yourself on that case? You see what the problem is, Jess?

"DEFENDANT MITCHELL: I see it, yes, sir."

On this record, we are persuaded the trial court adequately advised defendant of his right against self-incrimination prior to defendant's taking the witness stand, and that defendant took the witness stand knowing that by doing so he was waiving his privilege against self-incrimination.

No Error in Admitting Evidence
That Codefendant had Pled Guilty

Defendant contends the trial court erred in admitting evidence that Russell had pled guilty and instructing that Russell was an accomplice as a matter of law, without also instructing that Russell's guilty plea was not independent evidence that defendant was guilty. The contention is without merit.

The rule is settled that "[a] trial court is required to instruct sua sponte only on those general principles of law that are closely and openly connected with the facts before the court and necessary for the jury's understanding of the case. [Citation.]" (People v. Price (1991) 1 Cal.4th 324, 442.) The issue of the limited admissibility of evidence is not such a general principle of law. In People v. Collie (1981) 30 Cal.3d 43, 63, the court stated: "Although the trial court may in an appropriate case instruct sua sponte on the limited admissibility of evidence of past criminal conduct, we have consistently held that it is under no duty to do so. [Citations.]"

The fact that a defendant is pro se does not alter the rule. "The general rule is that a self-represented defendant is not entitled to any assistance or advice from the trial judge on matters of law, evidence or trial practice. [Citations.]" (People v. Jones (1992) 2 Cal.App.4th 867, 873.)

Here, defendant did not object when Russell testified that he (Russell) had pleaded guilty to the same crimes that were also charged against defendant. Likewise, defendant did not request a limiting instruction that would have informed the jury that Russell's guilty plea was not independent evidence of defendant's guilt.

We hold that defendant's failure to object and to request a limiting instruction waived the issue and precludes defendant from raising it for the first time on appeal.

Any Error in Giving CALJIC No. 2.11.5 is Waived

Defendant contends the trial court erred in giving unmodified CALJIC No. 2.11.5, which instructed the jury that it should not discuss or consider the reasons why a person other than the defendant was not being prosecuted. While conceding that the instruction was proper as applied to Eugene, defendant argues it was erroneous as applied to Russell because its effect was to direct the jury that it could not consider Russell's plea bargain in evaluating Russell's credibility. We disagree.

It People v. Sully (1991) 53 Cal.3d 1195, 1218, where it was contended that CALJIC No. 2.11.1, although properly given based on the evidence, was too general to the extent it could be viewed as applying to the appellant, who was a prosecution witness, but where no request was made for a limiting instruction, the court, in holding that appellant had waived any assignment of error, stated: "'A party may not complain on appeal that an instruction correct in law and responsive to the evidence was too general or incomplete unless the party has requested appropriate clarifying or amplifying language.'" (Citation omitted.)

Here, since defendant did not request an appropriate limiting instruction below, he is therefore precluded from claiming error on appeal. Again, "a self-represented defendant is not entitled to any assistance or advice from the trial judge on matters of law, evidence or trial practice. [Citations.]" (People v. Jones, supra, 2 Cal.App.4th at p. 873.)

No Error in Admitting Evidence of Texas Crimes

We also reject, for lack of merit, defendant's contention that the trial court erred in admitting evidence of a crime unrelated to the current charges which Russell claimed defendant had committed in Texas in 1991.

During his examination in chief, Russell testified that he first met defendant in Houston, Texas when defendant, in the company of other persons, was there for a visit. Apart from asking Russell when and where he first met defendant, with whom defendant was with, and how defendant came to Texas, the prosecutor did not ask Russell anything else about defendant's contacts or activities in Texas.

On cross-examination, defendant attempted to impeach Russell's credibility by showing that Russell had earlier made inconsistent statements to police investigators about their meeting in Houston. Defendant asked Russell whether they had in fact met in Houston, whether Russell had told investigators it was in 1992 rather than in 1991 when they first met, and whether Russell had told the investigators that defendant and his companions had flown, rather than driven, to Houston. Defendant also challenged Russell's claim that defendant's purpose in coming to California was to commit drug-dealer robberies with defendant.

Before redirect examination, the prosecutor argued to the court that defendant had "opened the door" to examination about "drug rip-offs," including whether defendant's purpose in going to Texas was to rob drug dealers. The trial court agreed the subject area had been opened up through defendant's questions about Texas, drug-dealer robberies, when defendant went to Texas and with whom, when he first met Russell, and why Russell came to California. When defendant argued he was only asking Russell to explain inconsistencies in Russell's testimony and statements, the court told him the questioning had not been narrow: "[Y]ou conducted a lot of examination concerning that type of an issue, what was going on in Texas, why you were there, what you did there, how long you stayed there, when you came back to California, when

Mr. Russell came to California, why he came to California, who he stayed with, what he did, did he work, did you work, et cetera."

On redirect examination, Russell testified, without objection from defendant, that defendant and his companions had come to Texas to rob drug dealers because Texas drug dealers were less wary of robbery and did not secure their money as carefully. Russell further testified that he had set up two drug dealers for robbery by defendant.

Pursuant to Evidence Code section 353, subdivision (a), a judgment may not be set aside on grounds of erroneous admission of evidence unless there appears of record a timely objection "so stated as to make clear the specific ground of the objection . . . ." Here, defendant's objection was only that the matter of drug-dealer robberies was beyond the scope of his cross-examination; there was no objection on Evidence Code section 352 or 1101 grounds. Accordingly, objections on those grounds were waived.

"It is well settled that when a witness is questioned on cross-examination as to matters relevant to the subject of the direct examination but not elicited on the examination, he may be examined on redirect as to such new matter." (People v. Kynette (1940) 15 Cal.2d 731, 752.) "Upon redirect examination it is proper to permit the witness to state facts and circumstances that tend to correct or repel any wrong impressions or inferences that might arise on matters drawn out on cross-examination." (Myers v. Rose (1938) 27 Cal.App.2d 87, 89.) "A trial court's exercise of discretion will not be disturbed unless it appears that the resulting injury is sufficiently grave to manifest a miscarriage of justice. [Citation.] In other words, discretion is abused only if the court exceeds the bounds of reason, all of the circumstances being considered. [Citation.]" (People v. Stewart (1985) 171 Cal.App.3d 59, 65.)

On this record, we conclude the trial court did not abuse its discretion in admitting, during redirect examination, without objection from defendant, evidence of a crime unrelated to the current charges which Russell claimed defendant had committed in Texas in 1991.

No Denial of Right of Confrontation

Defendant contends the trial court denied him his Sixth Amendment right of confrontation and cross-examination, and due process, by precluding him from inquiring "whether Mr. Russell hoped to gain from his testimony in this case any benefit in regard to matters pending against him in Texas." The contention is without merit.

Before Russell took the witness stand, the prosecutor informed the court outside the presence of the jury that "at one point . . . there was a request to extradite Mr. Russell out of Texas for a murder"; that the extradition request was no longer pending; and that he did not believe Russell had been convicted of murder in Texas. The prosecutor then moved to exclude any reference to Russell "as a suspect in a murder or him being extradited for murder or charged with murder or anything along those lines out of Texas in this case."

The following colloquy ensued: "MR. MITCHELL: In other words, that's saying I can't ask him has he ever committed similar crimes to this before?

"THE COURT: Well, that you can't ask in any event unless you have evidence to present to establish that conduct. Again, if he does testify, you have the right to offer evidence that would impeach his credibility. . . . And if Mr. Hood does not bring those out on direct, you can certainly bring those out on cross-examination because the relevance bears upon credibility.

". . . . .

"MR. MITCHELL: I just have one question then. Maybe you can direct to Mr. Hood then and we could answer this and then I wouldn't have any other reason to bring it up. Was any deal made with Mr. Russell pertaining to that Texas extradition situation.

"THE COURT: That's a very good point.

"MR. MITCHELL: Concerning—

"THE COURT: I understand exactly what you are saying. That's a very good point. If, in fact, there has been some assistance provided by the People in this particular case with respect to your pending matter in Texas and that's part of the motivation as to why Mr. Russell is testifying, then you could certainly go into it, if that be the case.

"MR. MITCHELL: That's why I am asking now, sir, to find out.

"THE COURT: Yes, that's a reasonable request because you do have a right to attempt to impeach credibility and to show a prejudice or bias or motivation as to why somebody is testifying. And if there was some type of arrangement made with respect to that by the People in this case, it certainly would be relevant."

Further down the colloquy, the exchange continued: "THE COURT: ... In the absence of some evidence that you might have, Mr. Mitchell, that the People in this case suggested to Mr. Russell in some fashion that they would assist him on his matters in Texas, whether it be the present extradition matter for violation of parole or whether it be this other matter where apparently there was a murder charge pending, in the absence of some evidence, did that play in his motivation to testify, I would rule that it's all legally inadmissible. [¶] If there is evidence that that was discussed and considered and formed a basis or the part of the basis for Mr. Russell to testify in this case, then it certainly would be admissible because it was relevant to show a motivation as to why he is testifying, to wit, he is trying to help himself on his pending matters in Texas and in exchange for that help, he is testifying in the fashion he is testifying in. [¶] But again, based on the representations made by the People and based upon the agreement they claim you have, there's apparently been no discussion of any whatsoever of any type involving the Texas matters.

"MR. MITCHELL: I would still be concerned that it appears to be suspicious that suddenly Mr. Russell wouldn't be charged with murder in another jurisdiction and he would suddenly become a witness in Santa Clara County.

"THE COURT: I can't answer that for you and I don't know anything about the Texas matters. I don't know anything about the Texas charge or why it was filed or why it was withdrawn. None of that is before the court. [¶] I am simply saying in the absence of any evidence that that played a factor in his deciding to testify, it's all irrelevant. If it did play a factor and it was suggested to him that perhaps the People could help him on those Texas matters, et cetera, then of course it would be relevant and you could examine him about it. . . .

". . . . .

"MR. MITCHELL: One other area that I want to cover about that is I didn't see in here any—anything about in the agreement about Mr. Russell's extradition to Texas for his probation violation. And I was just curious as to whether or not that was going to be something that would be done as a part of his deal with them, that he would go to Texas to serve his time that he's been offered here.

"THE COURT: If you feel that that's part of his motivation, that he wants to go to Texas to serve his time on this charge, you can ask him that question.

"MR. MITCHELL: Thank you, sir.

"THE COURT: If you feel that he is testifying in the fashion he is because he simply wants to get out of California and go to Texas and this is the fastest way he can do it and he is receiving assistance in that respect, you can ask him.

"MR. MITCHELL: Thank you, sir."

Clearly, on this record, there was no violation of defendant's right of confrontation and cross-examination, and due process. The court did not preclude defendant from cross-examining Russell on his motivation for changing his plea and testifying for the prosecution. Specifically, the court did not preclude defendant from asking Russell if Russell stood to benefit from testifying as he did.

The cross-examination restrictions imposed by the court did not amount to abuse of discretion. As stated in <u>Delaware</u> v. <u>Van Arsdall</u> (1986) 475 U.S. 673, 679: "It does not follow . . . that the Confrontation Clause of the Sixth Amendment prevents a trial judge from imposing any limits on defense counsel's inquiry into the potential bias of a prosecution witness. On the contrary, trial judges retain wide latitude insofar as the Confrontation Clause is concerned to impose reasonable limits on such cross-examination based on concerns about, among other things, harassment, prejudice, confusion of the issues, the witness' safety, or interrogation that is repetitive or only marginally relevant. . . . '[T]he Confrontation Clause guarantees an <u>opportunity</u> for effective cross-examination, not cross-examination that is effective in whatever way, and to whatever extent, the defense might wish.' [Citation.]"

No Error in Credit Card Fraud Instructions

Defendant contends count 6 must be reversed because the trial court failed to instruct that an essential element of the charged crime was that the credit card must have been stolen. We disagree.

At the time of the commission of the crime charged in count 6, section 484g provided: "Every person, who with intent to defraud, (a) uses for the purpose of obtaining money, goods, services or anything else of value an access card obtained or retained in violation of Section 484e or an access card which he or she knows is forged, expired, or revoked, or (b) obtains money, goods, services or anything else of value by representing without the consent of the cardholder that he or she is the holder of an access card or by representing that he or she is the holder of an access card and the card has not in fact been issued, is guilty of theft. If the value of all money, goods, services and other things of value obtained in violation of this section exceeds four hundred dollars ($400) in any consecutive six-month period, then the same shall constitute grand theft." (See Stats. 1986, ch. 1436, § 4.)

As should be noted, section 484g does not require proof that the credit card was stolen. All it requires is that the card was "obtained or retained in violation of Section 484e," and thereafter used with the knowledge that it was so obtained or retained. Section 484e, subdivision (a), on the other hand, provides that "[e]very person who acquires an access card from another without the cardholder's or issuer's consent or who, with knowledge that it has been so acquired, acquires the access card, with intent to use it or to sell or transfer it to a person other than the issuer or the cardholder is guilty of petty theft." Subdivision (c) of section 484e further provides that "[e]very person who sells, transfers, conveys, or receives an access card with the intent to defraud, or who acquires an access card with the intent to use it fraudulently, is guilty of grand theft."

The trial court's instruction to the jury read: "In order to prove this crime, each of the following elements must be proved: One, a person used an access card for the purpose of obtaining money, goods, services or anything else of value. Two, the person used the access card by representing without consent that he was the holder of the access card. And three, at the time of such use, the person had the specific intent to defraud."

Clearly, the instruction satisfied the elements of section 484g. Accordingly, there was no error.

We agree with defendant, however, that the count 6 conviction should be reduced from a felony to a misdemeanor. Section 484g plainly provides that a violation of that section is theft unless the value of all money, goods, services, and other things of value obtained exceeds $400 in any consecutive six-month period, in which case, the crime is grand theft.

Here, the wheels and tires which were ordered, and which had a retail value of $2,600, were never in fact delivered; they were not therefore "obtained" within the meaning of section 484g. As to the items that were actually purchased with the card, no evidence was presented to show that their combined value exceeded $400.

Respondent contends that the provision in section 484g defining as grand theft the obtaining of money, goods, services, et cetera, worth in excess of $400 is not the exclusive but only an alternative means of establishing grand theft. In support of this contention, respondent claims that because acquiring an access card with intent to defraud is already grand theft under section 484e, subdivision (c), use of a card so acquired cannot be less.

The flaw in this argument is that while section 484e is a means to commit a violation of section 484g, a violation of section 484e is a separate crime in itself. Hence, had defendant been separately charged with a violation of section 484e, subdivision (c), a conviction thereunder would have been grand theft, his misdemeanor conviction under section 484g would have been in addition thereto. But because defendant was not so separately charged, the People cannot here bootstrap the penalty for the greater crime not charged to the lesser crime that was charged.

Moreover, in construing criminal statutes, "[i]f the statutory language is ambiguous and susceptible to two plausible interpretations, we must, because this is a criminal statute, adopt the one more favorable to the defendant. [Citation.]" (People v. Bransford (1994) 8 Cal.4th 885, 895 (conc. and dis. opn. of Kennard, J.).)

Accordingly, on count 6, we must remand for resentencing.

Materiality a Jury Question

Defendant contends the trial court erred in instructing the jury with respect to count 10 that certain allegedly false statements in defendant's application for a California driver's license were material matters within the meaning of the elements of the crime of perjury, because such instruction removed the question of materiality from the jury. We agree.

In People v. Jimenez (1992) 11 Cal.App.4th 1611, 1622, this court, relying on People v. Lem You (1893) 97 Cal. 224, 228 (hereafter, Lem You), held that the issue of materiality in a perjury prosecution "is a question 'of law for the court, and not of fact for the jury.'" Although we were critical of that rule, noting that the continuing validity of that proposition has been put to question in light of modern due process requirements, we felt bound to apply it until Lem You was reversed. (11 Cal.App.4th at pp. 1622-1623.)

Recently, in People v. Kobrin (1995) 11 Cal.4th 416, 427, footnote 7, the Supreme Court, citing the recent opinion of the United States Supreme Court in U.S. v. Gaudin (1995) 515 U.S. ___ [115 S.Ct. 2310], expressly overruled Lem You. The Kobrin court held that (1) "'materiality' constitutes an element of the crime of perjury" (11 Cal.4th at p. 426); (2) the due process clause requires that the jury determine the question of materiality in a perjury prosecution (id. at pp. 423-424); and (3) the failure of the court to instruct the jury on materiality requires reversal per se because "it infects the structural integrity of the trial process" (id. at p. 428). Gaudin had held that materiality in a prosecution under 18 United States Code section 1001, which prohibits making false statements or representations of material fact to a federal department or agency, is a question of fact for the jury. (U.S. v. Gaudin, supra, 115 S.Ct. at p. 2314.)

Because the removal of the materiality issue from the jury is reversible per se, the trial court's error is incurable by harmless error analysis. (People v. Kobrin, supra, 11 Cal.4th at pp. 428-430.)

No Error in Imposing Restitution Fine of $5,000

Defendant contends the restitution fine of $5,000 must be reduced to the minimum of $200, or the case be remanded for a determination of his ability to pay. We disagree.

Although present law no longer requires a finding of ability to pay, this case is governed by former Government Code section 13967, subdivision (a), which provided in pertinent part that "if the person is convicted of one or more felony offenses, the court shall impose a . . . restitution fine of not less than two hundred dollars ($200), subject to the defendant's ability to pay, and not more than ten thousand dollars ($10,000)." (See Stats. 1992, ch. 682, § 4.)

There was no requirement under former Government Code section 13967, subdivision (a), that the trial court make an express determination on the record of a defendant's ability to pay. (People v. Frye) (1994) 21 Cal.App.4th 1483, 1485-1486.) Defendant's ability to pay could be implied form the record. (Ibid.) Further, the court was "not limited to considering a defendant's present ability but may consider a defendant's ability to pay in the future." (Id. at p. 1487.) The court could consider that as a prison inmate defendant would be compensated for performing work assigned to him. (Ibid.) On appeal, the trial court's finding of ability to pay will be upheld if supported by the record. (People v. Staley (1992) 10 Cal.App.4th 782, 785-786.)

Here, the court explicitly found defendant had ability to pay. At the sentencing hearing on June 16, 1994, the court stated: "With respect to the restitution fund fine, I do find you have an ability to pay. I do find that there is no question but that you will be involved in a work program in the Department of Corrections . . . . I know from your own statements and from the probation report and from the evidence that you are able-bodied, that you can work. You were physically fit per your own statements repeatedly; you keep yourself in condition. You don't abuse drugs or alcohol. You take care of yourself physically, so you certainly are able to work. You will work, I assume, and if you do work you will receive monies. Out of those monies the Department of Corrections will take an appropriate portion to pay to the restitution fund fine."

The trial court's finding of defendant's ability to pay is supported by the record. The fact alone that defendant's total term of imprisonment is 14 years indicates that defendant has that much time to work in prison to earn the $5,000 restitution fine. Accordingly, we find no abuse of discretion.

DISPOSITION

The judgment of conviction on count 10 is reversed. In all other respects, the judgment is affirmed. This matter is remanded to the superior court for resentencing on count 6 in the manner indicated in this opinion.

XV.
Tran v. Nguyen
(Unpublished)

Tran discusses the rule on appearances *in propria persona*. Although *Tran* is a civil case, the rule on self-representation is, for the most part, the same as in criminal cases. The fact that the litigant appearing on his own behalf is not a lawyer is no reason for the court to ease the rules of procedure and evidence in his favor. The self-representing litigant is held to the same standard of technical knowledge, competence, conduct, and performance as the lawyers practicing before the court. Ignorance cannot be rewarded by holding otherwise.

In California, punitive damages cannot be awarded without evidence of the defendant's financial condition. The reason is punitive damages should be large enough to hurt the defendant and teach him a lesson, and yet not too large to be disproportionate to the defendant's ability to pay. A punitive damage award of P20,000, for example, will not hurt a Filipino millionaire's pocket, and so will not serve the punitive purpose of the award, which is to deter him from repeating similar misconduct in the future. But the same award against a defendant who earns P15,000 a month is vastly disproportionate to his ability to pay, and will ruin him if allowed. The purpose of punitive damages is to teach the defendant a lesson, not to ruin him economically.

In California, if the action is based on a contract, the court cannot award attorney fees to the prevailing party unless the contract provides for the payment of attorney fees on actions arising from that contract. The fact that the breach required the plaintiff to sue and engage the services of counsel is not a basis to award attorney fees where the contract is silent on attorney fees.

Civil cases are also tried by jury. However, the parties may agree that the case be tried by the court. Where the case is tried by the court, the court, at the end of the trial, announces its tentative decision either by oral statement in open court in the presence of the parties, or by a written statement filed with the clerk. The court may designate a party, usually the prevailing party, to prepare the statement of decision, or it may prepare the statement of decision itself. If a party is designated by the court to prepare the statement of decision, the party so designated prepares the proposed statement of decision and the proposed judgment, and files it with the court, serving copies on all the parties, who may then serve and file objections to the proposed statement of decision or judgment. If the court approves the proposed statement of decision and judgment, it signs and files it as its statement of decision and judgment. The court may, of course, reject the proposed statement of decision and judgment and prepare its own statement of decision and judgment, or modify the proposed statement and file it as modified.

This practice of assigning a party, usually the prevailing party, to prepare a proposed statement of decision and judgment is not done in the Philippines. However, it is probably worth studying. It frees some valuable time of the court and allows the court to use that time to study and move on to other cases. No ethical problems are involved because the court's decision and judgment has already been made and publicly announced in the presence of all the parties. All the designated party does is merely write the *statement* of the court's decision and judgment in a manner that conforms to the court's announced decision and judgment. Moreover, the proposed statement of decision and judgment is served on all the other parties, who then are given the opportunity to file their objections. The court can always make changes or revisions to the proposed statement of decision and judgment, or even entirely reject it and prepare its own. The final statement of decision and judgment will still be the court's sole, exclusive, and final responsibility.

The opinion in *Tran v. Nguyen* follows:

Defendants Quyen V. Nguyen (hereafter, Quyen) and Kim Ngoc Le (hereafter, Le) appeal from a judgment awarding plaintiffs Hanh Duc Tran and Thanhtong Ton damages, attorney fees, and costs. We affirm.

BACKGROUND

Quyen owned 11 fourplexes in San Jose, but had the title to some of them registered to the names of other persons. In 1988, Quyen entered into an oral agreement with plaintiffs whereby he agreed to sell to plaintiffs all 11 fourplexes. Pursuant to that agreement, plaintiffs started making payments to Quyen and to others at Quyen's instruction.

While plaintiffs were making their payments, Quyen, without the knowledge and consent of plaintiffs, sold some of the four-plexes to other persons. Plaintiffs decided that if they could not buy the 11 units, they would buy only 3 of a certain model. Quyen sold four units to Ngai Nguyen (hereafter, Ngai).

Plaintiffs had paid Quyen $60,000 on the units that were sold to other persons. Quyen agreed to return this amount by assigning to plaintiffs certain promissory notes which Ngai had executed as part payment for the four units sold to him. These notes had been made payable to Le at Quyen's instruction.

Le signed the assignments in plaintiffs' favor. Quyen asked plaintiffs not to record the assignments yet because he was still negotiating with Ngai about other business deals. Without any reason to suspect Quyen's motives, plaintiffs accommodated Quyen's request.

Quyen and Le then negotiated with Ngai for an early payoff of the $60,000 notes. They offered to accept $22,000 as full payment of the $60,000 notes if Ngai would pay off the notes early. Ngai agreed to the early payoff by writing two checks: one to the order of Le, the other to the order of a certain Kim Nguyen. Le cashed her check and gave the money to Quyen. She thereafter instructed the title company to record a deed of reconveyance.

Plaintiffs filed the instant action against Quyen, Le, and Ngai for breach of promissory note, common count, fraud and deceit, cancellation of written instrument, and imposition of constructive trust.

Ngai cross-complained against plaintiffs, Quyen, and Le, for fraud, negligent misrepresentation, breach of fiduciary duties, conversion, and declaratory relief. Ngai's cross-complaint alleged, inter alia, that the condition of the properties was not as represented in the purchase contract; that Quyen concealed from him the fact that the properties did not conform to the requirements of certain housing codes and were located within a flood zone; that the termite work, which was completed by a company in which Quyen had an interest, was not satisfactory; and that Ngai expended approximately $76,036 to repair the properties.

At the mandatory settlement conference, plaintiffs and Ngai, in the presence of defendants, agreed to mutually dismiss with prejudice all causes of action which they had against each other, and in consideration of such covenant, Ngai assigned and transferred to plaintiffs all his existing claims and causes of action against defendants.

At the trial below, defendants appeared in propria persona. Judgment was rendered in favor of plaintiffs and against defendants. This appeal ensued.

CONTENTIONS

On appeal, defendants contend:

1. The trial court's award of punitive damages must be reversed.

2. The denial of defendants' right to a jury trial requires reversal of the court's judgment.

3. The assignment of defendant Ngai's cross-complaint to plaintiffs was improper.

4. The trial court's award of attorney fees was improper.

5. There is insufficient evidence to support the judgment.

6. The judgment should be reversed for the trial court's failure to issue a proposed judgment.

DISCUSSION

Appearance in Propria Persona

As stated, defendants appeared below in propria persona. Defendants' lack of counsel representation underpins their complaints in this appeal. For this reason, we consider it appropriate to address first the standard upon which defendants' in propria persona representation must be measured in resolving this appeal.

In Doran v. Dreyer (1956) 143 Cal.App.2d 289, the defendant, who had appeared in propria persona at the trial of the case, requested the appellate court "'in the best interests of justice'" to "'extend further latitude to appellant than would ordinarily be the case.'" The court of appeal responded: "This request misconceives the applicable rule. 'A litigant has a right to act as his own attorney [citation] "but, in so doing, should be restricted to the same rules of evidence and procedure as is required of those qualified to practice law before our courts, otherwise, ignorance is unjustly rewarded." [Citations.] . . . "A layman with resources who insists upon exercising the privilege of representing himself must expect and receive the same treatment as if represented by an attorney—no different, no better, no worse.""" (Id. at p. 290.)

Likewise, in Harding v. Collazo (1986) 177 Cal.App.3d 1044, 1056, where the appellant argued that as a litigant who appeared in propria persona he was somehow entitled to a more indulgent application of the rules than other litigants or attorneys, the court rejected the contention, stating: "His propria persona status afforded him no special treatment. 'When a litigant is appearing in propria persona, he is entitled to the same, but no greater, consideration than other litigants and attorneys [citations].' [Citations.]"

There is no reason why the standard of representation should be different in this case. Here, we are presented with a record that shows defendants to be well educated. Quyen has a master's degree in business administration from Golden Gate University, has been in this country since 1975, and is a licensed and experienced real estate broker. Not every American citizen is as well educated or as experienced in fields requiring some familiarity with the law. Le is also a licensed real estate agent.

Curiously, Quyen was initially represented by counsel. However, for reasons not shown in the record, Quyen substituted himself as his own counsel. Quyen's sophistication was apparent to the trial court. At the hearing of defendants' motion for a new trial, the court observed: "[D]on't describe this man as ignorant. This man is a very bright, sophisticated man . . . . This man knows what he is doing."

Furthermore, when this case was first assigned to the Honorable John S. McInerny for trial on the morning of April 13, 1992, plaintiff's counsel testified by declaration that "Judge McInerny went to great lengths, on the record, to explain to the in pro per defendants that this was a serious matter and that they should have legal counsel." Sutherland further declared that when the case was assigned to the Honorable Mark E. Thomas, Jr., for trial on the afternoon of April 13, 1992, Judge Thomas, at the commencement of trial, "informed the defendants that since they were representing themselves, they would be held to the same standard as an attorney."

In their memorandum in reply to plaintiffs' opposition, defendants did not dispute this declaration. We can therefore accept Sutherland's statement as a fair statement of the facts.

Having stated the standard by which defendants' in propria persona representation must be measured, we now proceed to address defendants' contentions.

Jury Trial

Defendants contend that they were denied their right to a jury trial. We find no merit to this contention.

The record shows that defendants were present at the settlement conference on April 8, 1992. The minutes of that proceeding reveal that the case was to be calendared for a nonjury trial which was estimated to be for one day. The minutes do not indicate who explicitly agreed to the court trial. It is clear, however, that defendants did not in any event object thereto. For failing to object, defendants are precluded from raising the issue on appeal. "It is the rule that even a serious error or impropriety is waived if it could have been cured had it been raised in time; otherwise, a party could remain quiet and speculate on the chance of a favorable verdict while holding the point in reserve in case the verdict goes against him. [Citations.]" (Sherwood v. Rossini (1968) 264 Cal.App.2d 926, 930-931.)

Moreover, defendants participated actively in the court trial without objection. Defendants' participation was the functional equivalent of express consent. "'[W]aiver may be shown by conduct; and it may be the result of an act which, according to its natural import, is so inconsistent with the intent to enforce the right in question as to induce a reasonable belief that such right has been relinquished.'" (Escamilla v. California Ins. Guarantee Assn. (1983) 150 Cal.App.3d 53, 58-59.) In Escamilla, the court stated that "'"a party cannot without objection try his case before a court without a jury, lose it and then complain that it was not tried by a jury."'" (Id. at p. 63, citation omitted.)

In any event, defendants have not demonstrated prejudice. Pursuant to article 6, section 13, of the California Constitution, "[n]o judgment shall be set aside, or new trial granted, in any cause, . . . for any error as to any matter of procedure, unless, after an examination of the entire cause, including the evidence, the court shall be of the opinion that the error complained of has resulted in a miscarriage of justice." There is "miscarriage of justice" if "it is reasonably probable that a result more favorable to the appealing party would have been reached in the absence of the error." (People v. Watson (1956) 46 Cal.2d 818, 836.)

"'"Defendants cannot play 'Heads I win, Tails you lose' with the trial court." Reversal of the trial court's refusal to allow a jury trial after a trial to the court would require reversal of the judgment and a new trial. It is then reasonable to require a showing of actual prejudice on the record to overcome the presumption that a fair trial was had and prejudice will not be presumed from the fact that trial was to the court or to a jury.' [Citation.] Prejudice by a nonjury trial cannot be presumed; on the contrary, it is presumed that the party had the benefit of a fair and impartial trial as contemplated by the Constitution. [Citation.]" (McIntosh v. Bowman (1984) 151 Cal.App.3d 357, 363.)

Defendants have not shown that had the matter been tried to a jury, it is reasonably probable that the result would have been more favorable to them.

Punitive Damages

Defendants contend that the award of punitive damages should be reversed because there was no meaningful evidence in the trial court of defendants' financial condition. Defendants rely on Adams v. Murakami (1991) 54 Cal.3d 105, 111, which held that evidence of a defendant's financial condition is a prerequisite to an award of punitive damages because the punitive damages award can be so disproportionate to the defendant's ability to pay that the award is excessive for that reason alone. The contention is without merit.

In its statement of decision, the court stated: "12. With regard to the issue of the amount of punitive and exemplary damages to be awarded under the Cross-Complaint, the Court's decision is that the sum of $203,252 is an appropriate award against Quyen V. Nguyen considering his participation and net worth and $1,000 is an appropriate award against Kim Ngoc Le considering her minimal participation and net worth. [¶] a. The court based its decision on the following facts: [¶] (1) The oral testimony of all witnesses pertaining to the conduct of Quyen V.

Nguyen and Kim Ngoc Le; [¶] (2) The oral testimony of Thanhtong Ton regarding Quyen V. Nguyen's net worth of approximately two million dollars; and [¶] (3) The oral testimony of Kim Ngoc Le regarding her net worth."

It is thus clear that the trial court in fact considered defendants' financial condition and net worth in awarding punitive damages. The only question is whether the trial court's conclusion is supported by substantial evidence. (Weisenburg v. Molina (1976) 58 Cal.App.3d 478, 490.)

Plaintiff Ton, upon whose testimony the trial court based in part its award of punitive damages, testified that Quyen had told her that he was the owner of land in Los Gatos on Lark Avenue, which was worth more than $6 million. Ton also testified that Quyen had taken her to North Valley and had shown her land which Quyen had told her was worth more than $1 million. Ton further testified that Quyen had told her that he had a house in San Francisco, one in San Leandro, and several houses in San Jose, and that he was worth several million dollars.

Additionally, the court was requested to take judicial notice of three grant deeds that had been recorded in favor of Quyen and his wife, and one deed of trust and full reconveyance thereof, covering one of Quyen's properties.

We find the foregoing evidence of Quyen's financial condition sufficient to support the trial court's award of punitive damages.

Nor was the award excessive as a matter of law. "In considering a contention that excessive damages were awarded, an appellate court will not disturb the verdict unless the sum awarded is so disproportionate to any reasonable amount warranted by the evidence so as to shock the conscience and suggest passion and prejudice on the part of the jury. [Citations.] Although the amount of an award of exemplary damages may seem unreasonable to an appellate court based upon a review of the evidence, it will not substitute its conclusion for that of the trier of fact if it is supported by substantial evidence. [Citations.]" (Weisenburg v. Molina, supra, 58 Cal.App.3d at p. 490.)

Because "exemplary damages are awarded to serve as an example or warning to others not to engage in conduct found to be proscribed by Civil Code section 3294 . . . [t]he amount of such damages is a matter generally within the discretion of the [trier of fact]. [Citation.]" (Emerson v. J. F. Shea Co. (1978) 76 Cal.App.3d 579, 594.) "[T]here is no fixed standard by which punitive damages can be determined . . . ." (Weisenburg v. Molina, supra, 58 Cal.App.3d at p. 490.)

Here, the punitive damage award was less than twice the amount of the compensatory damages awarded. Far greater ratios have been upheld by the courts. For example, in Devlin v. Kearny Mesa AMC/Jeep/Renault, Inc. (1984) 155 Cal.App.3d 381, the punitive damage award was 27 times the compensatory damage award; in Wetherbee v. United Ins. Co. of America (1971) 18 Cal.App.3d 266, the ratio was 190.5 to 1; and in Finney v. Lockhart (1950) 35 Cal.2d 161, the ratio was 2,000 to 1. While there is no mathematical formula to calculate punitive damages (Devlin v. Kearny Mesa AMC/Jeep/Renault, Inc., supra, 155 Cal.App.3d at pp. 388-389), "[g]enerally, the more reprehensible the act, the greater the appropriate punishment" (Walker v. Signal Companies, Inc. (1978) 84 Cal.App.3d 982, 997).

Assignment of Cross-Complaint

Defendants contend that Ngai's cross-complaint causes of action for fraud, negligent misrepresentation, breach of fiduciary duties, conversion, and declaratory relief are not assignable, and therefore the damages awarded to plaintiffs based thereon was reversible error. We disagree.

As stated, Ngai had assigned the causes of action in his cross-complaint to plaintiffs. The question is whether such assignment is valid. We hold it is.

Civil Code section 954 provides: "A thing in action, arising out of the violation of a right of property, or out of an obligation, may be transferred by the owner." In Osuna v. Albertson (1982) 134 Cal.App.3d 71, 80, the court held that this section applies to causes of action for fraud and negligent misrepresentation.

Osuna involved an assignment of rights in promissory notes and deeds of trust and of causes of action for fraud and deceit and negligent misrepresentation. In holding the assignment of the fraud and negligent misrepresentation causes of action valid, the court stated: ""Assignability of things in action is now the rule; nonassignability, the exception; and this exception is confined to wrongs done to the person, the reputation, or the feelings of the injured party, and to contracts of a purely personal nature, like promises of marriage." . . . [Citation.]'" (Osuna v. Albertson, supra, 134 Cal.App.3d at p. 82.)

Osuna distinguished causes of action for fraud and negligent misrepresentation involving promissory notes and deeds of trust from causes of action arising from legal malpractice, thus: "The distinction between assignable and nonassignable causes of action for fraud and deceit is well illustrated in Goodley v. Wank & Wank, Inc. (1976) 62 Cal.App.3d 389, in which plaintiff alleged he was the owner of a claim for legal malpractice against defendants arising out of erroneous advice given to a wife in dissolution of marriage proceedings. . . . [¶] 'Our view that a chose in action for legal malpractice is not assignable is predicated on the uniquely personal nature of legal services and the contract out of which a highly personal and confidential attorney-client relationship arises, and public policy considerations based thereon.'" (Osuna v. Albertson, supra, 134 Cal.App.3d at p. 82.)

In the instant case, property rights were involved because defendants, by means of fraud, deceit, and misrepresentation, succeeded in taking money from plaintiffs. In American T. Co. v. California etc. Ins. Co. (1940) 15 Cal.2d 42, 67, the court observed that "[i]t is, of course, well settled in California that the right to recover money or property obtained by fraud may be thus assigned." (See also Wikstrom v. Yolo Fliers Club (1929) 206 Cal. 461; Jackson v. Deauville Holding Co. (1933) 219 Cal. 498.)

The cases relied on by defendants (Goodley v. Wank & Wank, Inc. (1976) 62 Cal.App.3d 389; Jackson v. Rogers & Wells (1989) 210 Cal.App.3d 336; Kracht v. Perrin, Gartland & Doyle (1990) 219 Cal.App.3d 1019) are inapposite. Those cases involve legal malpractice claims which, as stated, are different from fraud actions arising from promissory notes.

Attorney Fees

Defendants contend that the award of attorney fees was improper, firstly, because there is no contract or statute in this case authorizing an award of attorney fees, and secondly, because there is insufficient evidence to support the award of attorney fees. We disagree.

The instant complaint includes causes of action based on both contract and tort. The contract causes of action arise from promissory notes and deeds of trust which expressly provide for the payment of attorney fees to the prevailing party. Likewise, the causes of action in the cross-complaint against defendants are based on misrepresentations concerning the condition of the properties which were the subject of a purchase contract containing a provision for the payment of attorney fees. Therefore, defendants' claim that the award of attorney fees is not authorized by contract is incorrect.

In <u>Perry</u> v. <u>Robertson</u> (1988) 201 Cal.App.3d 333, 343, where the defendant argued that the award of attorney fees was improper because the action, which was based on the defendant's negligence in drafting the written sales agreement, sounded in tort and was not an action on the contract, the court held that where "the trial court could reasonably determine from the pleading that the defendants' negligence occurred in the course of performance of the contract and was a direct breach of its <u>contractual</u> obligations," the court may properly award attorney fees.

The court explained: "'[T]he same act may be both a breach of contract and a tort. Even where there is a contractual relationship between parties, a cause of action in tort may sometimes arise out of the negligent manner in which the contractual duty is performed . . . .' [Citation.] Conversely, where a contract gives rise to a duty of care, negligence in the performance of the duty may give rise to a cause of action for breach of contract. [Citation.] When such a hybrid cause of action arises, the plaintiff may pursue both legal theories of recovery until an occasion for an election of remedies arises. [Citations.] . . . [¶] [] Defendants' central argument concerning the pleading is that, because it alleges that they were negligent, it must present only a legal theory in tort. This argument is fundamentally flawed. It selects the means of breach of contract as the determinant of its legal form. If the contract theory is negligence in the performance of contractual obligations, the allegation of negligence is integral to the statement of a cause of action for breach of contract. Moreover, even if the allegation of negligence were extrinsic to the contract cause of action, it does not follow that an extrinsic allegation destroys an otherwise complete set of allegations that state such a cause of action. [¶] The allegation of negligence is not an election of a tort remedy. An election does not occur by the assertion of an inconsistent allegation, but by the acceptance of an actual benefit from an alternative theory which would render unfair continued pursuit of the alternative. [Citation.]" (Perry v. Robertson, supra, 201 Cal.App.3d at pp. 340-341.)

Concerning the holding in Stout v. Turney (1978) 22 Cal.3d 718, which defendants cite in support of their argument, the Perry court remarked: "Defendants principally rely upon inapposite authority to support their position. They cite various cases that have denied an attorney's fees award under Civil Code section 1717 where the prevailing party has recovered on a legal theory of fraud in the inducement of a contract. [Citations.] This line of case law is based on the rationale that section 1717 is only meant to establish reciprocity of provisions for attorney's fees for enforcement of the contract. [Citation.] An action premised on fraud in the inducement seeks to avoid the contract rather than to enforce it; the essential claim is 'I would not have entered into this contract had I known the truth.' The duty not to commit such fraud is precontractual, it is not an obligation undertaken by the entry into the contractual relationship." (201 Cal.App.3d at pp. 342-343, fn. omitted.)

On the sufficiency of the evidence supporting the attorney fees award, the record indicates that Ngai had paid his counsel $13,000. This claim was included in the causes of action that Ngai had assigned to plaintiffs. In addition, plaintiffs were obligated to pay their own attorneys approximately $45,000. The total was therefore $58,000. No objection was made to the admission of this evidence. In the absence of any objection, this evidence was sufficient to support the award of $58,000 attorney fees.

Cost of Repairs

Defendants contend the evidence was insufficient to support the award of $96,372 for the cost of repairs. We disagree.

Among the rights which Ngai had assigned to plaintiffs was his right to recover the cost of repairs from defendants. Ngai had cross-complained that the units sold to him had been cited for a number of housing code violations and was subject to an order requiring corrections. At trial, Ngai testified that the total cost of repairs he had expended was $76,036. Van Nguyen, who was Ngai's property manager, also testified that the total cost of repairs was $76,636.05, and that the figure was taken from the year-end summary of expenses. This was sufficient evidence to support the trial court's finding. As stated in People v. Williams (1992) 4 Cal.4th 354, 369, "the testimony of any single witness 'is sufficient for proof of any fact.' [Citation.]"

Issuance of Proposed Judgment

Defendants contend that the judgment should be reversed because the trial court failed to issue a proposed judgment. The contention is without merit.

On June 10, 1992, following a motion for a new trial, the court issued the following order: "The Court is of the opinion that the judgment was signed prematurely. As defense counsel contends, a proposed judgment per Rule 232e should have been sent. The judgment is therefore set aside; however, the parties shall consider that judgment as a proposed judgment. Mr. Sutherland shall prepare a statement of decision."

Because the earlier judgment was set aside and corrected, the only issue is whether defendants were prejudiced by that judgment. We do not think so.

What happened here is not unprecedented. In National Secretarial Service, Inc. v. Froehlich (1989) 210 Cal.App.3d 510, 523, the court signed the judgment and statement of decision before considering defendants' objections. When the court realized the error, it vacated the prematurely signed judgment and ordered the prevailing party to present a new judgment for its signature. On appeal, the appellate court held the error was nonprejudicial. Said the court: "[A]ny error that might have been committed by the court in signing the judgment and filing the statement of decision on March 10th was cured when the court did in fact consider defendants' objections and issued its minute order accordingly. Contrary to defendants' argument there is no rule which entitled them to a formal hearing in this instance. In any event, any error, if there was one, clearly was not prejudicial to defendants." (Ibid.)

Here, defendants have likewise not shown how they were prejudiced by the error which the court subsequently corrected.

Sanctions

Plaintiffs' request for the imposition of monetary sanctions against defendants for prosecuting a frivolous appeal is denied. Code of Civil Procedure section 907 provides that "[w]hen it appears to the reviewing court that the appeal was frivolous or taken solely for delay, it may add to the costs on appeal such damages as may be just." Likewise, rule 26, subdivision (a), of the California Rules of Court states in part that "[w]here the appeal is frivolous or taken solely for the purpose of delay . . . the reviewing court may impose upon offending attorneys or parties such penalties, including the withholding or imposing of costs, as the circumstances of the case and the discouragement of like conduct in the future may require."

In In re Marriage of Flaherty (1982) 31 Cal.3d 637, 650, the court held that "an appeal should be held to be frivolous only when it is prosecuted for an improper motive—to harass the respondent or delay the effect of an adverse judgment—or when it indisputably has no merit—when any reasonable attorney would agree that the appeal is totally and completely without merit." In Cox v. County of San Diego (1991) 233 Cal.App.3d 300, 314, the court admonished that sanctions for frivolous appeals "should be used sparingly to deter only the most egregious conduct."

Here, although we have determined defendants' contentions to be without merit, we do not find the appeal to be so frivolous as to require the imposition of sanctions.

DISPOSITION

The judgment is affirmed.

XVI.
People v. Garza
(Unpublished)

Garza addresses issues relating to the disclosure of a police officer's surveillance location, and whether the failure of defense counsel to move for such disclosure results in ineffective assistance of counsel. A conviction resulting from ineffective assistance of counsel is reversible because it effectively nullifies the defendant's constitutional right to counsel. The constitutional right of the accused to the assistance of counsel implies the right to effective assistance. Assistance that is ineffective is no assistance at all, and makes the constitutional guarantee illusory.

The Philippines is starting to recognize the implications of the constitutional guarantee of right to counsel. In *People v. Liwanag, et. al.* (G.R. No. 120468. August 15, 2001), for example, the Philippine Supreme Court declared that the constitutional right to counsel means the right to effective assistance of counsel.

The citizens have the constitutional right to life, liberty, and the pursuit of happiness. So that this right may be enjoyed, the state is concomitantly obligated to protect it. The duty of the state to ensure a life of safety, peace, and freedom for its citizens, without fear of molestation or harm from criminal elements, in turn gives the state the inherent right to make laws and enforce them. Effective law enforcement sometimes requires the employment and use of confidential informants to supply the state with information necessary to track down criminals and bring them to justice. But confidential informants are effective only if their identities are protected and their safety not endangered. On the other hand, the individual has, under the constitution, the right to confront the witnesses against him and to call witnesses in his defense. What happens when the right, and the duty, of the state to enforce the laws clash with the individual's right of confrontation? The court will have to balance the need of the state for confidential information against the right of the defendant to confront the witnesses against him. Such a balancing exercise is sometimes difficult. *Garza* is an example.

In the Philippines, we have no jurisprudence on the right of the state to refuse disclosure of an officer's surveillance location as part of the confidentiality of privileged communications. When I was practicing law in the Philippines, an officer was invariably required on cross-examination to disclose his surveillance location. The court always considered the question relevant and there was no privileged communication consideration to balance the probative value of the evidence.

The opinion in *People v. Garza* follows:

Defendant Jaime Antonio Garza was charged by information with possession of cocaine for sale. (Health & Saf. Code, § 11351.) The information further alleged various prior felony convictions. A jury found defendant guilty of the new offense and, in a bifurcated proceeding, defendant admitted all the alleged priors. The trial court sentenced defendant to seven years in state prison, the sentence consisting of the middle term of three years on the new offense and four years for the priors.

Defendant argues on appeal that (1) he was denied effective assistance of counsel due to his trial counsel's failure to move for disclosure of the surveillance location; (2) the court committed reversible error by failing to give CALJIC No. 2.71 sua sponte; (3) the court prejudicially erred by giving CALJIC No. 2.11.5; and (4) the ordered drug program fee and restitution fine should be set aside.

In regard to the ineffective assistance of counsel claim, defendant separately filed during the pendency of this appeal a petition for a writ of habeas corpus. We resolved to consider that petition together with this appeal.

We affirm the judgment, remand for resentencing, and deny the habeas petition.

FACTS

San Jose Police Officer Anthony Ciaburro, a member of the Narcotic Enforcement Team, was conducting surveillance in the Nordale-Welch neighborhood about 9:20 p.m. on February 9, 1993. A call had been received by the police dispatchers around 7 p.m. about some drug activities in the area and several officers went to check it out. Ciaburro was about 40 or 50 feet away and across the street from two men standing next to each other on the sidewalk who were both attempting to flag down passing cars by yelling the word "coke," waving, motioning, and occasionally whistling at them as they drove by. It was dark, but the area was lit by amber street lights and Ciaburro had an unobstructed view of the two men. During the 20 to 30 minutes of his surveillance, and during which time he was in his uniform and on foot, Ciaburro did not see any actual sales take place.

Ciaburro broadcast a description of the two men and their activities on his two-way radio and signaled for the other officers to join him. He was picked up by Officers Michael Fernandez and Westphal in an unmarked police car around the corner from the two men. When the officers were still about 20 feet away from the two men and had yelled "Police," "Stop," defendant ran between two buildings. Ramirez, the other man who had been whistling and yelling, ran in another direction. Ciaburro and Fernandez chased defendant, who made a couple of turns and climbed over a cyclone fence. Defendant then went into an abandoned laundry room, slammed the door, and tried to hold it shut.

Ciaburro and Fernandez told defendant to open the door. When defendant did not open it, the officers forced the door open. The officers discovered defendant alone in the room, pulled him out after a struggle, and handcuffed him. Fernandez searched defendant and found four small bindles of cocaine (weighing about 1/2 gram each) inside a piece of paper in defendant's right front jacket pocket. No weapon, money, or pager was found on him. The laundry room and surrounding area were also searched but no other contraband or money was found. However, $20 in various bills was later found on Ramirez.

Ciaburro had testified in court several times before as an expert on whether contraband retrieved from a suspect was for personal use or for sale. He testified here that, even removing the factor of having seen defendant flag down cars and shouting "coke," he would not consider the four bindles defendant had on him as possessed for personal use rather than for sale. Four 1/2-gram bindles of cocaine, each costing $40 on the street, would last a typical user longer than one day. Also, if somebody wanted to buy a large quantity, they would get a better deal if it was all packaged together rather than in separate bags.

Fernandez was qualified at the trial as an expert on the recognition of cocaine and when it is possessed for personal use or sale. He testified that based on his training and experience each of the four bindles found on defendant contained a usable amount of cocaine, and the entire amount was possessed for sale. Usually a purchaser buys only one bindle. If somebody was using so heavily as to buy four bindles of cocaine at one time, they would not buy it in individual packages. Fernandez further testified that although packaging materials, scales, and ledgers are not usually found on persons arrested for street sales of cocaine, money and a pager often (but not always) are. Often one person will hold the money and another person will hold the contraband. If no sales had been made, no money would be found. Defendant did not appear to be under the influence of any drug at the time of his arrest, nor did he have items or implements (such as a straw or rolled up bills) that could be used to ingest cocaine. However, taking away the observations made by Ciaburro, Fernandez testified his opinion "could have gone either way."

Fernandez later compared the 12 bindles of cocaine that were discarded by Ramirez when he was running away from the police with the 4 bindles found on defendant. The packaging of the bindles was very similar. Fernandez and Officer Estrabao each prepared a report of the incident but Ciaburro did not, even though he was the only officer who actually witnessed the activity by the men on the sidewalk.

Defendant did not testify in his defense. However, Ramirez, after he was convicted of possession for sale of cocaine as a result of this incident, testified for defendant.

Ramirez testified that defendant was not with him on the night of February 9, 1993. He further testified that while he was walking by himself that night carrying an envelope containing 12 bindles of cocaine in a big package and 4 bindles in a smaller package, he ran into a policeman who told him to stop. Ramirez continued to run and threw the envelope containing the cocaine on the sidewalk. Ramirez said he saw the officer pursuing him pick up the envelope. Ramirez denied yelling, whistling, or trying to sell drugs to passing cars.

XVI. *Ineffective Assistance of Counsel*

DISCUSSION
Ineffective Assistance of Counsel

Defendant contends the failure of his trial counsel to move for the disclosure of the surveillance location denied him effective assistance of counsel. We disagree.

Pursuant to Evidence Code section 1040, subdivision (b),[22] "[a] public entity has a privilege to refuse to disclose official information, and to prevent another from disclosing official information, if the privilege is claimed by a person authorized by the public entity to do so . . . ." "Official information" is "information acquired in confidence by a public employee in the course of his or her duty and not open, or officially disclosed, to the public prior to the time the claim of privilege is made." (§ 1040, subd. (a).)

In In re Sergio M. (1993) 13 Cal.App.4th 809, 813, this court held that "surveillance location is information to which this privilege can apply. [Citations.]"

The standard which the trial court must apply when the defendant in a criminal proceeding demands disclosure of the source of the official information is provided by section 1042. Subdivision (d) of that section requires the defendant to show that the informant is a "material witness on the issue of guilt."

However, the test of materiality is not simple relevance; it is whether the nondisclosure might deprive defendant of his or her due process right to a fair trial. (People v. Walker (1991) 230 Cal.App.3d 230, 236.) Under section 1042, subdivision (d), "[t]he court shall not order disclosure, nor strike the testimony of the witness who invokes the privilege, nor dismiss the criminal proceeding, if the party offering the witness refuses to disclose the identity of the informant, unless, based upon the evidence presented at the hearing held in the presence of the defendant and his counsel and the evidence presented at the in camera hearing, the court concludes that there is a <u>reasonable possibility that nondisclosure might deprive the defendant of a fair trial</u>." (Emphasis added.) The requirement of a reasonable possibility that the

---

[22] Further statutory references in this case are to the Evidence Code unless otherwise stated.

nondisclosure might deprive defendant of a fair trial is the "crucial standard." (People v. Alderrou (1987) 191 Cal.App.3d 1074, 1080.)

In People v. Walker, supra, 230 Cal.App.3d at page 238, the court held that because "the informant's identity and surveillance location issues are analogous," section 1042 is also "the appropriate standard for determining the materiality of a surveillance location."

Here, defendant argues that "[w]hether or not Ciaburro could actually observe what he claimed to have seen Mr. Garza do and say is unquestionably material evidence," because "[t]his case boiled down to a credibility contest between the officers and Mr. Ramirez who testified that all 16 cocaine bindles were his and that Mr. Garza was not assisting him in attempting to sell cocaine on the street." However, defendant does not show how his right to a fair trial was prejudiced by the nondisclosure of the surveillance location.

In Price v. Superior Court (1970) 1 Cal.3d 836, 843, the court stated that the defendant's burden to establish materiality under section 1042 is discharged """when defendant demonstrates a reasonable possibility that the anonymous informant whose identity is sought could give evidence on the issue of guilt which might result in defendant's exoneration."""

To meet the requirement of reasonable possibility of exoneration, the court in People v. Walker, supra, 230 Cal.App.3d at page 238, required some showing that there was some point within the area surveilled that the officer could not have observed the defendant because of some obstruction. In Anderson v. U.S. (D.C.App. 1992) 607 A.2d 490, 497, the court even went further: "We therefore hold that the defendant is obligated to show not only that there are locations in the area from which the view is impaired or obstructed, but also that there is some reason to believe that the officer was making his observations from such a location. Without some reason so to believe, the existence of obstructed locations is logically irrelevant."

In the instant case, the facts show that Ciaburro was equipped with a two-way radio which he used to communicate with the other officers while conducting his surveillance. In fact, during the surveillance Ciaburro broadcast to the other officers detailed descriptions of Garza and Ramirez and their activities. Evidently, if Ciaburro's view had been obstructed by anything or if Ciaburro had been at a location beyond hearing distance from defendant and Ramirez, Ciaburro would not have been able to describe defendant and Ramirez to the other officers and monitor their activities. It is not therefore reasonably possible that had Ciaburro's location been disclosed, the disclosure would have resulted in defendant's exoneration.

To the contrary, such a disclosure might have incriminated defendant even more. "[A]n informant is not a 'material witness' nor does his nondisclosure deny the defendant a fair trial where the informant's testimony although 'material' on the issue of guilt could only further implicate rather than exonerate the defendant." (People v. Alderrou, supra, 191 Cal.App.3d at pp. 1080-1081.)

Because there is here no showing that disclosure had a reasonable possibility of resulting in defendant's exoneration, defendant's ineffective counsel claim cannot succeed.

Regardless, assuming that trial counsel's failure to demand disclosure amounted to ineffective assistance of counsel, the lack of adequate assistance was harmless under the facts. The evidence is uncontradicted that at the time of his arrest defendant had on his person four bindles of cocaine. Ciaburro and Fernandez testified that four bindles of cocaine in defendant's possession were sufficient to show that the possession was for sale. Defendant presented no contradicting evidence. Ciaburro further testified that even removing from the evidence his observations from the surveillance location, he would still consider the four bindles in defendant's possession as being possessed for sale.

We agree the remaining evidence was sufficient to support defendant's conviction.

The case of People v. Montgomery (1988) 205 Cal.App.3d 1011, relied on by defendant, is distinguishable. In that case,"[t]he only direct evidence supporting the verdict of sale of marijuana was the observation by Officer Weir from the surveillance location in issue." (Id. at p. 1023.) Here, as pointed out, even if the surveillance evidence was excluded, the remaining evidence was enough to support defendant's conviction.

In any event, we do not find Montgomery's analysis convincing. Montgomery's analysis ended at the determination that disclosure was "material on the issue of guilt or innocence." (205 Cal.App.3d at

p. 1022.) Montgomery did not proceed to determine whether the disclosure would have resulted in a reasonable possibility of exoneration. Hence, to the extent that Montgomery might be read to require only "relevance on the issue of guilt or innocence," without also requiring reasonable possibility of exoneration, we decline to follow it. Because location is always material in every evidence dispute involving police surveillance, were we to adopt such analysis we would be requiring trial courts to strike testimony in every case in which a confidential surveillance location is used. The Legislature could not have intended such an absurd result.

In light of the conclusions we have reached on the surveillance location issue, defendant's petition for a writ of habeas corpus cannot be sustained.

CALJIC No. 2.71

Defendant contends that with respect to his alleged shouting of "coke," the trial court committed reversible error by failing sua sponte to instruct the jury to view the admission with caution, pursuant to CALJIC No. 2.71. We agree the trial court erred in failing to give the cautionary instruction, but hold the error was harmless.

CALJIC No. 2.71 states: "An admission is a statement made by [the] defendant other than at [his] trial which does not by itself acknowledge [his] guilt of the crime(s) for which such defendant is on trial, but which statement tends to prove [his] guilt when considered with the rest of the evidence. [¶] You are the exclusive judges as to whether the defendant made an admission, and if so, whether such statement is true in whole or in part. If you should find that the defendant did not make the statement, you must reject it. If you find that it is true in whole or in part, you may consider that part which you find to be true. [¶] [Evidence of an oral admission of [the] defendant should be viewed with caution.]"

In People v. Stankewitz (1990) 51 Cal.3d 72, 93-94, it was held that trial courts have the sua sponte duty to instruct pursuant to CALJIC No. 2.71 whenever there is presented at trial evidence of defendant's oral admission.

Evidence that defendant was yelling "coke" was clearly evidence of admission. It was an oral statement tending to prove defendant's guilt when considered with the rest of the evidence.

However, the omission to instruct on CALJIC No. 2.71 was harmless. The evidence was strong regarding defendant's intent to sell the cocaine: he was in possession of four 1/2-gram bindles of cocaine; he was whistling at and motioning for passing cars to stop; and there were uncontradicted expert testimonies that four 1/2-gram bindles of cocaine were more than enough for personal use.

CALJIC No. 2.11.5

Defendant contends the trial court prejudicially erred in instructing the jury pursuant to CALJIC No. 2.11.5. The contention is without merit.

CALJIC No. 2.11.5 reads: "There has been evidence in this case indicating that a person other than defendant was or may have been involved in the crime for which the defendant is on trial. [¶] There may be many reasons why such person is not here on trial. Therefore, do not discuss or give any consideration as to why the other person is not being prosecuted in this trial or whether [he] has been or will be prosecuted. Your [sole] duty is to decide whether the People have proved the guilt of the defendant[s] on trial."

Defendant argues the trial court erred in giving this instruction because the instruction "advised the jury that they could give no consideration to Mr. Ramirez's admission of guilt." Defendant misreads the instruction. There is nothing in the instruction which can be construed as precluding the jury from considering Ramirez's testimony that defendant was uninvolved. As stated in People v. Farmer (1989) 47 Cal.3d 888, 918: "[T]he instruction does not tell the jury it cannot consider evidence that someone else committed the crime. [Citation.] It merely says the jury is not to speculate on whether someone else might or might not be prosecuted."

Restitution Fine

Finally, defendant challenges the legality of the $100 drug program fee (Health & Saf. Code, § 11372.7, subd. (a)) and $100 restitution fine (Gov. Code, § 13967, subd. (a)) imposed by the court, arguing that he lacks the ability to pay either one. We reject this challenge.

The record shows that both the drug program fee and the restitution fine were contained in the probation report. This notwithstanding, defendant did not object to either item, nor did he request a hearing on his ability to pay. In People v. Foster (1993) 14 Cal.App.4th 939, 944, the court held that the defendant's failure to object to the restitution condition in the trial court waived the objection on appeal. Although Foster involved restitution to the victim, we see no reason why the rule should not be applied to restitution fines.

Likewise, we see no reason why the rule should not apply to drug program fees. As stated in People v. Saunders (1993) 5 Cal.4th 580, 589-590: "'"An appellate court will ordinarily not consider procedural defects or erroneous rulings, in connection with relief sought or defenses asserted, where an objection could have been, but was not, presented to the lower court by some appropriate method . . . . The circumstances may involve such intentional acts or acquiescence as to be appropriately classified under the headings of estoppel or waiver . . . . Often, however, the explanation is simply that it is <u>unfair to the trial judge and to the adverse party</u> to take advantage of an error on appeal when it could easily have been corrected at the trial."' [Citation.] '"The purpose of the general doctrine of waiver is to encourage a defendant to bring errors to the attention of the trial court, so that they may be corrected or avoided and a fair trial had . . . ."' [Citation.] '"No procedural principle is more familiar to this Court than that a constitutional right," or a right of any other sort, "may be forfeited in criminal as well as civil cases by the failure to make a timely assertion of the right before a tribunal having jurisdiction to determine it." [Citation.]' [Citation.]" (Footnote omitted.)

Respondent claims that the trial court improperly imposed a restitution fine of $100 because the statutory minimum is $200. Respondent's point is well taken. Effective September 14, 1992, Government Code section 13967, subdivision (a), has been amended to increase the minimum restitution fine to $200. (See Stats. 1992, ch. 682, § 4.)

DISPOSITION

The judgment is affirmed. The matter is remanded for resentencing on the amount of the restitution fine, with direction to comply with Government Code section 13967, subdivision (a). The petition for a writ of habeas corpus is denied.

XVII.
People v. Lang
(Unpublished)

Lang addresses the question of when a witness is unavailable for the purpose of admitting a previously recorded statement in lieu of his personal testimony in court, and what constitutes harmless error.

Because there is no trial by jury in the Philippines, in-court identification does not pose the same admissibility problems in the Philippines as it does in the United States.

The doctrine of harmless error, so common in the United States, has not been developed in Philippine jurisprudence. It is rarely, if at all, seen in the appellate opinions of Philippine courts. In the Philippines, appellate briefs assign errors supposedly committed by the trial courts, but do not show that the commission of those errors requires reversal. Likewise, when an appellate court finds error, there is no further discussion whether the error is prejudicial enough to require reversal, or whether it is a harmless error that should not affect the outcome of the appeal.

In California, as in the rest of the United States, it is not enough to show error. The error must be further shown to be prejudicial, requiring reversal. However, there are errors that are inherently prejudicial and reversible. For such errors, no harmless error analysis is required. Among the inherently harmful errors are errors of constitutional dimension. Denial of the defendant's right to counsel, for example, cannot be harmless, and is always reversible.

Lang also discusses issues relating to the right of a defendant to confrontation. A defendant's right to confrontation can be implicated when a witness who testified at the preliminary hearing is unavailable at trial. The question is whether the witness's testimony at the preliminary hearing is admissible at trial. This issue is better appreciated when it is considered that the purpose of the preliminary hearing is merely to establish probable cause to hold the accused for trial, whereas the purpose of the trial is to establish the guilt of the accused beyond a reasonable doubt. Because only probable cause needs to be established at a preliminary hearing, a common tactical practice of lawyers is for the defense counsel not to conduct extensive cross-examination so as not to show too much of his trial card. He usually wants to save his best cross-examination points for the trial in chief. This is good defense strategy. The problem, however, as demonstrated in *Lang*, is when the witness becomes unavailable at trial. The inadequate preliminary hearing cross-examination could hurt the defense. *Lang* grapples with this question.

The opinion in *People v. Lang* follows:

Defendant Thomas Walker Lang appeals from three judgments of conviction. We affirm.

PROCEDURAL AND FACTUAL BACKGROUND

For convenience, we will identify the appealed judgments by the case numbers assigned to them in the superior court.

1. Case No. CR-5577

In case no. CR-5577, defendant was charged by information with attempted murder (Pen. Code, §§ 187, 664; count 1)[23] and assault with a deadly weapon (§ 245, subd. (a); count 2). The information further alleged that with respect to count 1, defendant used a deadly weapon (§ 12022, subd. (b)); with respect to both counts, defendant intentionally inflicted great bodily injury (§ 12022.7).

Defendant moved to suppress evidence on the ground that his detention was illegal (§ 1538.5). The court denied the motion.

The facts underlying case no. CR-5577 are as follows. On September 30, 1991, at about 11:30 p.m., Michael Morgan, a citizen of Ireland legally residing in the United States, was at the Blue Lagoon Bar in Santa Cruz. There, he met another Irishman who was seated with defendant and three other persons, one of whom was a woman. At 1:50 a.m., which was the bar's closing time, Morgan was invited by defendant and defendant's companions to go with them to a party supposedly at a house on the boardwalk. Morgan accepted the invitation. Up to that time, Morgan had consumed about a bottle of low-alcohol champagne and two or three beers.

---

[23] Further statutory references in this case are to the Penal Code unless otherwise stated.

At a liquor store on Laurel and Pacific streets, Morgan bought another bottle of champagne. A man from the Midwest, who was with defendant's group, also bought beer. Defendant stayed outside the store.

Some 45 minutes later, three companions of defendant, who had not been with them since leaving the Blue Lagoon Bar, rejoined defendant, Morgan, and the man from the Midwest at the end of Pacific Street. The group sat down to drink behind the Palomar Restaurant and Bar.

After Morgan had drunk about one-fourth of the champagne bottle, defendant started arguing with the man from the Midwest over the last beer. Defendant got on top of the Midwest man, and the two wrestled on the ground. Morgan stood up and said: "What is going on?" and "Take it easy."

Defendant turned toward Morgan, produced a knife, and attacked Morgan with the knife. The knife, which had a blade four to six inches wide, cut Morgan's left hand between the thumb and the index finger. Morgan turned and ran away. Defendant pursued him. Morgan felt something strike him in the shoulder and twice on the back. Morgan thought he was being punched. Morgan continued to run out of the area until he reached Washington Street where he "stayed low for about five minutes." He later returned to Pacific Street because he had left his backpack there and wanted to retrieve it; he also wanted to find out what had happened to the man from the Midwest. Morgan found everyone gone.

At approximately 3:50 a.m., Officer Green was on routine patrol at Laurel and Washington streets. Green saw Morgan waving at him. Green approached Morgan. Green observed that Morgan's hand was bleeding. Morgan told Green he needed a ride to a hospital.

Morgan told Green that he had been attacked by four white men and that his injury was the result of that attack. Morgan described one of his assailants as about five feet eleven inches tall, black-haired, and wearing a bandanna. Later, Morgan told Detective Kaleas that he had not told the truth the first time to Green because he was afraid "defendant might be connected with a gang or be a gang member" since defendant was with other people when the crime was committed.[24] Morgan

---

[24] The parties stipulated that there was no evidence that defendant was involved with a gang.

explained he was concerned about his own safety because he had "been stabbed four times with a knife."

Green testified that Morgan appeared dizzy, the speech was slow, and was moving "real slow." Morgan complained that his back was hurting. Green walked around to look at Morgan's back and saw holes and blood in Morgan's sweater. Realizing that Morgan might have been stabbed, Green radioed for paramedic assistance.

Minutes later, Green observed three or four people standing at the corner of Laurel and Cedar streets. Green asked Officers Serafin and Goodwin, who had arrived in separate patrol cars, to contact the persons because those persons could be "witnesses or possible witnesses."

As Serafin's and Goodwin's cars approached the group, the persons dispersed in different directions. Serafin followed one, but lost him. Goodwin followed a woman and a man who was trailing the woman. The man turned out to be defendant. As Goodwin passed defendant, Goodwin saw defendant throw a metallic, palm-sized object into the front yard of a house. Goodwin maneuvered his vehicle to block defendant's path, exited the vehicle, and grabbed defendant. Defendant's right hand was bleeding profusely. Green observed a cut on the knuckle of the small finger. The wound appeared to have reached the bone.

Goodwin retrieved the object that defendant threw. It was a closed folding knife four inches long. Defendant admitted to the police that the knife was his.

At trial, a forensic pathologist expert testified that in his opinion the cut in defendant's finger was consistent with defendant's right hand sliding down onto the blade if the knife were to hit something hard, such as a bone, while held in a particular manner.

2. Cases Nos. CR-5536 and CR-6484

In case no. CR-5536, defendant was charged by information with robbery of James Cotter (§ 211; count 1); assault by means of force likely to produce great bodily injury on Cotter (§ 245, subd. (a); count 2); robbery of James Heagerty (§ 211; count 3); robbery of Charles Lindsay (§ 211; count 4); robbery of John Doe, an unidentified Hispanic male in the Metro Center's restroom (§ 211; count 5); attempted robbery of John Doe, another unidentified male in a bathroom stall in Metro

Center's restroom (§§ 211, 664; count 6); attempted robbery of Aaron Myers (§§ 211, 664; count 7); and misdemeanor battery (§ 242) on Jeremy Whitener. As to counts 1 and 2, the information further alleged intentional infliction of great bodily injury (§ 12022.7).

Defendant initially pleaded guilty to the Cotter robbery count and admitted the enhancing allegation. However, this plea was subsequently vacated on the basis that the court had not advised defendant that he was ineligible for probation.

In case no. CR-6484, the Santa Cruz grand jury returned a true bill against defendant on five counts of forcible intimidation of victims Whitener, Lindsay, and Heagerty (§ 136.1). The court ordered counts 3 and 5 combined with count 2.

The facts underlying cases nos. CR-5536 and CR-6484 are as follows. On the evening of January 23, 1992, while 14-year-old Charles Lindsay and his friend James Heagerty were outside Taco Bell near Metro Center looking for adults willing to buy beer for them, they were approached by defendant and Stanley Huffman, who both smelled of alcohol and acted drunk. Defendant told Heagerty and Lindsay that he had an earlier encounter with someone who had a "tazer." He asked Heagerty if he had a taser, saying that if Heagerty had one, he would take care of him right there. Heagerty replied he had no taser.

The four, joined by two or three more persons, later heckled a passerby, after which they proceeded to nearby Metro Center where they continued to loiter. After a while, defendant and Huffman announced they were going to the restroom. Later, after the other persons had also left, Lindsay said he had to use the restroom. Heagerty accompanied Lindsay to the restroom.

Inside the restroom, Heagerty and Lindsay witnessed defendant and Huffman repeatedly hitting another person (John Cotter) "[i]n the head, in the rib cage and in the shoulder areas." Cotter fell down. While Cotter was down, defendant and Huffman kicked Cotter in the head until Cotter was unconscious "in a pool of blood larger than himself." Cotter was "torn up." The beating "knocked all [of Cotter's] front teeth loose." Cotter suffered lacerations in the head "which required 12 stitches."

During the attack on Cotter, Huffman ordered Lindsay to hold the restroom door and not move. Lindsay did as ordered. At one point, Lindsay announced that somebody was trying to get in. Defendant and Huffman told Lindsay to keep holding the door and not let anybody in. Lindsay and Heagerty stood against the wall "scared out of our minds" and "frozen still" while watching defendant and Huffman take turns kicking Cotter. Defendant and Huffman went through Cotter's pockets, but removed nothing.

Defendant kicked open a stall occupied by a "hippie" and asked the man if he had money. When the man said he had none, defendant and Huffman dragged the man out of the stall and demanded money again. Defendant struck the man in the head and threw him up against the wall. Defendant and Huffman warned the man to not tell anybody what he had seen.

A Hispanic male by the urinals kept saying that he could not speak English. Defendant handled the Hispanic "roughly" and asked him in Spanish for his money. The man gave defendant $40 or $50. Defendant told the man in Spanish that he would kill him if he told anybody what had happened.

Defendant and Huffman pushed Lindsay and Heagerty out the restroom door, saying: "Let's go." Heagerty said this was too "heavy" for him, and that he and Lindsay were leaving. Defendant and Huffman replied: "No, you are not. You are coming with us."

Defendant and Huffman walked Lindsay and Heagerty to the Taco Bell restroom. Inside the restroom, defendant and Huffman washed themselves clean of the blood on their persons. Lindsay and Heagerty said they were leaving. Defendant and Huffman blocked the restroom door and said "No." Defendant warned Lindsay and Heagerty that they would be killed if they said anything to the police.

Defendant and Huffman talked about their need to change clothes and "not look the same." They asked Lindsay to give them his flannel shirt; Lindsay refused. They demanded Heagerty to give them his leather jacket. Heagerty refused, saying "my best friend died in this thing." Heagerty offered his shirt instead. Defendant took it.

The four left the restroom and ordered some food. Lindsay and Heagerty asked to leave again, but defendant and Huffman would not allow them to. Defendant and Huffman walked Lindsay and Heagerty to a liquor store across the street. Defendant and Huffman asked Heagerty to give them his jacket; again, Heagerty refused. Defendant and Huffman pushed Lindsay and Heagerty to an area behind the liquor store and beat them there. Lindsay gave his flannel shirt to defendant and Huffman to stop them from taking Heagerty's jacket. But as Heagerty fell to the ground, Huffman got Heagerty's jacket. Heagerty and Lindsay ran to Heagerty's car, drove to Heagerty's home, and called the police.

On the same evening as the Cotter-Heagerty-Lindsay incident, Aaron Myers and Jeremy Whitener ate at Taco Bell and then walked to the Metro Center. As Myers and Whitener were walking, defendant and Huffman appeared. Defendant and Huffman started yelling obscenities at Myers and heckled him about his military status. Myers, a Marine on leave, ignored defendant and Huffman.

Defendant and Huffman attacked Myers. Defendant asked Myers to give him $10. When Myers responded he did not have $10, defendant said: "Well, if you don't give us $10, we will commence to beat your ass." Defendant threw punches at Myers, one of which hit Myers on his upper lip.

Defendant and Huffman ran to Whitener, approaching him from the rear. Myers yelled to Whitener to watch his back. Whitener ducked, but defendant's punch hit Whitener in the ear.

The trial on the indictment trailed the trial on the informations. Following the trial on the informations, the jury found defendant guilty on all counts; it also found the enhancing allegations to be true.

Thereafter, defendant pleaded guilty to the indictment in case no. CR-6484.

Defendant's motion to reduce the attempted robbery charge in the Myers case on the basis of insufficient evidence, grant a new trial in case no. CR-5577, and vacate his pleas in case no. CR-6484, were all denied.

The trial court sentenced defendant to an aggregate prison term of 22 years and 4 months. The sentence that is relevant to this appeal is the sentence in case no. CR-6484 imposing two consecutive terms of three years.

CONTENTIONS

On appeal, defendant contends:

1. The People failed to carry the burden of proving that Morgan was unavailable to testify at trial. Therefore, the transcript of Morgan's testimony at the preliminary examination was inadmissible. This error was not harmless beyond a reasonable doubt, and reversal of the conviction in case no. CR-5577 is required.

2. Since Proposition 115 limited the scope of cross-examination at preliminary hearings, defendant did not have a meaningful opportunity to cross-examine either Morgan or Heagerty. Therefore, their prior testimony was inadmissible at trial even if the prosecution showed due diligence in attempting to secure their presence.

3. The trial court erred in rejecting defendant's proffered instructions on the intent necessary to establish attempted murder in case no. CR-5577.

4. The trial court erred in admitting Morgan's in-court identification of defendant. The identification was tainted by a previous suggestive identification procedure.

5. The trial court committed error by denying defendant's motion under section 1538.5 as to probable cause to arrest defendant after the Morgan incident.

6. The evidence was insufficient to support a finding of enhancement for infliction of great bodily injury as to the attack on Morgan, and that finding must be reversed.

7. The trial court committed reversible error in admitting evidence of Morgan's "concern for his physical safety" over defendant's timely objection under Evidence Code section 352.

8. The trial court erred in refusing defense instructions on the reliability of accomplice testimony. Heagerty and Lindsay had aided defendant and Huffman in the commission of the various crimes in the Metro Center restroom, and could have been considered accomplices.

9. The evidence was insufficient to convict defendant of the attempted robbery of Myers, and the conviction on that count must be reversed.

10. There was insufficient evidence to support the robbery conviction on Lindsay, and the conviction must be reversed.

11. There was insufficient evidence to support the attempted robbery conviction on the unknown Hispanic man, and the conviction must be reversed.

12. The court below erred in sentencing defendant to two consecutive terms of three years in case no. CR-6484 in violation of section 1170.1, subdivision (a).

13. The use of CALJIC No. 2.90 violated defendant's federal right to due process and to a jury trial because the instruction includes the terms "moral certainty" and "moral evidence," which are confusing and can be construed to understate the requirement of proof beyond a reasonable doubt.

DISCUSSION
Unavailability for Trial

Defendant contends the trial court erred in finding that Morgan was unavailable to testify within the meaning of Evidence Code section 240. Defendant further contends that the error was not harmless because Morgan was the only eyewitness to the incident whose testimony might have contributed to the convictions. We disagree.

The record shows that during the preliminary hearing on the morning of October 17, 1991, Morgan was in court. Morgan observed defendant during the session. When the preliminary hearing resumed in the afternoon, Morgan did not appear. As a result, the court dismissed the charges against defendant.

The court issued a bench warrant for Morgan's arrest. Morgan was arrested and booked on a charge of contempt of court, then released.

The prosecutor subpoenaed Morgan to his office a number of times to determine how cooperative he was. When Morgan appeared each time, the district attorney, convinced that Morgan was "going to continue to assist in the program," refiled the case.

At the second preliminary examination, Morgan appeared and identified defendant. Morgan testified that defendant attacked him and stabbed him in the back and shoulder with a knife. The magistrate ordered Morgan to appear at defendant's arraignment in superior court. Morgan appeared as ordered. Following arraignment, the trial court set defendant's trial for April 13, 1992, and ordered Morgan to appear on that date. Morgan said "Okay."

Morgan did not appear when the case was called for trial. Earlier, the prosecutor had received a letter from Morgan dated April 2, 1992, and postmarked April 13, 1992, stating that circumstances were such that he had to leave the country; that he was already in the British Isles; that he felt he had done his duty; and that he was sorry he would not be available to attend further court proceedings.

Marty Krauel, an inspector with the district attorney's office, attempted to locate Morgan from November 23, 1992, until the matter was assigned for trial on February 1, 1993.

Krauel made telephone calls attempting to locate Morgan from addresses and phone numbers listed in the case file. When the calls failed to locate Morgan, Krauel requested assistance from the United States Immigration Service (hereafter, Immigration). Krauel learned from Immigration that Morgan was a resident alien who entered the United States from Ireland in 1989. Krauel further learned that while resident aliens are required to keep a "passbook," they are "not required to maintain any factual record of either entering or leaving the country."

Immigration had no information on where Morgan might be located, but gave Krauel the telephone numbers of Morgan's parents and brother. Krauel telephoned Morgan's brother in Chicago. Morgan's brother told Krauel that Morgan was in Ireland and "unavailable."

Krauel contacted the immigration service in Ireland and the Ireland telephone information service to request assistance in locating Morgan. Neither office could provide Krauel with any useful information.

Krauel ran record checks with the FBI, the CI&I, and the DMV. The results were the same: no information.

On these facts, we are persuaded that the efforts exerted by the prosecution to locate Morgan constituted "reasonable diligence" within the meaning of Evidence Code section 240, subdivision (a)(5).

In People v. Jackson (1980) 28 Cal.3d 264, 311-312, the court stated that unavailability under Evidence Code section 240, subdivision (a)(5), "may be established by showing that the declarant is 'Absent from the hearing and the proponent of his statement has exercised reasonable diligence but has been unable to procure his attendance by the court's process.' [Citation.]"

In People v. Hovey (1988) 44 Cal.3d 543, 562, the court stated that while "[t]he prosecution must make a good faith effort and exercise reasonable diligence to procure the witness's appearance," good faith efforts "do not include pursuing futile acts not likely to produce the witness for trial."

Hovey also held that "the question of due diligence is a factual one depending on the circumstances in each case, and that the trial court's determination of the issue will not be disturbed in the absence of a showing of an abuse of discretion. [Citations.]" (44 Cal.3d at p. 563.) Recently, however, in People v. Cummings (1993) 4 Cal.4th 1233, 1296, the court stated that "independent review might be appropriate."

We are persuaded, however, that under either standard the prosecution had exercised reasonable diligence.

Defendant argues that because Morgan was a resident alien, the prosecution should have obtained a federal subpoena pursuant to 28 United States Code section 1783 to compel Morgan's appearance.[25] We disagree.

28 United States Code section 1783, subdivision (a), provides in pertinent part: "A court of the United States may order the issuance of a subpoena requiring the appearance as a witness before it, or before a person or body designated by it, of a national or resident of the United States who is in a foreign country, . . . if the court finds that particular testimony . . . is necessary in the interest of justice . . . ."

In arguing that a federal subpoena should have been applied for, defendant cites People v. St. Germain (1982) 138 Cal.App.3d 507, which held that compliance with 28 United States Code section 1783, subdivision (a), was required to show reasonable diligence in procuring a witness's attendance by court process.

St. Germain is distinguishable. There, the resident alien, Ms. Smith, was a national of Curacao. However, at the time of the trial Smith

---

[25] We had granted defendant's request to take judicial notice of 28 United States Code section 1783, although that request was unnecessary in light of Evidence Code sections 451 and 459. Defendant's citation to that statute would have been sufficient.

was living neither in the United States nor in Curacao, but in a third country, Holland. The prosecution's attempt in trying to produce Smith as a witness consisted of writing a letter to inform her of her trial date and asking her to call collect to advise if she was "'available to come to San Francisco or if you are unable to come.'" (138 Cal.App.3d at p. 516, fn. 5.) Smith called the district attorney's office to advise that she was unable to come because of financial and other reasons.

The St. Germain court held that the prosecution did not exercise due diligence with respect to Smith because there was no attempt "'to procure his attendance by the court's process,'" pursuant to Evidence Code section 240, subdivision (a)(5). The court reasoned that "[t]he prosecutor had available the remedy of a subpoena to be issued by the federal courts requiring the appearance as a witness before a 'body designated by it'—here the superior court jury—'of a national or resident of the United States who is in a foreign country. . . .' [Citation.]" (138 Cal.App.3d at p. 517.)

St. Germain characterized the attempt to procure the witness's attendance "by the court's process" as the sine qua non that was "completely missing" from the proof adduced by the prosecution.

Here, on the other hand, the "court's process" was not missing. The record shows that following arraignment the court set the case for trial on April 13, 1992, and ordered Morgan to appear on that date. Morgan said "Okay." The court's order was no less a "court process" than a subpoena, and was by no means less compulsive. It was in every respect the equal of any written subpoena. Therefore, resort to a federal subpoena under 28 United States Code section 1783 was superfluous. Defendant has not shown what a federal subpoena could have done to compel Morgan's attendance that the trial court's oral order in this case could not do. To suggest that Morgan was more likely to obey a federal than a state court order is speculative.

Moreover, in St. Germain, Smith's foreign address was known to the prosecution. Requesting a federal subpoena was therefore feasible. Here, on the other hand, no one knows Morgan's foreign address. Assuming a federal court would have issued a roving international subpoena to one whose foreign address is unknown, it has not been suggested how such a subpoena could be served to serve its purpose.

St. Germain is further distinguishable in yet another respect. There, the witness left the United States not for the purpose of returning to his homeland but to live in a third country. Here, on the other hand, Morgan returned to his country of citizenship.

The question whether the United States can require by federal subpoena the citizen of another country living in his own country to appear before a state court in this country involves questions of sovereignty and international law. We are not cited to any authority or rule of international law that could compel Morgan, on these facts, to leave his country and testify before our courts.

The United States Supreme Court recognized this problem in Mancusi v. Stubbs (1972) 408 U.S. 204. In that case, a witness (Holm) had been born in Sweden but had become a naturalized American citizen. At the time of the defendant's second trial (defendant's conviction in the first trial was overturned on federal habeas corpus on the basis that defendant did not have effective assistance of counsel), Holm had returned to Sweden and had taken up permanent residence there. Over defense objection, the Tennessee trial court admitted into evidence Holm's testimony in the first trial, reasoning that Holm was unavailable as a witness. In rejecting the argument that Tennessee might have obtained Holm as a trial witness by attempting to invoke 28 United States Code section 1783, the United States Supreme Court, observing that Holm was not merely absent from the State of Tennessee but was a permanent resident of Sweden, stated: "We have been cited to no authority applying this section to permit subpoena by a federal court for testimony in a state felony trial, and certainly the statute on its face does not appear to be designed for that purpose." (Id. at p. 212.)

In a footnote, the court observed that the 1964 amendment to 28 United States Code section 1783 authorized a subpoena to bring a witness "before a person or body designated by" the District Court, but declined to decide whether such amendment "would afford assistance to state authorities on the facts represented by this case" because the amendment "was not available to the Tennessee authorities for Stubbs' 1964 trial." (408 U.S. at p. 212, fn. 2.) Because Holm had returned to Sweden, the court stated that "the State of Tennessee, so far as this record shows, was powerless to compel his attendance at the second trial, either through its own process or through established procedures depending on the voluntary assistance of another government. [Citation.]" (Id. at p. 212.)

But even in California, St. Germain has not been followed. The court in People v. Watson (1989) 213 Cal.App.3d 446, 453, declined to follow it. In avoiding the St. Germain result, the Watson court stated that "[a] federal subpoena . . . is not the sine qua non for all cases, and particularly those where the witness has been served with a valid state subpoena." (Ibid.)

Watson, like this case and Mancusi, involved a witness who was a legal resident of this country but had returned to his country of origin (Argentina). The instant case is even a stronger case for the non-application of 28 United States Code section 1783 in that in Watson the foreign address of the witness was known to the prosecution. In fact, the prosecution in Watson had been in contact with the witness at the witness's foreign address. Therefore, unlike here where the foreign address of the witness is unknown, service of a federal subpoena was possible. Nevertheless, the Watson court held that 28 United States Code section 1783 did not apply because the service of a state subpoena on the witness before his return to his native country rendered unnecessary further resort to a federal subpoena.

We conclude the trial court did not err in holding that Morgan was unavailable as a witness within the meaning of Evidence Code section 240, subdivision (a)(5).

Right of Confrontation

Defendant contends that because Proposition 115 limited the scope of cross-examination at preliminary hearings, he did not have a meaningful opportunity to cross-examine either Morgan or Heagerty; therefore, their prior testimony was inadmissible at trial even if the prosecution showed due diligence in attempting to secure their presence. We disagree.

Section 866, subdivision (b), which was added by Proposition 115, states: "It is the purpose of a preliminary examination to establish whether there exists probable cause to believe that the defendant has committed a felony. The examination shall not be used for purposes of discovery."

We first note that defendant did not object below to the admission of Morgan's and Heagerty's preliminary examination testimonies on constitutional grounds. The trial court was not therefore provided with opportunity to consider the argument as a basis for excluding those testimonies. Consequently, the objection is waived on appeal. "A verdict or finding shall not be set aside, nor shall the judgment or decision based thereon be reversed, by reason of the erroneous admission of evidence unless: [¶] (a) There appears of record an objection to or a motion to exclude or to strike the evidence that was timely made and so stated as to make clear the specific ground of the objection or motion . . . ." (Evid. Code, § 353.)

Regardless, we do not think that Proposition 115 has outlawed use at trial of prior preliminary examination testimony when the witness is unavailable under Evidence Code section 1291. In People v. Cudjo (1993) 6 Cal.4th 585, 618, the court stated: "Both the state and federal Constitutions guarantee criminal defendants the right to confront the witnesses against them. [Citations.] The right of confrontation is not absolute, however; in particular, it does not preclude the prosecution from proving its case through the prior testimony of a witness who is unavailable at trial, so long as the defendant had the right and the opportunity to cross-examine the witness during the earlier proceeding at which the witness gave this testimony. [Citations.]"

In People v. Zapien (1993) 4 Cal.4th 929, 975, the court explained: "Frequently, a defendant's motive for cross-examining a witness during a preliminary hearing will differ from his or her motive for cross-examining that witness at trial. For the preliminary hearing testimony of an unavailable witness to be admissible at trial under Evidence Code section 1291, these motives need not be identical, only 'similar.' [Citation.] Admission of the former testimony of an unavailable witness is permitted under Evidence Code section 1291 and does not offend the confrontation clauses of the federal or state Constitutions— not because the opportunity to cross-examine the witness at the preliminary hearing is considered an exact substitute for the right of cross-examination at trial [citation], but because the interests of justice are deemed served by a balancing of the defendant's right to effective cross-examination against the public's interest in effective prosecution. [Citations.]"

To the same effect is People v. King (1969) 269 Cal.App.2d 40, 47: "While it is true that '[a] preliminary hearing is ordinarily a much less searching exploration into the merits of a case than a trial, simply because its function is the more limited one of determining whether probable cause exists to hold the accused for trial' [citation], nevertheless the interest and motive for the cross-examination of a prosecution witness in both proceedings are similar."

Here, notwithstanding the restrictive language of Proposition 115, defendant in fact conducted extensive cross-examinations of Morgan and Heagerty. At no instance during Morgan's and Heagerty's testimonies did the prosecutor object to any question propounded by defendant, and at no instance did the magistrate limit the scope of defendant's cross-examinations of Morgan and Heagerty on the basis of Proposition 115. All questions that defendant wanted asked were asked, and Morgan and Heagerty answered them all. Defendant cannot therefore complain that his right to confront Morgan and Heagerty was in fact adversely affected by Proposition 115 limitations. Defendant has not indicated what area in Morgan's and Heagerty's testimonies he wanted to cross-examine but could not because of Proposition 115.

We conclude that the admission of Morgan's and Heagerty's preliminary examination testimonies did not, under the facts of this case, deprive defendant of his right of confrontation under the state and federal constitutions.

Specific Intent to Kill Instructions

On the attempted murder count, defendant offered the following instructions on specific intent to kill: "Specific intent to kill is a necessary element of attempted murder. It cannot be inferred merely from the commission of another dangerous crime such as the commission of the offense of assault with a deadly weapon. Thus, proof of an assault with a deadly weapon does not itself provide the basis for an inference of an intent to kill."

"In a charge of attempted murder, the defendant must specifically contemplate the taking of human life. Even though the act of the defendant is such as would be murder if death occurred, nevertheless, if the defendant does not intend to kill, the defendant is not guilty of any attempt to commit murder."

The trial court refused both instructions, ruling that CALJIC No. 8.66 was adequate. The court stated that the proposed instructions were an accurate statement of the law, and defense counsel was free to argue those points, but the instructions were argumentative and unnecessary.

The trial court committed no error in refusing the requested instructions.

Regarding the first requested instruction, defendant correctly stated that "[s]pecific intent to kill is a necessary element of attempted murder." However, such a statement merely rephrased the language of CALJIC No. 8.66 that in order to prove the crime of murder, or an attempt thereof, the prosecution must prove the elements of the crime, one of which is: "The person committing such act harbored express malice aforethought, namely, a specific intent to kill unlawfully another person." Therefore, this part of the requested instruction was superfluous.

The rest of the first requested instruction, taken by itself, may at first glance appear acceptable in the sense that a specific intent to kill cannot arguably be inferred merely from the commission of another dangerous crime, such as the commission of the offense of assault with a deadly weapon. However, a close reading of that part of the requested instruction shows it to be misleading and confusing. The misleading terms are "cannot" and "merely." "Cannot" tells the jury it is not possible to find otherwise, and that would be wrong; "merely" is vague. To instruct that a specific intent to kill "cannot" be inferred "merely" from the commission of another dangerous crime would suggest that a dangerous crime may be committed without any attending circumstances—an impossibility. Since no crime can be committed in a vacuum, the commission of another dangerous crime considered in the circumstances under which it was committed may in fact be sufficient to show a specific intent to kill.

The second requested instruction suffers from the same fault. The statement that "[i]n a charge of attempted murder, the defendant must specifically contemplate the taking of human life," is correct as far as it goes. However, the rest of the requested instruction is both confusing and misleading, and even incorrect. Although the statement "[e]ven though the act of the defendant is such as would be murder if death occurred" correctly covers a situation where murder may be found from acts demonstrating implied malice, the other statement that "if the defendant does not intend to kill, the defendant is not guilty of any attempt to commit murder" suggests that intent to kill may exclude implied malice, in that while implied malice may be sufficient to establish murder, it is not sufficient to establish attempted murder.

For these reasons, the trial court did not err in refusing the requested instructions.

In-court Identification

Defendant contends the trial court erred in admitting into evidence Morgan's identification of defendant at the preliminary examination. The contention is without merit.

The record shows that at the second preliminary examination on February 7, 1992, Morgan identified defendant as one of the persons he was with, first, at the Blue Lagoon Bar in downtown Santa Cruz and, later, behind the Palomar Restaurant and Bar. Defendant contends this in-court identification was tainted by a previous suggestive identification procedure in that on October 17, 1991, when Morgan was in the courtroom for the first preliminary hearing, Morgan had asked Detective Kaleas if defendant, who was the only person in the jury box, was the man, and that Kaleas had told Morgan defendant was the man who they thought had assaulted him.

It has been held, however, that while "any one-on-one confrontation is inherently suggestive," such circumstance does "not suggest that an in-court identification of a person clearly identified as a criminal defendant accused of the crime of which the witness was a victim violates due process, even though the defendant be the only person of his or her race in the courtroom." (People v. Palmer (1984) 154 Cal.App.3d 79, 88.) Because in-court identifications, even if suggestive, do not raise due process issues, the question is not one of admissibility but weight. As observed in Palmer, a case involving the identification of the only black person in the courtroom: "The reliability of these in-court identifications should be evaluated in light of the psychological influences inherent in being asked to identify the only black person in the courtroom, under the direct prompting of the district attorney and subject to the stares of 12 persons 'tried and true' sitting in the jury box." (Ibid.)

In Evans v. Superior Court (1974) 11 Cal.3d 617, 625, the court suggested that the proper procedure a defendant should take whenever the issue of eyewitness identification becomes material is to request "a pretrial lineup in which witnesses to the alleged criminal conduct can participate." Here, defendant made no such request.

In any event, we do not think the in-court identification of defendant was impermissibly suggestive. The courtroom colloquy was as follows: "Q. [by prosecutor] Now, the three of you were the ones invited?

"A. [Morgan] Yes.

"Q. And who did the inviting?

"A. The three other people. It was two guys and one girl.

"Q. Are any one of the latter three people here in court?

"A. Yes.

"Q. Who is that?

"A. The person seated over here with the orange suit.

"THE COURT: The defendant, for the record."

As the colloquy indicates, Morgan did not identify defendant as the person who stabbed or attacked him. That was not the prosecution's question. Rather, Morgan simply identified defendant as one of the persons who invited him that night. Clearly, there was nothing improper to the question or Morgan's answer. Morgan was with defendant and defendant's companions for hours; i.e., from the time he joined defendant's group at the Blue Lagoon Bar to the time they continued their drinking behind the Palomar Restaurant and Bar. Morgan could therefore competently identify in court any person he was with that night.

Whether the person Morgan identified in court as one of those he was with that night was also the person who stabbed him is a matter that the jury could infer from the rest of Morgan's testimony, as well as from the other evidence adduced in the case.

On these facts, we conclude the trial court committed no error in denying defendant's objection to Morgan's in-court identification.

Legality of Detention

Defendant contends he was illegally detained after the Morgan incident and therefore the trial court erred in denying his section 1538.5 motion to suppress all "fruits" of that detention. The contention is without merit.

It is settled that "in the absence of probable cause, police may stop and/or briefly detain a person if they have specific and articulable facts causing them to suspect that criminal activity has taken place, is taking place or is about to occur, and that the person they intend to stop or detain is involved in that activity. [Citations.]" (People v. Ross (1990) 217 Cal.App.3d 879, 884.) Whether the suspicion is reasonable is determined according to the particular facts of each case. (Terry v. Ohio (1968) 392 U.S. 1, 16.)

Here, Morgan reported to Green that he had been robbed and attacked with a knife somewhere in the area. Green saw apparent stab wounds in Morgan's back. Morgan told Green he was attacked by four men and that one of them had black hair and wore a bandanna. Green radioed for assistance.

Two officers, Goodwin and Serafin, arrived to assist Green. Minutes later, the officers saw the silhouettes of four people standing near a Foster Freeze store. Goodwin and Serafin drove in separate cars to where the persons were, while Green stayed with Morgan. The persons ran away. Goodwin followed two of them. One of the two was defendant.

Goodwin saw defendant throw a palm-sized metallic object into a yard. Goodwin turned his patrol car into an alley to block defendant's route. Defendant stopped. Goodwin stepped out of his patrol car. He observed blood on defendant's hands and a bandanna hanging out of defendant's pocket. Goodwin detained defendant, pat searched him, handcuffed him, and placed him in the back of his patrol car. Goodwin then retrieved the object which defendant had thrown into the yard. The object turned out to be a folding knife covered with fresh blood.

Defendant admitted ownership of the knife. The cut in defendant's small finger was in the same position as wounds that Goodwin had seen on the knuckles of perpetrators of other stabbing cases involving the same kind of knife.

It has been held: "A proceeding under section 1538.5 to suppress evidence is a full hearing on the issues before the superior court sitting as finder of fact. [Citations.] The power to judge credibility of witnesses, resolve conflicts in testimony, weigh evidence and draw factual inferences, is vested in the trial court. On appeal all presumptions favor proper exercise of that power, and the trial court's findings—whether express or implied—must be upheld if supported by substantial evidence. [Citations.]" (People v. Superior Court (Keithley) (1975) 13 Cal.3d 406, 410.) Where the facts are undisputed, the question becomes one of law and the appellate court will make its own determination. (People v. Flores (1979) 100 Cal.App.3d 221, 228.)

We are convinced that on these facts, regardless of whether we view the issue as one calling for the application of the substantial evidence rule or of the independent determination rule, the conclusion will be the same: defendant's detention was reasonable; therefore, the trial court did not err in denying defendant's motion to suppress.

Sufficiency of Evidence of Great Bodily Injury

Defendant contends that as to the attack on Morgan, the evidence was insufficient to support the trial court's finding of great bodily injury within the meaning of section 12022.7. We disagree.

In arguing insufficiency of the evidence, defendant relies on the testimony of Dr. Weaver that Morgan's wounds were "not too significant." The reliance is misplaced. Defendant reads Dr. Weaver's words out of context. Dr. Weaver testified that he had examined Morgan's injuries consisting of the following: (1) a cut in his hand about an inch and a half long; (2) a laceration on the posterior area of the left shoulder about an inch long and three inches deep; (3) a laceration to the left of his spine at the base of the neck about one inch long and one inch deep; and (4) a laceration about halfway down his back that was two inches long and three inches deep. Dr. Weaver also stated that he had estimated Morgan's blood loss to be "about two cups." Dr. Weaver was then asked what he thought of the wound in the area of the spine that was three inches deep. It was to that question that Dr. Weaver answered: "Well, in this gentleman, it turned out to be not too significant." However, Dr. Weaver explained that the wound could have been serious under certain conditions; e.g.: if it had punctured something inside, causing extensive internal bleeding; if it had punctured Morgan's lung; if it had damaged the spinal cord, causing paralysis; if the lung had collapsed; or if there had been infection. Dr. Weaver stated that all these were "potential serious injuries," but because "fortunately, all these things were intact," the particular wound inquired about "turned out to be not too significant."

Clearly, Dr. Weaver did not mean "not too significant" to preclude a finding of great bodily injury within the meaning of section 12022.7. He used that language in the context of the seriousness of the injury's threat to Morgan's life or bodily function. But "great bodily injury" does not require serious threat to life or bodily function.

Section 12022.7, subdivision (d), defines great bodily injury as a "significant or substantial physical injury." In People v. Escobar (1992) 3 Cal.4th 740, 747-750, the court held that for an injury to be "great bodily injury" within the meaning of section 12022.7, it need not be characterized by permanent, prolonged, or protracted disfigurement, impairment, or loss of bodily function. Thus, the court upheld the trial court's finding that the injuries suffered by the rape victim in that case— extensive bruises and abrasions over her legs, knees and elbows, injury to her neck, and vaginal soreness which impaired her ability to walk— came within section 12022.7's definition of great bodily injury. The court observed that the victim's injuries were not inherent in the offense of rape.

Further, Escobar held that the question whether the injury is great bodily injury "is essentially a question of fact, not of law" (3 Cal.4th at p. 750) and that "'it is the trier of fact that must in most situations make the determination.' [Citation.]" (Id. at p. 752.)

In the instant case, Dr. Weaver's characterization of one of Morgan's injuries as "not too significant" was an opinion. Although an expert opinion, it was not binding on the jury. Unlike the jury, Dr. Weaver did not have the benefit of the court's instruction on the legal meaning of "great bodily injury." Because the jury had been instructed on the legal definition of "great bodily injury," it could have reasonably disregarded Dr. Weaver's opinion and concluded that all the injuries that Morgan had received, taken together, constituted great bodily injury within the meaning of section 12022.7.

The case of People v. Martinez (1985) 171 Cal.App.3d 727, relied on by defendant, is distinguishable. In Martinez, there was only one "minor laceration-type injury in the middle of [victim's] back" which witnesses had characterized as "little." The wound did not require medical treatment. In fact, the prosecutor in that case had conceded that the wound was insubstantial and had even asked the court to strike the allegation of great bodily injury. Such is not the fact pattern here. Here, there were four wounds, two of which were three inches deep; three of the wounds were at the back; the wounds resulted in the loss of about two cups of blood; all the wounds required medical treatment and suturing; and all carried potentials for infection and complications.

We conclude there is substantial evidence to support the jury's finding of great bodily injury.

Evidence of Morgan's Concern About his Physical Safety

Defendant contends the trial court committed reversible error in admitting evidence of Morgan's "concern for his physical safety" over his timely objection under Evidence Code section 352. The contention is without merit.

The record shows that at the second preliminary examination on February 7, 1992, the prosecutor asked Morgan a series of questions relating to why he did not come back to the courtroom in the afternoon of the first preliminary hearing, and why he told a different story to Officer Green on the night of the incident as to how he received his injuries. Morgan explained that he was "scared for my—myself" and was "concerned about my own welfare." Defendant did not object to the earlier questions that covered about two pages of transcript, but finally objected on the ground of relevance to the question whether Morgan "at the present time" wanted the defendant to know his whereabouts. The court overruled the objection.

At the pretrial hearing on February 10, 1993, to redact Morgan's preliminary examination transcript, defendant objected to the above-described line of questions on relevancy and Evidence Code section 352 grounds. The court overruled the objection.

Defendant argues on appeal that while the evidence relating to Morgan's physical safety was highly prejudicial to defendant, its probative value was nil; therefore, the trial court abused its discretion in admitting the challenged testimony into evidence.

We first note that no Evidence Code section 352 objection was made at the preliminary examination. Defendant's failure to raise the objection at that time barred him from raising the objection at any subsequent time. (Evid. Code, § 353, subd. (a).) Had defendant made a timely objection, the questions might have been rephrased to overcome any Evidence Code section 352 claim of prejudice. (1 Witkin, Cal. Evidence (3d ed. 1986) § 802, p. 772.)

Regardless, the trial court's determination that a challenged evidence is more probative than prejudicial will be disturbed on appeal only upon a clear showing of abuse of discretion. (People v. Terry (1970) 2 Cal.3d 362, 403.) Defendant has not done so. The relevance of the challenged evidence is apparent to explain why Morgan told Green a different story concerning how he received his injuries, and why Morgan was reluctant to point out defendant to Detective Kaleas during the first preliminary hearing. Indeed, Morgan's fear for his physical safety could even explain why he left the country and made himself unavailable as a witness. Although the parties stipulated that there was no evidence that Lang belonged to a gang, the fact is Morgan was afraid that defendant might belong to one because defendant was in the company of other persons when the incident happened.

On the other hand, defendant's claim that the evidence was highly prejudicial because it suggested that defendant "may have threatened or intimidated Morgan," is refuted by Morgan's admission that he had not in fact "received any threats in this case."

Defendant's argument that the trial court failed to make an explicit determination that the probative value of the questioned evidence outweighed the potential for prejudice is also without merit. In People v. Garceau (1993) 6 Cal.4th 140, 179, the court held that the requirement that the court state on the record that it had weighed prejudice against probative value is satisfied where "[t]he record, including the trial court's comments, sufficiently establishes that the court weighed and rejected the arguments of defense counsel. [Citations.]"

Here, the record shows that when defendant raised the Evidence Code section 352 issue, defense counsel and the prosecutor devoted two and a half pages of transcript to argue why the questioned evidence was or was not more prejudicial than probative. When the prosecutor was arguing that any perceived prejudice was "minor" compared to the issue of Morgan's credibility, the court interrupted to ask if there was "any recross on that?" The court's interruption demonstrated that it was following counsel's argument and was weighing both sides of the question. The prosecutor answered the court: "[n]ot recross, but . . . redirect," and invited the court "to read '56' and the beginning of '57' to decide this whole issue because it has some bearing on it." Only after the court had presumably reviewed the indicated portions of the record did the court overrule defendant's Evidence Code section 352 objection.

We conclude this record sufficiently establishes that the trial court had weighed the issue of prejudice against probative value before it concluded that the evidence was admissible.

Accomplice Testimony Instructions

Defendant contends that Heagerty and Lindsay had aided defendant and Huffman in the commission of various crimes in the Metro Center restroom; consequently, they could have been considered accomplices and the trial court erred in refusing defense instructions on the reliability of accomplice testimony. We disagree.

An accomplice is "'one who is liable to prosecution for the identical offense charged against the defendant on trial' [citation]." (People v. Rodriguez (1986) 42 Cal.3d 730, 758.) In People v. Hoover (1974) 12 Cal.3d 875, 879, the court stated: "In order to be charged with the identical offense as the defendant it would be necessary for the witness to be considered a principal under the provisions of section 31, which includes '[a]ll persons concerned in the commission of a crime . . . whether they directly commit the act constituting the offense, or aid and abet in its commission, or not being present, have advised and encouraged its commission. . . .' . . . [I]n order to bring [a witness] within the definition of an accomplice . . . it had to be demonstrated that he acted with 'guilty knowledge and intent with regard to the commission of the crime.' [Citations.]"

Moreover, "[t]he defendant must establish accomplice status by a preponderance of the evidence. [Citation.]" (People v. Anderson (1987) 43 Cal.3d 1104, 1138.) "Mere presence, knowledge of the crime or failure to attempt to prevent it does not suffice to make one an aider or abettor and, therefore, an accomplice [citation]." (People v. Moran (1974) 39 Cal.App.3d 398, 413.)

Here, although there was evidence that Heagerty and Lindsay, together with defendant, Huffman, and others, had "heckled" a passerby, and that Lindsay had held the restroom door upon being ordered by Huffman, there was no evidence that defendant's and Huffman's criminal purpose was known to Heagerty and Lindsay before Heagerty and Lindsay entered the restroom, or that the heckling of the passerby aided and abetted the commission of the crimes by defendant and Huffman inside the restroom.

As to Lindsay's holding the restroom door, the evidence is uncontradicted that Lindsay was ordered to do so by Huffman and that Lindsay obeyed Huffman's order because he was afraid. It is likewise uncontradicted that defendant and Huffman did not allow Heagerty and Lindsay to leave when Heagerty and Lindsay repeatedly asked to do so.

The court could therefore reasonably conclude that Lindsay and Heagerty did not act with guilty knowledge and intent with regard to the crimes that were committed in the restroom, and hence were not accomplices.

It has been held that where the facts are in dispute as to the knowledge and intent of the alleged accomplice, the question is one of fact for the jury. (People v. Gordon (1973) 10 Cal.3d 460, 466-467.) However, when the facts are "clear and undisputed" the court may determine that "the witness is or is not an accomplice as a matter of law. [Citations.]" (People v. Rodriguez, supra, 42 Cal.3d at p. 759.)

Here, because the facts were not in dispute, the trial court correctly treated the question as one of law.

Defendant argues that although Lindsay claimed that he had held the restroom door because he was afraid, "another possible inference is that he aided and abetted the commission of the crimes that took place there." There is no merit to this argument. An inference is a deduction that flows from an established fact (Evid. Code, § 600, subd. (b)); therefore, it cannot of itself raise a question of fact.

Sufficiency of Attempted Robbery Evidence (Myers)

Defendant contends that the evidence was insufficient to convict defendant of the attempted robbery of Myers. Defendant argues that at most the offense committed against Myers was attempted extortion. We disagree.

As defendant correctly points out, the salient distinction between robbery and extortion is that in robbery the property is taken against the will of the owner; whereas, in extortion the property is taken with the owner's consent, albeit coerced or unwillingly. (Cf. In re Stanley E. (1978) 81 Cal.App.3d 415, 420.)

Here, Myers clearly did not consent to the taking of his money, and defendant went beyond coercion to attempt to take Myers's money. Defendant actually attacked Myers. The evidence shows that defendant cold-cocked Myers in the side of the neck, which caused Myers to almost fall down. When Myers righted himself from the blow, defendant and Huffman backed Myers across the street, isolating him from Whitener. Defendant then demanded money, threatening to beat Myers's "ass" if he did not so do. When Myers refused to give, saying he had no money, defendant renewed the attack.

These facts clearly constitute substantial evidence to support the finding of attempted robbery.

Sufficiency of Robbery Evidence (Lindsay)

Defendant contends there was insufficient evidence to support the conviction of robbery on Lindsay. He claims that "[n]either Huffman nor Lang ever demanded Lindsay's shirt, nor did they threaten Lindsay if he failed to turn it over," and that "Lindsay willingly gave up his shirt to Huffman." The contention is without merit.

The evidence shows that while inside the Taco Bell restroom defendant and Huffman decided that they had to change clothes to look different. Defendant and Huffman then demanded to have Heagerty's leather jacket. Heagerty refused, saying "my best friend died in this thing." Later, behind the liquor store, Lindsay himself was beaten by defendant and Huffman. Huffman also punched Heagerty, and defendant and Huffman tried to remove Heagerty's jacket. To prevent further harm to his friend, Lindsay gave his flannel shirt to Huffman.

It is clear that the taking of Lindsay's shirt was accomplished by means of force or fear. Demand is not an element of robbery. (§ 211.) It is enough that the property is taken by means of force or fear. (People v. Prieto (1993) 15 Cal.App.4th 210, 215.)

Here, 14-year-old Lindsay had earlier witnessed what defendant and Huffman had done to their victims in the Metro Center restroom. And Lindsay was witnessing what defendant and Huffman were doing to Heagerty to take Heagerty's jacket. Lindsay did not want to see further harm to his friend. To stop defendant and Huffman from further beating Heagerty, Lindsay offered to give his flannel shirt. The jury could clearly find that Lindsay gave his shirt for "fear of an immediate and unlawful injury to the person or property of anyone in the company of the person robbed at the time of the robbery." (§ 212, subd. 2.) The jury could also find that Lindsay's shirt was taken by force because defendant and Huffman had beat him behind the liquor store.

We conclude the trial court's finding of robbery with respect to the taking of Lindsay's shirt is supported by substantial evidence.

Sufficiency of Attempted Robbery Evidence (Hispanic Man)

Defendant contends there was insufficient evidence to support the attempted robbery conviction on the unknown Hispanic man, arguing that "there was no evidence Lang was not acting with this man's consent or under a claim of right." The contention is devoid of merit.

Defendant had handled the Hispanic man "roughly" in asking for his money. Heagerty's preliminary examination testimony stated that the Hispanic man had received from defendant "the same treatment" as the man in the stall received. That man in the stall had been "socked in the head" and thrown up against the wall.

The jury could thus reasonably conclude that force was used to take the Hispanic man's money.

Consecutive Sentencing

Defendant contends the trial court erred in sentencing defendant to two consecutive terms of three years in case no. CR-6484, in violation of section 1170.1, subdivision (a). We disagree.

In support of this contention, defendant points out that in case no. CR-6484, he was convicted on his guilty plea of three counts of violation of section 136.1 (intimidation of witnesses). He argues that section 1170.1, subdivision (a), limits subordinate terms for consecutive offenses which are not violent felonies to five years. He states that section 667.5, subdivision (c), defines violent felonies in 15 [sic] categories, and that violations of section 136.1 are not among the violent felonies therein defined. Defendant then argues that because his convictions in case no. CR-6484 are not for violent felonies, they are subject to the section 1170.1, subdivision (a), five-year limitation for subordinate terms.

It is true that pursuant to section 1170.1, subdivision (a), the total of subordinate terms for consecutive offenses which are not violent felonies, as defined in section 667.5, subdivision (c), shall not exceed five years. However, section 1170.1, subdivision (a), does not apply where the matter comes under the operation of section 1170.15. The language of section 1170.15 is plain and needs no interpretation: "Notwithstanding the provisions of subdivision (a) of Section 1170.1 which provide for the imposition of a subordinate term for a consecutive offense of one-third of the middle term of imprisonment, if a person is convicted of a felony, and of an additional felony which is a violation of Section 136.1 or 137 and which was committed against the victim of, or a witness or potential witness with respect to, or a person who was about to give material information pertaining to, the first felony, or of a felony violation of Section 653f which was committed to dissuade a witness or potential witness to the first felony, the subordinate term for each consecutive offense which is a felony described in this section shall consist of 100 percent of the middle term of imprisonment for the felony for which a consecutive term of imprisonment is imposed, and shall include 100 percent of any enhancements imposed pursuant to Section 12022, 12022.5, or 12022.7. . . ." (Emphasis added.)

It is thus clear that for section 1170.15 to apply the felonies need not be violent; it is enough that the additional felonies are for violations of section 136.1 "committed against the victim of, or a witness or potential witness with respect to, or a person who was about to give material information pertaining to, the first felony." (§ 1170.15.) That is the situation here. Consequently, by imposing 100 percent of the 3-year middle term on counts 2 and 4 of case no. CR-6484, the trial court merely applied the mandatory language of section 1170.15. The trial court committed no error.

Reasonable Doubt Instruction

Finally, defendant challenges the constitutionality of CALJIC No. 2.90, based upon Cage v. Louisiana (1990) 498 U.S. 39 and Sandoval v. California (No. 92-9049, cert. granted Sept. 28, 1993). The United States Supreme Court has now upheld this instruction. (Victor v. Nebraska (1994) ___ U.S. ___, 114 S.Ct. 1239.)

DISPOSITION

The judgment is affirmed.

XVIII.
People v. Jones
(Supreme Court opinion published at 10 Cal.4th 1102)

Our court issued two opinions in *Jones*. The first opinion was issued in the regular course of the appeal; that is, following the briefing and the oral argument. That opinion was certified by our court for partial publication. Partial publication means publication of parts of the opinion only. These are the parts of the opinion that contribute something new to the existing body of law and jurisprudence. Parts of the opinion that do not so contribute are omitted in the publication.

Two main issues were raised in *Jones*. The first was the claimed violation of the Fourth Amendment to the United States Constitution. The Fourth Amendment protects individuals against unreasonable searches and seizures. We have the same guarantee in the Philippine Constitution. The first opinion was published for its discussion of the Fourth Amendment issue.

In *Jones*, the defendant (Jones) was searched in a public place (street). He was asked to strip his pants down so that the police officer could see if he was hiding contraband in his crotch area. The officer had stopped Jones for speeding, and, observing symptoms of substance abuse, pat-searched him. The officer felt what seemed like a baggie in Jones's crotch area. The question in *Jones* was whether the officer's public search of Jones's genitals was a violation of the Fourth Amendment.

After we decided *Jones*, the defendant filed a petition for review with the California Supreme Court. The Supreme Court granted review, but not on the search and seizure issue, which it left undisturbed. The Supreme Court granted review only on the limited issue of whether the defendant's contention that the trial court had erred in imposing the payment of various fees as a condition of probation was cognizable on appeal. Our court had declined to reach that issue, reasoning that the defendant had not included that issue in his notice of appeal, and the non-inclusion precluded us from considering it. The probation discussion was the part of the first opinion that was not published. The Supreme Court disagreed with our decision not to reach the probation issue, and held that the rule requiring the specification of issues in the notice of appeal "is intended to determine only whether an appeal should proceed and not what issues the reviewing court may consider." *People v. Jones* (1995) 10 Cal.4th 1102, 1110.) Since the notice of appeal on the search and seizure issue had made the appeal operative, our court could therefore reach the probation issue that the defendant had briefed. The Supreme Court transferred the case back to us for a determination of that issue. The California Supreme Court opinion may be found at 10 Cal.4th 1102.

We then issued a second opinion addressing the issue of whether the trial court had erred in imposing the payment of various fees as a condition of probation. We found no error. Accordingly, we affirmed the trial court on that issue as well.

The two *Jones* opinions are reproduced below. Only the published part is reproduced in the first opinion. The probation part, which was not published, appears in the second opinion.

The first opinion in *Jones* follows:

I. PROCEDURAL BACKGROUND

Defendant Wendale Levette Jones was charged by information with possession of cocaine base for sale (Health & Saf. Code, § 11351.5; count 1), transporting cocaine base (Health & Saf. Code, § 11352, subd. (a); Pen. Code, § 1203.073, subd. (b)(6); count 2), and misdemeanor driving on a suspended license (Veh. Code, § 14601.1, subd. (a); count 3).

Defendant moved to suppress evidence pursuant to Penal Code section 1538.5.[26] The court denied the motion. Defendant then entered a guilty plea on all counts.

The court granted probation. Among other conditions of probation, the court imposed a restitution fine of $100, laboratory fees of $50 on each of counts 1 and 2, a drug education program fee of $100, and probation supervision fees not exceeding $20 per month. The court also ordered defendant to pay $150 attorney fees.

We affirm.

---

26 Further statutory references in this case are to the Penal Code unless otherwise stated.

II. FACTS

On January 11, 1992, at 3:27 a.m., San Jose Police Officer Knox stopped defendant for speeding. Defendant did not have a driver's license. A radio check disclosed that defendant's driving license had been suspended and that defendant had a "small" outstanding warrant in Fresno County.

Knox asked defendant to step out of his car and approach the patrol car. Defendant told Knox that he had been using narcotics that evening. Knox also observed in defendant symptoms of substance abuse. Knox arrested defendant for being under the influence of a controlled substance.

As Knox was handcuffing defendant, another officer arrived at the scene. When Knox pat-searched defendant, he felt no weapons but felt what was "obviously a baggie of some type . . . down the front of [defendant's] pants." Knox decided to determine what was in the baggie.

Knox uncuffed defendant and asked him to pull his pants forward so that Knox "could see down them." Defendant unfastened his pants, exposing his underwear to Knox. Knox shined his flashlight at the underwear, but saw nothing. Knox told defendant to pull the underwear away from his body, which defendant did. Knox shined his flashlight at the crotch area inside defendant's underwear and saw a plastic baggie. Knox told defendant to remove the baggie. Defendant did so. Observing crack cocaine inside the baggie, Knox seized the baggie.

Knox did not touch defendant's skin, pants, or underwear. Defendant's pants were never removed. The period of time during which defendant's pants were unfastened lasted "a couple of minutes at the most." At the place where defendant was searched, which was on the south side of Santa Clara Street across from the construction site for the San Jose Arena, Knox did not see any person in or around any of the buildings except the other officer who was standing further back on the sidewalk. Knox did not recall any traffic in the area. Knox's patrol car was between defendant and the street.

III. CONTENTIONS

On appeal, defendant contends:

1. The public strip search of defendant's genitalia violated defendant's Fourth Amendment right to be free from unreasonable searches of his person, and thus the cocaine seized from his crotch area must be suppressed.

2. The public strip search of defendant's genitalia violated his due process rights as it "shocks the conscience," and thus the cocaine seized from his crotch area must be suppressed.

3. The trial court improperly imposed fees as conditions of probation by failing to make a determination of defendant's ability to pay or to pronounce them in the oral judgment.

IV. DISCUSSION

A. Standard of Review

Where, as here, a section 1538.5 motion to suppress evidence is heard de novo, the standard of review is as stated by the court in People v. Loewen (1983) 35 Cal.3d 117, 123: "The trial court's factual findings relating to the challenged search or seizure, 'whether express or implied, must be upheld if they are supported by substantial evidence.' [Citation.] '"The trial court also has the duty to determine whether, on the facts found, the search was unreasonable within the meaning of the Constitution." [Citation.] Because "that issue is a question of law," the appellate court is not bound by the substantial evidence standard in reviewing the trial court's decision thereon. Rather, . . . in such review it is "the ultimate responsibility of the appellate court to measure the facts, as found by the trier, against the constitutional standard of reasonableness." [Citation.] On that issue, in short, the appellate court exercises its independent judgment.' [Citations.]"

In this case, the facts are undisputed. The lone testimony of Knox is uncontested. Therefore, the question before us is one of law. Accordingly, we must exercise our independent judgment.

B. Reasonableness of Search

Defendant first contends that the public strip search of his genitalia violated his Fourth Amendment right to be free from unreasonable searches of his person, and thus the cocaine seized from his crotch area must be suppressed. The contention is without merit.

Firstly, we must state that the Fourth Amendment issue in this case does not turn on the characterization of the search as a public strip search or something else. Fourth Amendment issues are not a matter of "incantation[s]" or characterizations. (Katz v. United States (1967) 389 U.S. 347, 353.) In Katz, the United States Supreme Court declined to adopt the parties' formulation of the issue as one turning on the question of whether a telephone booth is a "constitutionally protected area" because "the correct solution of Fourth Amendment problems is not necessarily promoted by incantation" of certain phrases. (Id. at p. 350.) The court noted that attaching great significance to the characterization of a telephone booth as a "constitutionally protected area" merely deflected attention from the problem presented in that case, which was whether the search was unreasonable under the Fourth Amendment. As in Katz, the question here is whether the search, by whatever characterization, was a reasonable search under the Fourth Amendment.

In Winston v. Lee (1985) 470 U.S. 753, 758-759, the United States Supreme Court explained the meaning and scope of the Fourth Amendment, thus: "The Fourth Amendment protects 'expectations of privacy,' [citation] — the individual's legitimate expectations that in certain places and at certain times he has 'the right to be let alone—the most comprehensive of rights and the right most valued by civilized men.' [Citation.] Putting to one side the procedural protections of the warrant requirement, the Fourth Amendment generally protects the 'security' of 'persons, houses, papers, and effects' against official intrusions up to the point where the community's need for evidence surmounts a specified standard, ordinarily 'probable cause.' Beyond this point, it is ordinarily justifiable for the community to demand that the individual give up some part of his interest in privacy and security to advance the community's vital interests in law enforcement; such a search is generally 'reasonable' in the Amendment's terms."

Here, there is no question that, as a general proposition, defendant had a reasonable expectation of privacy in his genitalia. However, when defendant used his crotch area to conceal contraband, he forfeited his Fourth Amendment protection. "The human body is not . . . a sanctuary in which evidence may be concealed with impunity. [Citation.] Appropriate procedures to retrieve such evidence are neither 'unreasonable' per se under the Fourth Amendment, nor violations of 'due process' procedures guaranteed by the Fifth and Fourteenth Amendments. [Citations.]" (People v. Scott (1978) 21 Cal.3d 284, 293.)

In United States v. Robinson (1973) 414 U.S. 218, 235, the court held that where the custodial arrest of a person is lawful, "a full search of the person is not only an exception to the warrant requirement of the Fourth Amendment, but is also a 'reasonable' search under that Amendment." In such a case, the search "requires no additional justification." (Ibid.)

The court explained: "A police officer's determination as to how and where to search the person of a suspect whom he has arrested is necessarily a quick ad hoc judgment which the Fourth Amendment does not require to be broken down in each instance into an analysis of each step in the search. The authority to search the person incident to a lawful custodial arrest, while based upon the need to disarm and to discover evidence, does not depend on what a court may later decide was the probability in a particular arrest situation that weapons or evidence would in fact be found upon the person of the suspect. A custodial arrest of a suspect based on probable cause is a reasonable intrusion under the Fourth Amendment; that intrusion being lawful, a search incident to the arrest requires no additional justification. It is the fact of the lawful arrest which establishes the authority to search, and we hold that in the case of a lawful custodial arrest a full search of the person is not only an exception to the warrant requirement of the Fourth Amendment, but is also a 'reasonable' search under that Amendment." (United States v. Robinson, supra, 414 U.S. at p. 235, emphasis added.)

The court quoted with approval Charles v. United States (9th Cir. 1960) 278 F.2d 386, 388-389: "'Once the body of the accused is validly subjected to the physical dominion of the law, inspections of his person, regardless of purpose, cannot be deemed unlawful, unless they violate the dictates of reason either because of their number or their manner of perpetration.'" (United States v. Robinson, supra, 414 U.S. at pp. 237-238, fn. 1.)

Justice Powell's concurring opinion was equally terse: "[A]n individual lawfully subjected to a custodial arrest retains no significant

Fourth Amendment interest in the privacy of his person. . . . [T]he custodial arrest is the significant intrusion of state power into the privacy of one's person. If the arrest is lawful, the privacy interest guarded by the Fourth Amendment is subordinated to a legitimate and overriding governmental concern. No reason then exists to frustrate law enforcement by requiring some independent justification for a search incident to a lawful custodial arrest. This seems to me the reason that a valid arrest justifies a full search of the person, even if that search is not narrowly limited by the twin rationales of seizing evidence and disarming the arrestee. The search incident to arrest is reasonable under the Fourth Amendment because the privacy interest protected by that constitutional guarantee is legitimately abated by the fact of arrest." (United States v. Robinson, supra, 414 U.S. at pp. 237-238.)

Robinson was applied in Gustafson v. Florida (1973) 414 U.S. 260, 266: "We hold, therefore, that upon arresting petitioner for the offense of driving his automobile without possession of a valid operator's license, and taking him into custody, Smith was entitled to make a full search of petitioner's person incident to that lawful arrest. Since it is the fact of custodial arrest which gives rise to the authority to search, it is of no moment that Smith did not indicate any subjective fear of the petitioner or that he did not himself suspect that the petitioner was armed. Having in the course of his lawful search come upon the box of cigarettes, Smith was entitled to inspect it; and when his inspection revealed the homemade cigarettes which he believed to contain an unlawful substance, he was entitled to seize them as 'fruits, instrumentalities, or contraband' probative of criminal conduct. [Citations.]"

Although no further justification is necessary when the search of the person is conducted as an incident to a lawful custodial arrest, the search in this case was in fact further justified by its factual reasonableness. For even "balancing the need to search against the invasion which the search entails," pursuant to Terry v. Ohio (1968) 392 U.S. 1, 21, it is clear that what Knox felt as an "obvious" plastic baggie "down the front" of defendant's pants reasonably invited the search. Given that defendant had told Knox that he had been using narcotics that evening, and given the presence of symptoms of substance abuse that Knox had observed in defendant, which together led Knox to conclude that defendant was under the influence of drugs, Knox could reasonably believe that the baggie in defendant's front contained contraband and that defendant was using his crotch area to hide the baggie.

And although the place was public, the totality of the circumstances under which the search was made did not make the search unreasonable under the Fourth Amendment. As the trial court observed: "The lateness of [the] night, locale of the search, and scope and manner of the search resulted in a brief and minimal intrusion under the circumstances."

Defendant admits that the search could have been validly conducted in the privacy of the police station. The fact that it could have been so conducted did not invalidate the search that was actually made. As the People point out, defendant's suggestion merely argues "a choice among reasonable alternatives."

It is true that in Schmerber v. California (1966) 384 U.S. 757, the court stated that "the mere fact of a lawful arrest does not end our inquiry," because whatever the validity might be of the considerations that led to the Robinson/Gustafson analysis, "they have little applicability with respect to searches involving intrusions beyond the body's surface." (384 U.S. at p. 769, emphasis added.) The Schmerber court reasoned that "[t]he interests in human dignity and privacy which the Fourth Amendment protects forbid any such intrusions on the mere chance that desired evidence might be obtained. In the absence of a clear indication that in fact such evidence will be found, these fundamental human interests require law officers to suffer the risk that such evidence may disappear unless there is an immediate search." (Id. at pp. 769-770.)

Schmerber is distinguishable. In that case, the defendant was hospitalized following an auto accident. A police officer smelled liquor and observed other symptoms of drunkenness. The officer placed the defendant under arrest and directed a physician to take a blood sample. The defendant did not give his consent.

Here, on the other hand, there was no "intrusion beyond the body's surface." Knox did not even touch defendant's body.

In any event, the court in Schmerber did not find the blood extraction unreasonable under the facts. To the contrary, the court held that "the attempt to secure evidence of blood-alcohol content in this case was an appropriate incident to petitioner's arrest" and that "the test chosen to measure petitioner's blood-alcohol level was a reasonable one." (384 U.S. at p. 771.)

The case of Illinois v. Lafayette (1983) 462 U.S. 640, relied on by defendant, is inapposite. That case involved an inventory search, not search of the defendant's person. As stated by the court, the issue in that case was "whether, at the time an arrested person arrives at a police station, the police may, without obtaining a warrant, search a shoulder bag carried by that person." (Id. at p. 641.) In holding that the police may, the court stated that "[t]he justification for such searches does not rest on probable cause, and hence the absence of a warrant is immaterial to the reasonableness of the search." (Id. at p. 643.) The justification, rather, is the recognition that an "inventory search is not an independent legal concept but rather an incidental administrative step following arrest and preceding incarceration." (Id. at p. 644.) The justification covers a "range of governmental interests," which includes deterring false claims by the arrested persons as to the items taken from them; inhibiting theft or careless handling of articles taken from arrested persons by the police; and protecting arrested persons from injuring themselves with dangerous instruments that might be concealed in innocent-looking articles taken from their possession. (Id. at p. 646.)

Also distinguishable is People v. Laiwa (1983) 34 Cal.3d 711. In that case, the officer saw the defendant in a parking lot. The defendant was making movements which made the officer conclude that the defendant was under the influence of PCP. The officer detained the defendant, tested him for certain distinctive eye movements, then arrested him when the test proved positive. The officer took from the defendant a closed tote bag, opened and searched it, and found a cigarette containing PCP. The officer testified that he searched the tote bag for inventory purposes. The issue was whether the validity of the search could be upheld as an "accelerated booking search." The court held it could not be so upheld, noting that since the bag had been removed from defendant's possession, there was no necessity to search the bag in the premises. "There will be ample opportunity for the proper officials to discharge these duties when the arresting officers deliver the prisoner into their custody." (Id. at pp. 726-727.)

In contrast, the baggie in this case was still in defendant's possession. The purpose of the search was precisely to determine what was in the baggie, and to remove it from defendant's possession if it contained evidence of the crime.

C. Section 4030

Defendant also contends that the search of his crotch area violated section 4030. That section provides, in relevant part, that "[n]o strip search . . . may be conducted without the prior written authorization of the supervising officer on duty" (subd. (f)), and that "[a]ll strip . . . searches shall be conducted in an area of privacy so that the search cannot be observed by persons not participating in the search" (subd. (m)).

Because the issue in this appeal is the propriety of the denial of defendant's motion to suppress, section 4030 is impertinent in light of People v. Wade (1989) 208 Cal.App.3d 304. That case held that while a violation of section 4030 may be a basis for criminal prosecution or an action for civil damages, it is not a ground to exclude evidence under the Fourth Amendment. The court reasoned that nowhere in section 4030 "has the Legislature provided for suppression of evidence obtained without section 4030 compliance . . . . [Citation.] And in this post-Proposition 8 era, absent such a pronouncement by the Legislature, state courts are powerless to suppress evidence unless federal law so requires. [Citation.]" (208 Cal.App.3d at p. 308.)

Evidently, the question of what is unreasonable under the Fourth Amendment is not for each individual state to determine. As stated in California v. Greenwood (1988) 486 U.S. 35, 43-44: "Individual States may surely construe their own constitutions as imposing more stringent constraints on police conduct than does the Federal Constitution. We have never intimated, however, that whether or not a search is reasonable within the meaning of the Fourth Amendment depends on the law of the particular State in which the search occurs." Noting that respondent's argument in that case was "no less than a suggestion that concepts of privacy under the laws of each State are to determine the reach of the Fourth Amendment," the court said: "[w]e do not accept this submission." (Ibid.)

D. No Due Process Violation

Defendant next contends that the public strip of his genitalia violated his due process rights as it "shocks the conscience," and thus the cocaine seized from his crotch area must be suppressed. In arguing this point, defendant relies on Rochin v. California (1952) 342 U.S. 165, 172, which held that police conduct which "shocks the conscience" and offends "even hardened sensibilities" violates the Due Process Clause of the Fifth and Fourteenth Amendments. The contention is without merit, and the reliance on Rochin is misplaced.

In Rochin, deputy sheriffs physically forced open defendant's mouth, then pumped his stomach to retrieve morphine capsules that defendant had swallowed. The court stated that the methods employed were "too close to the rack and the screw to permit of constitutional differentiation" (342 U.S. at p. 172) and violated due process because allowing such methods would "afford brutality the cloak of law" (id. at p. 173).

The facts of this case do not compare to those of Rochin. As noted, Knox did not even touch defendant.

Regardless, because we have concluded that the search here was a valid search incident to defendant's lawful arrest, it did not offend due process. (People v. Scott, supra, 21 Cal.3d at p. 293.)

E. Fees as Probation Conditions

(Omitted. See second opinion for the determination of this question.)

V. DISPOSITION

The judgment is affirmed.

The pertinent part of the second *Jones* opinion follows:

On September 8, 1994, the Supreme Court granted review in this case on the limited issue of "whether appellant's claims regarding conditions of probation are cognizable on appeal in view of California Rules of Court, rule 31(d), and the contents of his notice of appeal."

On August 10, 1995, the Supreme Court filed its decision, holding that rule 31(d) "does not govern the cognizability of noncertificate issues in an operative appeal," and that "rule 31(d) did not render defendant's probation condition claims noncognizable." (Opinion, p. 12).) In so holding, the Supreme Court reversed our opinion "insofar as it holds rule 31(d) renders defendant's claims regarding probation conditions noncognizable on appeal," and transferred the cause back to us "for decision on the remaining issues." (Opinion, p. 12.)

Because review was denied on issues other than the cognizability on appeal of defendant's claims regarding conditions of probation, our judgment on those other issues is now final and may no longer be disturbed. Parts I through IV-D of this opinion are the parts which the Supreme Court did not review. Part IV-E is the part that addresses the probation condition issues that we here decide.

I. PROCEDURAL BACKGROUND

(Omitted. Same as first opinion.)

II. FACTS

(Omitted. Same as first opinion.)

III. CONTENTIONS

(Omitted. Same as first opinion.)

IV. DISCUSSION
A. Standard of Review

(Omitted. Same as first opinion.)

B. Reasonableness of Search

(Omitted. Same as first opinion.)

C. Section 4030

(Omitted. Same as first opinion.)

D. No Due Process Violation

(Omitted. Same as first opinion.)

E. Fees as Probation Conditions

Defendant contends the trial court improperly imposed a drug education fee, a probationary supervision fee, and attorney fees as conditions of probation because it failed to determine defendant's ability to pay these fees. (AOB 26) The contention is without merit.

There is no requirement that the trial court make an express determination on the record of a defendant's ability to pay. (People v. Frye (1994) 21 Cal.App.4th 1483, 1485-1486.) A defendant's ability to pay can be implied from the record. (Ibid.) Further, the trial court is "not limited to considering a defendant's present ability but may consider a defendant's ability to pay in the future." (Id. at p. 1487.) On appeal, the trial court's finding of ability to pay will be upheld if supported by the record. (People v. Staley (1992) 10 Cal.App.4th 782, 785-786.)

Here, defendant's ability to pay is clear from the record. Before ordering payment of the $100 drug education fee and the $20 monthly probation supervision fee, the court announced: "I will recommend work furlough in this case." (RT 10/14/92, p. 11) By stating that it would recommend defendant for a work furlough, the court impliedly determined that defendant can work, and therefore can earn. A finding that a defendant can work and earn is an implied finding of ability to pay, at least in the future. As stated in People v. Staley, supra, 10 Cal.App.4th at p. 783: "'[A]bility to pay' a drug program fee does not require existing employment or cash on hand. Rather, a determination of ability to pay may be made based on the person's ability to earn where the person has no physical, mental or emotional impediment which precludes the person from finding and maintaining employment once his or her sentence is completed."

Defendant also claims the trial court did not order the payment of attorney fees or a laboratory analysis fee of $100 in the oral pronouncement of judgment. The claim is belied by the record. The reporter's transcript explicitly shows that at sentencing the trial court orally ordered defendant to pay "a $50 laboratory fee for each of the counts in count 1 and 2" and a $150 attorney fees for "public defender services." (RT 10/14/92, pp. 11, 11-12)

There is also no factual basis to defendant's claim that the trial court had ordered payment of attorney fees as a condition of probation. (AOB 31) The record shows that the trial court ordered payment of the $150 attorney fees not as a condition of probation, but as an unconditional part of defendant's sentence. This is clear from the following colloquy, which transpired after the court had advised defendant of the conditions of his probation:

"THE COURT: Any further conditions requested?

"MR. TUCCI [probation officer]: No, Your Honor.

"THE COURT: I need to set a surrender date. And did you say the 18th was your birthday?

"MR. JONES: Yes.

"THE COURT: You are ordered to surrender for the sentencing on January 20 at 9:00 a.m. Do you accept your probation?

"MR. JONES: Yes.

"THE COURT: Thank you very much. And for the public defender services in this matter, you are ordered to pay $150.

"MR. JONES: When do I have to pay this?" (RT 10/14/92, pp. 11-12)

As the colloquy discloses, the court ordered payment of the $150 attorney fees after it had imposed the last condition of probation and had been told by the probation officer that there were no further conditions of probation to consider.

Because payment of the attorney fees determined in this case was not a condition of probation but an unconditional part of defendant's sentence, we need not reach the issue whether ordering payment of attorney fees as a condition of probation is constitutionally prohibited. (AOB 31)

Finally, defendant contends the abstract of judgment incorrectly indicates a $100 laboratory analysis fee as a condition of probation in that the trial judge only ordered a $50 fee in his oral pronouncement of judgment. (AOB 32) Defendant misreads the record. The reporter's transcript shows that the trial court ordered defendant to pay as a condition of probation "a $50 laboratory fee for <u>each</u> of the counts in count 1 and 2." (RT 10/14/92) (Emphasis added.) A fee of $50 for each count is equal to $100 for two counts.

We conclude the trial court impliedly found that defendant had the ability to pay the challenged fees as a condition of probation, and that such implied finding is supported by the record. We further conclude that the abstract of judgment correctly reflects the trial court's oral pronouncement of judgment with respect to the attorney and laboratory fees imposed.

V. DISPOSITION

The judgment is affirmed.

XIX.
DVD CCA v. Bunner
(Unused Draft)

Bunner was the last case I worked on before my retirement in July 2001. I retired shortly after I had submitted the following memorandum to Justice Premo. After my retirement, I learned that the panel came up with an opinion that was different from what I had proposed. The panel voted to reverse the trial court and to dissolve the preliminary injunction. DVD CCA filed a petition for review with the California Supreme Court. The Supreme Court granted review, following which, it reversed the Court of Appeal and remanded the matter for further proceeding consistent with the guidelines it had set forth, which were: "On remand, the Court of Appeal must therefore 'make an independent examination of the entire record' (*Bose Corp. v. Consumers Union of U.S., Inc.* (1984) 466 U.S. 485, 499), and determine whether the evidence in the record supports the factual findings necessary to establish that the preliminary injunction was warranted under California's trade secret law (see *Lindsay v. City of San Antonio* (5th Cir. 1987) 821 F.2d 1103, 1107-1108 [noting that appellate courts must independently review factual findings relevant to the resolution of any First Amendment issues]). If, after this examination, the court finds the injunction improper under California's trade secret law, then it should find that the trial court abused its discretion. (See *ibid.* [holding that, in determining whether the 'issuance of a preliminary injunction constitutes an abuse of' discretion under the First Amendment, the reviewing court must independently review the factual findings subsumed in the constitutional determination]; see also *Gallo v. Acuna, supra,* 14 Cal.4th at p. 1109 [holding that preliminary injunctions are reviewed 'under an abuse of discretion standard'].) Otherwise, it should uphold the injunction." On remand, the court of appeal, independently reviewing the record, reversed the trial court and dissolved the preliminary injunction on the basis that it was improperly issued under California's trade secret law.

Although my memorandum in *Bunner* did not become the court's opinion, I am including the memorandum in this collection so

I can share with my Philippine readers some of the issues I grappled with in the case. In my memorandum, I recommended remand to allow the trial court to develop a fuller and more adequate record because I did not think that the record before us was sufficient to permit the court to conduct an independent review.

I do not think the issues in *Bunner* have ever been explored in the Philippines, or discussed in the country's legal literature.

My memorandum in *DVD CCC v. Bunner* follows:

FACTUAL AND PROCEDURAL BACKGROUND

Plaintiff DVD Copy Control Association, Inc. (DVD CCA) is a trade association of businesses involved in the digital versatile disc (DVD) industry. DVDs are five-inch-diameter discs used to store massive amounts of data. Full-length motion pictures in digital form can be stored in one DVD. Motion pictures stored in DVDs can be played back with much-enhanced audio and visual clarity.

Motion pictures stored in DVDS are protected from unauthorized use by the encryption of a "content scramble system," or CSS, that scrambles the pictures contained in the DVD. To decrypt, unscramble, and play back the motion pictures in the DVD, CSS requires the use of appropriately configured hardware, such as a DVD player or a computer DVD drive. However, while CSS permits playback of the motion pictures, it does not permit copying them. CSS is distributed pursuant to a licensing system that makes DVD CCA the sole licensing entity.

Each licensee from DVD CCA receives a "master key" in the CSS decryption software that matches a "key" in a DVD software. The matching of the two "keys" when the disc is played permits decryption of the motion picture. The license agreement requires the licensee to maintain the confidentiality of CSS, and prohibits reverse engineering.

In October 1999, a computer program named "DeCSS" was posted on the Internet by a 15-year old Norwegian named Jon Johansen. Thereafter, DeCSS appeared on numerous other websites, including the website of defendant Andrew Bunner (Bunner). DeCSS permits the unauthorized decryption and copying of DVDs. DVD CCA asserts that DeCSS was illegally created by a third party hacker who reverse engineered software created by a CSS licensee.

In December 1999, DVD CCA filed the instant complaint for injunctive relief against Bunner and the other defendants, alleging misappropriation of trade secrets. The complaint alleges that Bunner and the other defendants failed or refused to remove DeCSS from their websites despite demands by DVD CCA that they do so. (App., Vol. 1, p. 1) DVD further alleges that "the DeCSS program has the capability to defeat DVD encryption software and, as a result, the DeCSS program allows users to illegally pirate the copyrighted motion pictures contained on DVD videos — activity which is fatal to the DVD video format and the hundreds of computer and consumer electronics companies whose businesses rely on the viability of this digital format." (App., Vol. 1, p. 15)

The requested injunctive relief sought to enjoin Bunner and the other defendants from disclosing the DeCSS program or other proprietary CSS technology on their websites or elsewhere, and from linking their websites to other websites that disclosed DeCSS or other CSS technology. (App., Vol. 1, p. 19).

On December 29, 1999, the trial court denied DVD CCA's request for a temporary restraining order, but ordered the defendants, including Bunner, to show cause why the requested preliminary injunction should not be granted. (App., Vol. 1, p. 163-164)

On January 7, 2000, defendants McLaughlin and Bunner filed their memorandum of points and authorities in opposition to the order to show cause. (App., Vol 2, p. 173)

On January 13, DVD CCA filed its reply to McLaughlin's and Bunner's opposition. (App., Vol. 3, p. 598)

On January 21, 2000, the trial court issued a preliminary injunction enjoining defendants from "[p]osting or otherwise disclosing or distributing, on their websites or elsewhere, the DeCSS program, the master keys or algorithms of the Content Scrambling system ("CSS") or any other information derived from this proprietary information." (App., Vol. III, p. 711-712) However, the court refused to enjoin the defendants from linking their websites to other websites that contain the protected information on the ground that the links were indispensable to Internet access and a website owner could not be held liable for the content of other websites. (App., Vol. III, p. 716)

The court issued the preliminary injunction based on the following findings: First, CSS is DVD CCA's trade secret, and that, for nearly three years prior to the posting of CSS on defendants' websites, DVD CCA had exerted reasonable efforts to maintain the program's secrecy. Second, the evidence was "fairly clear" that the trade secret had been obtained through a reverse engineering procedure that violated the terms of the CSS license agreement. The court stated there was sufficient circumstantial evidence to show that the reverse engineering had been performed wrongfully after a third party had "clicked" on the DVD CCA license agreement that prohibits reverse engineering. The court stated that, based on defendants' boasting in various websites about their disrespect for the law, it could be inferred that defendant knew that the trade secret had been obtained through improper means. Third, the balancing of equities favored DVD CCA. The court determined that while the harm to defendants in being compelled to remove trade secret information from their websites was "truly minimal," the current and prospective harm to DVD CCA was irreparable in that DVD CCA would lose the right to protect CSS as a trade secret and to control unauthorized copying of DVD content.

The court stated that trade secret status should not be deemed destroyed merely by posting on the Internet, because, "[t]o hold otherwise would do nothing less than encourage misappropriators of trade secrets to post the fruits of their wrongdoing on the Internet as quickly as possible and as widely as possible thereby destroying a trade secret forever." (App., Vol. III, p. 715) The court added that "[o]ur system currently places high importance on protecting such intellectual property, and this Court must enforce such protections with all appropriate and available means." (Vol. III, p. 715)

Following the filing of Bunner's opening brief, we granted leave to the following amici curiae to file their briefs.

The American Committee for Interoperable Systems and the Computer & Communications Industry Association jointly filed their brief in support of Brunner's appeal.

The Institute of Electrical and Electronics Engineers, Inc. — United States Board (IEEE-USA) filed its brief in support of Bunner.

The Recording Industry Association of America (RIAA), the Motion Picture Association of America (MPAA), the American Film Marketing Association (AFMA), the Association of American Publishers (AAP), the Business Software Alliance (BSA), the Interactive Digital Software Association (IDSA), the National Music Publishers' Association (NMPA), the American Society of Composers, Authors, and Publishers (ASCAP), Broadcast Music, Inc. (BMI), the American Federation of Musicians of the United States and Canada (AFM), the Professional Photographers of America (PPA), the Producers Guild of America (PGA), the Directors Guild of America (DGA), the Writers Guild of America, West, Inc. (WGA), the Screen Actors Guild, Inc. (SAG), the American Federation of Television and Radio Artists (AFTRA), and the Video Software Dealers Association (VSDA), filed their joint brief in support of DVD CCA.

DISCUSSION
Standard of Review

The standard of review governing preliminary injunction orders is as summarized in Paradise Hills Associates v. Procel (1991) 235 Cal.App.3d 1528, 1537-1538: "To issue a preliminary injunction, the trial court must consider two interrelated factors. First, the court must evaluate whether the plaintiff is likely to prevail on the merits at trial. Second, the court must weigh the interim harm to the plaintiff if the injunction is denied against the harm to the defendant if the injunction is issued. [Citation.] [¶] On appeal, we 'merely determine whether the trial court "exceeded the bounds of reason" in determining [plaintiff] has a "reasonable probability of prevailing on the merits" and that the "balance of hardships" favors [plaintiff]. We can reverse the order only if appellant demonstrates an abuse of discretion in resolving these two issues. [Citation.]' [Citation.]"

However, not all orders granting preliminary injunction are entitled to such deferential review. "[A]ny prior restraint on expression bears a heavy presumption against its constitutional validity." (Wilson v. Superior Court (1975) 13 Cal.3d 652, 657, emphasis added.) "An injunction limiting citizens' rights of speech must be narrowly drawn." (Chico Feminist Women's Health Center v. Scully (1989) 208 Cal.App.3d 230, 247.) "[T]he reviewing court in free speech cases must make an independent examination of the whole record." (L. A. Teachers Union v. L. A. City Bd. of Ed. (1969) 71 Cal.2d 551, 557, emphasis added.) "[I]n cases raising First Amendment issues we have repeatedly held that an appellate court has an obligation to make an independent examination of the whole record in order to make sure that the judgment does not constitute a forbidden intrusion on the field of free expression." (Bose Corp v. Consumers Union of U.S., Inc. (1984) 466 U.S. 485, 499, quotation marks and citation omitted.) "[T]he rule of independent review assigns to judges a constitutional responsibility that cannot be delegated to the trier of fact, whether the factfinding function be performed in the particular case by a jury or by a trial judge." (Bose at p. 501.)

"In the case of a prior restraint on pure speech, the hurdle is substantially higher [than for an ordinary preliminary injunction]: publication must threaten an interest more fundamental than the First Amendment itself. Indeed, the Supreme Court has never upheld a prior restraint, even faced with the competing interest of national security or the Sixth Amendment right to a fair trial. For similar reasons, the standard of review is different. The decision to grant or deny an injunction is reviewed for abuse of discretion. We review First Amendment questions de novo." (Proctor & Gamble Co. v. Bankers Trust Co. (6th Cir. 1996) 78 F.3d 219, 226-227; Nebraska Press Ass'n v. Stuart (1976) 96 S.Ct. 2791, 2803-2804 [the Sixth Amendment right of a criminal defendant to a fair trial does not outrank the First Amendment right of the press to publish information]; New York Times Co. v. U.S. (1971) 403 U.S. 713, 718-726 ["national security" interest in suppressing classified information in the Pentagon Papers did not outrank First Amendment right of press to publish this classified information].) Even "[d]eference to a legislative finding cannot limit judicial inquiry when First Amendment rights are at stake." (Landmark Communications, Inc. v. Virginia (1978) 435 U.S. 829, 843.)

Thus, in order to determine the appropriate standard of review, we must first decide whether the trial court's preliminary injunction involved a restraint on defendant's First Amendment right to free expression. If so, we exercise independent review. If not, we review the injunctive order under a deferential abuse of discretion standard.

First Amendment Issues

Bunner contends that the issuance of the preliminary injunction is barred by the First Amendment to the United States Constitution. He argues that the preliminary injunction violates his First Amendment rights because: (1) DeCSS is expression protected by the First Amendment; (2) the preliminary injunction is a prior restraint on his freedom of expression; (3) the trial court erred in balancing the hardships because it ignored his constitutional injury caused by the injunction and overvalued the DVD CCA's purely economic and proprietary interest; and (4) the DVD CCA is unlikely to prevail on the merits because the court is unlikely to issue a prior restraint against the exercise of First Amendment rights.

The threshold issue is whether DeCSS is pure speech within the meaning of the First Amendment. A determination that it is not moots the other points in the argument.

In United States v. O'Brien (1968) 391 U.S. 367, the United States Supreme Court defined the extent of First Amendment protection in cases where a course of conduct involves both speech and non-speech elements. In O'Brien, the defendant (O'Brien) burned his certificate of registration for the military draft to express his opposition to the war in Vietnam and the military draft. Prosecuted for violation of the 1965 Amendment to section 12(b)(3) of the Universal Military Training and Service Act, O'Brien argued that he was merely exercising his First Amendment right. In rejecting the argument, the Supreme Court stated: "O'Brien first argues that the 1965 Amendment is unconstitutional as applied to him because his act of burning his registration certificate was protected 'symbolic speech' within the First Amendment. His argument is that the freedom of expression which the First Amendment guarantees includes all modes of 'communication of ideas by conduct,' and that his conduct is within this definition because he did it in 'demonstration against the war and against the draft.' We cannot accept the view that an apparently limitless variety of conduct can be labeled 'speech' whenever the person engaging in the conduct intends thereby to express an idea. However, even on the assumption that the alleged communicative element in O'Brien's conduct is sufficient to bring into play the First Amendment, it does not necessarily follow that the destruction of a registration certificate is constitutionally protected activity. This Court has held that when 'speech' and 'nonspeech' elements are combined in the same course of conduct, a sufficiently important governmental interest in regulating the nonspeech element can justify incidental limitations on First Amendment freedoms. To characterize the quality of the governmental interest which must appear, the Court has employed a variety of descriptive terms: compelling; substantial; subordinating; paramount; cogent; strong. Whatever imprecision inheres in these terms, we think it clear that a government regulation is sufficiently justified if it is within the constitutional power of the Government; if it furthers an important or substantial governmental interest; if the governmental interest is unrelated to the suppression of free expression; and if the incidental restriction on alleged First Amendment freedoms is no greater than is essential to the furtherance of that interest. We find that the 1965 Amendment to s 12(b)(3) of the Universal Military Training and Service Act meets all of these requirements, and consequently that O'Brien can be constitutionally convicted for violating it." (Id. at pp. 376-377.)

Burning a certificate of registration and posting information in an Internet web site are distinguishable activities. However, both are forms of expression. The physical act of burning a piece of paper is merely symbolic of the message it carries, which, in O'Brien's case, was repudiation of what the certificate stood for, and O'Brien's opposition to the Vietnam war. The message in O'Brien was clearly more dominant than the medium. However, this dominance of the speech element did not deter the O'Brien court from finding that the presence of the non-speech element (the act of burning the certificate) was enough to remove the conduct from First Amendment protection. In terse language, the high court declared: "We cannot accept the view that an apparently limitless variety of conduct can be labeled 'speech' whenever the person engaging in the conduct intends thereby to express an idea." "[W]hen 'speech' and 'nonspeech' elements are combined in the same course of conduct, a sufficiently important governmental interest in regulating the nonspeech element can justify incidental limitations on First Amendment freedoms." (Ibid.)

Does the act of posting information in an Internet web site for the purpose of allowing access to a protected trade secret fall under the "limitless variety of conduct" that can be mixed with speech to remove the totality of the conduct from First Amendment protection? On this record, we are unable to say.

The record before us is undeveloped. There is, as yet, no discovery. Many of the things we need to know to make a reasoned determination are not in the record. We cannot, for instance, determine just exactly what the expressive content of DeCSS is.

Bunner does not deny that DeCSS has a functional content. Indeed, Bunner concedes so in his reply brief. Bunner claims, however, that the functional element of DeCSS does not deprive it of First Amendment protection. (ARB 14, fn. 7)

The functional component of DeCSS is not hard to see. It includes the delivery to the user of DeCSS of instructions on how to decrypt CSS so that access can be gained to the movies contained in the DVD. But other than the set of descrambling instructions, the record does not tell us what expressive elements there are in DeCSS that are of such social value as to deserve First Amendment protection.

It is axiomatic that while the First Amendment protects a wide range of expression running from pure entertainment to political speech (Schad v. Borough of Mount Ephraim (1981) 452 U.S. 61, 65), not every expression is protected. Speech without any redeeming social value, such as obscenity and fighting words, receive no First Amendment protection. (Roth v. U.S. (1957) 354 U.S. 476, 484.) As stated in Chaplinsky v. State of New Hampshire (1942) 315 U.S. 568, 571-572: ") "[I]t is well understood that the right of free speech is not absolute at all times and under all circumstances. There are certain well-defined and narrowly limited classes of speech, the prevention and punishment of which has never been thought to raise any Constitutional problem. These include the lewd and obscene, the profane, the libelous, and the insulting or 'fighting' words . . . It has been well observed that such utterances are no essential part of any exposition of ideas, and are of such slight social value as a step to truth that any benefit that may be derived from them is clearly outweighed by the social interest in order and morality."

Does a decryption program, such as DeCSS, come under this exception of speech without any redeeming social value? The record provides no answer.

In Bernstein v. U.S. Department of Justice (9th Cir. 1999) 176 F.3d 1132, 1136-1137, we find the following historical overview of cryptography: "Cryptography is the science of secret writing, a science that has roots stretching back hundreds, and perhaps thousands, of years. [Citation.] For much of its history, cryptography has been the jealously guarded province of governments and militaries. In the past twenty years, however, the science has blossomed in the civilian sphere, driven on the one hand by dramatic theoretical innovations within the field, and on the other by the needs of modern communication and information technologies. As a result, cryptography has become a dynamic academic discipline within applied mathematics. It is the cryptographer's primary task to find secure methods to encrypt messages, making them unintelligible to all except the intended recipients: [¶] Encryption basically involves running a readable message known as "plaintext" through a computer program that translates the message according to an equation or algorithm into unreadable 'ciphertext.' Decryption is the translation back to plaintext when the message is received by someone with an appropriate 'key.' [Citation.] The applications of encryption, however, are not limited to ensuring secrecy; encryption can also be employed to ensure data integrity, authenticate users, and facilitate nonrepudiation (e.g., linking a specific message to a specific sender). [Citation.] It is, of course, encryption's secrecy applications that concern the government. The interception and deciphering of foreign communications has long played an important part in our nation's national security efforts."

As to how encryption works, the court explained in Junger v. Daley (6th Cir.2000) 209 F.3d 481, 482-483: "Encryption is the process of converting a message from its original form ('plaintext') into a scrambled form ('ciphertext'). Most encryption today uses an algorithm, a mathematical transformation from plaintext to ciphertext, and a key that acts as a password. Generally, the security of the message depends on the strength of both the algorithm and the key. [¶] Encryption has long been a tool in the conduct of military and foreign affairs. Encryption has many civil applications, including protecting communication and data sent over the Internet. As technology has progressed, the methods of encryption have changed from purely mechanical processes, such as the Enigma machines of Nazi Germany, to modern electronic processes. Today, messages can be encrypted through dedicated electronic hardware and also through general-purpose computers with the aid of encryption software. [¶] For a general-purpose computer to encrypt data, it must use encryption software that instructs the computer's circuitry to execute the encoding process. Encryption software, like all computer software, can be in one of two forms: object code or source code. Object code represents computer instructions as a sequence of binary digits (0s and 1s) that can be directly executed by a computer's microprocessor. Source code represents the same instructions in a specialized programming language, such as BASIC, C, or Java. Individuals familiar with a particular computer programming language can read and understand source code. Source code, however, must be converted into object code before a computer will execute the software's instructions. This conversion is conducted by compiler software."

Encryption is thus more of a process than speech, more of a function than expression. It is the shield to the message, not the message itself. In a DVD, encryption is the lock that secures the copyrighted movies contained in the DVD from unauthorized access. The movies are the expressive content of the DVD. CSS is the encryption shielding the movies in the DVD from unauthorized viewing and copying.

In DeCSS, what is the expressive content? Clearly, because DeCSS breaks the shield that protects the movie contents of the DVD, the use of DeCSS permits the user to access the same message—the same expression of ideas—that CSS protects, which is the copyrighted movies in the DVD. But other than the movies that CSS protects, what other ideas of social value does DeCSS express? Whatever those ideas are, are they of sufficient redeeming social value to deserve First Amendment protection? We do not know. The record does not tell us.

John Gilmore, in his declaration in opposition to the order to show cause why the preliminary injunction should not be granted, stated simply that "[t]he DeCSS software for Windows . . . permit compressed video images to be copied from a DVD disc onto a hard drive." (AA 276)

Bunner, also in his declaration in opposition to the order to show cause why the preliminary injunction should not be granted, stated that "providing others with access to the 'deCSS' program, and thereby enabling 'Linux' users to play 'DVDs,' was important because it would make 'Linux' more attractive and viable to consumers, thereby making 'Linux' a more viable and accepted Operating System platform," adding that he "felt that providing the source code of the 'deCSS' program on the Internet was an important and effective way to ensure programmers would have access to the information needed to add new features, fix existing defects and, in general, improve the 'deCSS' program." (AA 287)

John Hoy, the president of DVD CCA, stated in his reply declaration, that he had performed tests to determine whether DeCSS included the Xing "master key." Hoy described the tests he performed, as follows: "First, I took a DVD disc of a motion picture and played it on the DVD drive or a personal computer ('PC') to determine that the PC and DVD drive actually worked. The motion picture played properly on the PC. Second, using the DeCSS program which had been posted on October 6, 1999, I copied the digital images from the DVD disc onto the hard drive of the same PC. Again, the motion picture played properly, thus proving that DeCSS could descramble the digital images from the DVD disc. Third, I then 'zeroed out' (i.e., nullified) the Xing 'master key' in the DVD ROM buffer memory and, using the same DeCSS program, copied the digital data from the DVD disc and the other 'master keys' onto the hard drive of that PC. When I attempted to use the copied digital data, a message appeared on the computer screen stating that the motion picture could not be played. Finally, I 'zeroed out' all of the other 'master keys' in the DVD ROM buffer memory, but activated the Xing 'master key' only. Using the same DeCSS program, I copied the digital data from the DVD disc and the Xing key onto the computer's hard drive. When I attempted to play the motion from the hard drive this time, it played properly. From this experiment, I concluded that the October 6, 1999 posting contained both the CSS technology and only the Xing 'master key.'" (AA 480)

Hoy's tests merely established the functional element of DeCSS. It showed nothing about DeCSS's expressive content, other than the same copyrighted movies that CSS was supposed to make inaccessible. Moreover, in exhibit A of Hoy's reply declaration, which was filed under seal in the trial court and transmitted to this court as a sealed document, the answer given to the question "[h]ow do I select audio stream," which appeared in an apparent Internet exchange, was: "You don't. DeCSS is just a decryptor, nothing else." (Confidential Appendix of Sealed Documents, p. 495.)

However, because Hoy's account of his tests, and the results thereof, appears only in his reply declaration and was not subjected to cross-examination in a confrontational proceeding, such as a deposition or a regular trial, we cannot give it determinative weight, given the fact that the trial court has made no finding thereon; we are not a finder of fact; and there are serious First Amendment issues riding on the question.

Because we cannot determine from this record whether DeCSS is pure speech or not pure speech, we cannot determine what standard of review to apply. Because we cannot determine what standard of review to apply, we cannot determine whether the preliminary injunction granted below was properly granted or not.

It thus becomes necessary for us to return this case to the trial court for further proceedings for a full determination of the factual issues relating to the speech and non-speech elements of DeCSS. Until the trial court can make that determination on an adequate record, any preliminary injunction granted is premature, and should be dissolved.

Trade Secret Issues

In light of our conclusion to remand on the basis of the inadequacy of the record for a determination of the First Amendment issues raised in this appeal, it is not necessary to reach the trade secret issues. However, we believe that the trial court and the parties would be better served if we made certain observations on the state of the record as it relates to trade secret issues. As in the case of the question whether DeCSS is pure speech or not pure speech, the record is likewise inadequate on the issue of whether there was piracy of DVD CCA's trade secret.

There is no question that the CSS program protecting the motion picture content of the DVD from piracy is DVD CCA's trade secret. The trial court made this finding, and Bunner does not dispute such finding in this appeal. As a trade secret, CSS is entitled to protection under California's Uniform Trade Secrets Act. There is also no question that the movies contained in the DVDs are copyrighted. As such, they are entitled to the protection of the Copyright law.

In Computer Assocs. Int'l, Inc. v. Altai, Inc. (2d Cir. 1992) 982 F.2d 693, 717, it was observed: "Trade secret protection . . . remains a 'uniquely valuable' weapon in the defensive arsenal of computer programmers. [Citation.] Precisely because trade secret doctrine protects the discovery of ideas, processes, and systems which are explicitly precluded from coverage under copyright law, courts and commentators alike consider it a necessary and integral part of the intellectual property protection extended to computer programs. [Citations.]"

A trade secret, like a copyright, is intellectual property. As such, there is a constitutional basis for the laws that protect it. Article 1, section 8, of the United States Constitution explicitly empowers Congress "[t]o promote the Progress of Science and useful Arts, by securing for limited Times to Authors and Inventors the exclusive Right to their respective Writings and Discoveries."

Because there is a constitutional mandate to protect the exclusive right of inventors to the use of their discoveries, sweeping First Amendment claims to the unauthorized use by third parties of those discoveries cannot be accepted. "The First Amendment is not a license to trammel on legally recognized rights in intellectual property." (Dallas Cowboys Cheerleaders, Inc. v. Scoreboard Posters, Inc. (5th Cir. 1979) 600 F.2d 1184, 1188.)

Accordingly, injunctions to prevent misappropriation of intellectual property have been sustained, and are quite common. As the Dallas Cowboys Cheerleaders court observed: "Preliminary injunctions are a common judicial response to the imminent infringement of an apparently valid copyright. [Citations.]" (Id. at p. 1187.) In Masonite Corp. v. County of Mendocino Air Quality Management Dist. (1996) 42 Cal.App.4th 436, the court enjoined the disclosure of "emission factors" which had acquired the status of trade secrets. In

Courtesy Temp. Serv., Inc. v. Camacho (1990) 222 Cal.App.3d 1278, 1291, the court enjoined the employees from using the agency's customer list and related information, reasoning that the agency's customer list was a protectable trade secret under the Uniform Trade Secrets Act (Civ. Code, § 3426 et seq.). In American Credit Indemnity Co. v. Sacks (1989) 213 Cal.App.3d 622, 638, the court enjoined a former employee who had started a business of her own from using the plaintiff's customer list because that list fell within the definition of trade secrets under the Uniform Trade Secrets Act. In MAI Sys. Corp. v. Peak Computer, Inc. (9th Cir. 1993) 991 F.2d 511, injunction was granted to prevent copyright infringement and unfair competition with the computer systems manufacturer. The court held that there is copying for purposes of the copyright law when a computer program is transferred from its permanent storage device to a computer's random access memory (RAM).

Indeed, California's Uniform Trade Secrets Act (Civ. Code, § 3426.2, subd. (a)) specifically provides that "[a]ctual or threatened misappropriation may be enjoined." "Misappropriation" has been defined as: "[a]cquisition of a trade secret or another by a person who knows or has reason to know that the trade secret was acquired by improper means;" or "[d]isclosure or use of a trade secret of another without express or implied consent." (Civ. Code, §3426.1, subd. (b).) "Improper means," in turn, has been defined to include "theft, bribery, misrepresentation, breach or inducement of a breach of a duty to maintain secrecy, or espionage through electronic or other means. Reverse engineering or independent derivative alone shall not be considered improper means." (Civ. Code, § 3426.1, subd. (a).) Because misappropriation of trade secrets is unlawful, it may properly be restrained. Civil Code section 3426.2, subdivision (a), is clear that "[a]ctual or threatened misappropriation may be enjoined."

In finding "improper means" in the acquisition by Bunner of DVD CCA's trade secrets, the trial court pointed to "fairly clear" circumstantial evidence showing that DVD CCA's trade secrets were obtained by reverse engineering by Johansen, stating: "Although the parties dispute the who and how, the evidence is fairly clear that the trade secret was obtained through reverse engineering. The Legislative comment to the

Uniform Trade Secret Act states, 'Discovery by "reverse engineering," that is, by starting with the known product and working backward to find the method by which it was developed,' is considered proper means. The only way in which the reverse engineering could be considered 'improper means' herein would be if whoever did the reverse engineering was subject to the click licence [sic] agreement which preconditioned installation of DVD software or hardware, and prohibited reverse engineering. Plaintiff's case is problematic at this pre-discovery state. Clearly they have no direct evidence at this point that Mr. Jon Johansen did the reverse engineering, and that he did so after clicking on any licence [sic] agreement. However, in trade secret cases, it is a rare occasion when the plaintiff has a video of an employee walking out with trade secrets, or an admission of a competitor that they used improper means to obtain Plaintiff's intellectual property. In most situations, Defendants try to cover their tracks with considerably more effort that the Defendants did herein. The circumstantial evidence, available mostly due to the various defendants' inclination to boast about their disrespect for the law, is quite compelling on both the issue of Mr. Johansen's improper means and that Defendants' knowledge of impropriety. [¶] Defendants make the additional argument that even if Johansen clicked on the license agreement, such an agreement contravenes Norwegian law. This Court is not well positioned to interpret Norwegian Law, and Defendant's own expert, even if this Court could consider expert testimony on a question of legal interpretation, states that the issue has not been conclusively decided in Norway. Defendants have not sufficiently supported their argument that the licence agreement, like the one at issue here, would be disallowed by Norwegian Law, although they may at some point be able to do so." (AA, III, 702-703)

  The paucity of the record on the issue of whether the misappropriation of DVD CCA's trade secret was committed by improper means leaves us without a sufficient record to determine whether improper means were used to misappropriate DVD CCA's trade secret. First, as the trial court observed, there is no clear evidence of who actually reverse engineered CSS. Second, assuming that it was Johansen who reverse engineered CSS, the question of whether Johansen's reverse engineering was valid in Norway is material to the issue of whether the procedure is "improper" means within the meaning of California's Uniform Trade Secrets Act.

The trial court declined to find what the law of Norway is on reverse engineering. That omission is unfortunate. Although we can take judicial notice of Norwegian law, pursuant to Evidence Code sections 452 and 454, it has been held that "[w]hile we may take judicial notice of foreign law, we are not required to do so unless the parties so request and provide adequate data for our inquiry." (Ehret v. Ichioka (1967) 247 Cal.App.2d 637, 644.) We do not have in this record adequate data to satisfy our inquiry.

The experts disagree on what Norwegian law is, and the conflicting opinions have not been placed in the crucible of discovery and full trial.

Accordingly, we also remand this issue for further inquiry.

CONCLUSION

We conclude that until such time when the record is sufficiently developed to permit a fair determination of the injunctive issues raised, the preliminary injunction should be dissolved.

DISPOSITION

This matter is remanded to the trial court for further proceedings consistent with this opinion. Pending discovery and trial on the permanent injunction, the trial court is ordered to dissolve the preliminary injunction.

We declare no prevailing party. The parties shall bear their respective costs on appeal.